Amy Corzine is a writer, editor and former teacher from the US whose interest in the natural rhythm of life has been inspired by explorations on both sides of the Atlantic. She now resides in Britain.

The Secret Life of the Universe

The Quest for the Soul of Science

Amy Corzine

WATKINS PUBLISHING

LONDON

This edition published in the UK 2008 by
Watkins Publishing, Sixth Floor, Castle House,
75–76 Wells Street, London W1T 3QH

1 3 5 7 9 10 8 6 4 2

Designed and typeset by Paul Saunders

Printed and bound in Great Britain

British Library Cataloguing-in-Publication Data Available

ISBN: 978-1-905857-65-4

www.watkinspublishing.co.uk

CONTENTS

Dedicated to my late parents,
who are now elsewhere in the universe.

Author Note

The author apologizes for any errors or omissions and has taken every care to acknowledge sources. If she has omitted anyone, she apologizes and will, if informed, make corrections to any future editions.

ACKNOWLEDGEMENTS

Writing a book is a leap of faith, and I am grateful to the interviewees and individuals mentioned herein for their inspiration and support before and during this great leap of mine. Many others contributed to its creation, too many to name, but a few people who helped at strategic moments were Professor John C Poynton of the Society for Psychical Research, Eric Swanson, Uri Geller, and Jim Lyons of the British Society of Dowsers, who sent me in interesting directions, 'ex'-physicist David Crawford who corrected me on some fine points regarding science, musician Vicki Tofts who loaned me some significant books and artist/painter Martyn Lucksford, who gave me lots of information on recessed windows! Kudos also should go to Palden Jenkins, who achieved the well-nigh impossible accomplishment of editing this book with minimal disturbance to its author and to Shelagh Boyd for most carefully catching errors and lightening the text's footnotes. To publisher Michael Mann and poet Jay Ramsay, thank you for your faith in me. Finally, to the guardians of a very special secret garden, the contemplation of which helped me crystallize precisely what I wanted to say, I must offer my most sincere gratitude.

INTRODUCTION

I N OUR NEW GLOBALLY-CONSCIOUS Earth, we are meeting multiple reflections of each other. Needs, desires and limitations
we hold in common are reflected like millions of mirrors by our
technological forms of communication, from the internet to television, films and music. We learn about ourselves through the
stories we hear about others.

Yet somehow we are more distant from ourselves than ever
before. Our storytellers are no longer mere mortals sitting in our
parlours or standing on a stage. They are now superhuman images
on the giant screen – bigger than us, out of reach and out of touch.
We cannot see the faraway ramifications of our small, insignificant
actions, our pointless jobs. So we travel great distances to see,
acquire, rise above, control and ultimately lose everything.

Amid the chaos of our disagreements, we must remind ourselves that ours is a planet filled with people wishing to have
happier lives, many of whom hope to make a better world but have
different perspectives on how this may be achieved. India's ancient
epic The Mahabharata describes life as a battle, and many people
believe the world will always be thus.

Battles take many different forms, but the most serious conflicts
we face today may not be those between nations, religions, cultures
and races. They may be those inside us. If we do not overcome,
or at least better manage, our all-too-human vices, our internal
battles could turn into a mass battle for survival on a planet of
dwindling resources.

Perhaps the only way to overcome the fear behind individual internal battles is to perceive the universe as something that can be managed, and in a manner that will sustain and support life. We could start by managing our little part of Earth this way.

We occupy an illusory realm, Buddhists and Hindus say. This material world appears to be solid, but is not. Within and behind all apparently solid and 'real' forms are energy fields, patterns and structures studied by physicists, medical researchers and parapsychologists. These lie behind all that exists, behind what we know as life.

Still, we must deal with the world as we perceive it. Between the poles of our many differences, we may find a balance between extremes. My hope with this book is to plant a seed that will contribute to finding this balance, a seed that may sprout other seeds that will grow and multiply.

Contemplating this is much like the old Asian story about a frog at the bottom of a well, looking up at the sky ... a sky that changes with the weather, a weather caused by all sorts of forces that a frog will never understand.

AMY CORZINE

Essex, England, 2007

1

MAN'S CONNECTION TO THE UNIVERSE

There is an invisible way across the sky,
Birds travel that way, the Sun and Moon
And all the stars travel that path by night.

KATHLEEN RAINE

PERHAPS I SHOULD BEGIN with an ending. At the end of his book, *Gifts of Unknown Things*, about communal organic magic on an Indonesian island, Lyall Watson conveys how the universe continually replenishes itself. The dancing island's most special dancer loses her powers to bring under control the natural elements and heal her community's problems, and so the force needed by the island moves to another child. Thus life goes on, ever replacing what is lost.

One of my early glimpses of this came many years ago when I attended the last lecture in the professorial career of the late Indian philosopher-writer Raja Rao. He had almost single-handedly drawn me out of a post-adolescent depression by conveying, through the philosophies of Hinduism and Buddhism, a quality until then missing from my experience. Summing up his career as well as his talk, he asked, 'What is the end?' Accustomed to his abbreviated circular inversions, I queried, 'The beginning?' I will never forget his liquid eyes as he replied, 'And every beginning is an end. Both exist in each moment.'

Buddhist lamas often describe existence as being like the reflection of the moon upon water. Some people say the universe is infinite, unfathomable, while scientists plot their way through it, step by step, making material use of its mysteries in a way that visionaries and mystics do not.

As Sufi writer Reshad Feild once told me, it is all old information. There is nothing new to find. It is just a matter of 'uncovering' it. And what are we uncovering? Michio Kaku, in his book *Visions*, suggests that scientists are discovering what will soon enable us to become masters of matter itself. Ironically this poses the greatest threat yet faced by humanity, while at the same moment presenting it with the greatest gift of power we have ever had.

The possibility we might function as 'masters of matter' ensnares our concept of what we know as 'God'. Does the universe contain a force that is separate from visible, material bodies, enabling living creatures to be alive and awake? Is this a power we will ever be able to harness?

We are not in control of everything, often not even ourselves. So how are we connected to this vast universe? Does an ocean of microscopic vibrations link everything like some invisible web? Are we part of some vast field of energy or consciousness? Theoretical physics has brought us back to a perception of reality resembling that of many of the world's past natural philosophers, scientists and pagans. For followers of Wicca or Wyrd, all that we are, and all that happens, is based on past actions.

> The metaphor of the 'Web of Wyrd' [illustrates] how the actions of individuals can have widespread effects … If we imagine the universe as a big spider's web and … that each node where two strands meet represents an event (or a person, or a life) we can visualize the interconnectedness of things.[1]

Our predecessors left behind medical systems and lifetimes of research based upon the notion that everything affects everything else. Prehistoric man may well have perceived things that we in our physically comfortable modern world have never known.

Today's leaders may accept string theory – Brian Greene

states that 'the fundamental ingredients of nature [are] tiny one-dimensional filaments called strings' – and the notion in quantum mechanics that we live multi-dimensionally, perhaps even many different lives at the same time. Yet they will not consider the possibility that humanity is not at the pinnacle of its development. Our current lifestyle and way of perceiving may not actually be superior to that of our forebears.

Physicists have begun to wonder whether some unknown substance links everything in an inter-lacing web. They are seeking a particle they think may be the key to discovering a background energy that makes material reality possible.

Science is the study of the nature of existence, material or non-material (such as social patterns and behaviour). It utilizes the scientific method, which involves proposing a hypothesis and testing it, using any form of experimentation that can be repeated. Hypotheses are proven through repeatable experiments.

Ancient healing systems were built upon such trial-and-error research, without the extensive documentation that modern science demands. Research was based upon the notion that we are affected by our environment as much as we affect it. The idea that we are part of an invisible web is not at all new.

This may be seen in traditional art. Consider the 'eternal knot' symbol that appears worldwide from Tibet to Ireland. Interlocking infinity symbols, circles and spirals were popular as stone carvings, and are visible on ancient monuments like Newgrange in Ireland and the pyramids in Egypt.

Perhaps one truly 'cannot think a thought without the troubling of a star'. Given the right conditions, perhaps the flapping of a butterfly wing really can make an earthquake happen on the other side of the Earth, as chaos theorists have suggested.

Physicists know that our interdependence functions on infinitesimal levels. We are unified at levels we do not see. The strings of other creatures' circumstances draw us into their spheres no matter how we avoid them.

One day I saw a very gentle Western Buddhist lama kill a fly without meaning to. At the precise moment the lama set down a box, the fly flew directly beneath it. The lama's wish to be kind to all creatures did not stop him from killing an innocent insect. This illustrates how, no matter what we do, spontaneous coincidences and disasters occur. Microscopic living things exist that we cannot avoid harming, even while motionless and just breathing.

Theoretical physicists propose that an interlacing sea of energy lies behind material objects. Their applied-science partners constantly probe this unknown universe. Because of them, we have the complex machinery we use in everyday life, and medicines and surgical procedures that keep us alive longer. But also because of them, terrible things are being done to living creatures in the name of science.

Technology is applied science, not science per se. Science has been blamed for the atomic bomb, but technologists and technology were responsible for it. Since we may be harmed by things like atomic bombs, it is important that we learn as much as we can about how science is being applied.

It was obvious to people in the past that their actions had an immediate effect upon their surroundings, and vice versa. Their lives depended upon how they interacted with the natural world around them.

According to David Peat in *Blackfoot Physics*, American Indians developed an indigenous science based upon 'generations of painstaking observations and upon a perception that looks into the heart of things' with the senses and feelings, not just the mind. This kind of science is based upon 'knowledge that is given by the plants and animals to the two-legged'. When changes take place, 'they do so within an acknowledged web of relationship' where all things are subject to the forces of chance. What Indians term the trickster may surprise them and transform what they perceive.

The reduction of Man's importance in the universe

Early Man did not separate himself from his surroundings. He was inextricable from nature and all he encountered. Later on, human beings developed a geocentric view – that is, all planets and the

Sun revolved around the Earth. Man was his Creator's most important creation in the universe.

British physicist Bernard Carr maintains that Man's importance in the universe was reduced over time. It started in Europe during the Renaissance with the observation of Nicolaus Copernicus (1473– 1543) that Earth and planets near us revolved around the Sun. Subsequently, in 1610, Galileo Galilei (1564–1642) demoted the Sun's importance in humanity's conception of the universe by saying that suns other than our own exist.

Previous scientists had spent their time theorizing about the universe, but Galileo, alongside his English contemporary Francis Bacon (1561–1626), began trying to find out how things actually worked by conducting experiments in earnest. Galileo discovered the basic laws behind acceleration and falling bodies. He demonstrated that intuition is sometimes incorrect. What we sense is true is often not what is actually happening. Human beings were chagrined to hear that even their senses were no longer trustworthy. Accepted beliefs about the universe were being shaken by their roots. Eventually Galileo was seized by the Inquisition for declaring that the Earth revolved around the Sun, forced by the ruling theologians of his day to recant or face imprisonment and worse.

Humanity's adventure into the discovery of how this universe works could not be stopped. After Galileo, the seeds of scientific experimentation were unleashed. The most famous and avid experimenter of this period was mathematician and physicist Sir Isaac Newton (1642–1727), born in England the year that Galileo died. He became so successful after strictly following Galileo's habit of conducting experiments to test hypotheses that other scientists followed suit. This testing and retesting of material things in repeatable controlled trials became what we now call 'the scientific method'. Modern science was born.

Galileo's observation that planets revolve around the Sun made a great impression on the French philosopher and mathematician René Descartes (1506–1650). He decided to question everything, even his own existence, which is how he came up with the dictum, 'I think, therefore I am'. His idea that the universe was a giant machine was possibly inspired by his visit to Versailles, where automata filled its royal gardens.

Newton took this notion further and, in 1687, published his *Principia*, a text about how the cosmos functions like a machine. He believed that God had created this universal machine for Man, who was therefore important, but had no free will. As Carr states:

> Mechanism was soon stripped of its divine aspects and before long Man was generally perceived as being completely irrelevant to the functioning of the Universe.[2]

If all things operate according to the workings of a machine, they simply complete whatever action their first movement has set in motion. Newton said there are three laws of motion:

1. Inertia – when moving at constant speed, any object stays still or keeps moving in a straight line, unless pushed or pulled by a force.

2. When a force is applied to an object moving in a straight line at constant speed, its velocity changes at a rate proportional to the force that is applied, and in the direction in which that force is applied; also, the heavier or bigger an object, the more force is required to move it.

3. An object maintains its position with a force that is equal and opposite to any force applied to it to make it move. Objects on top of each other – like a pot sitting upon the ground – have forces that cancel each other out so that they remain where they are.

Since Newton's time we have discovered that we can say relatively little about our universe with absolute certainty. For the past three centuries, physicists have searched for universal laws. Experiments have grown ever more subtle until our present time, when physicists are exploring subatomic regions. They now know things exist that they can't see. They know invisible things are present because they can see their effects. As Carr says, with the creation of atomic theory came the first hints that our experience of the small is just as limited as our experience of the large.

Since the last century, physicists have been trying to create what they term 'a unified theory' of laws to resolve the conflicting observations they have made regarding the large and small levels of existence, space and time. Thus far, they have been unable to do so. A battle now rages between them, usually regarding the often opposing theories of general relativity and quantum physics. Albert Einstein (1879–1955) died without resolving this conflict, expressing only the opinion that 'God does not play dice'.

Until Einstein, most physicists followed the theories of Newton, whose law of gravitation is especially important in the search for this single theory of everything. Newton thought that universal laws existed, and that these could be applied throughout space and time. His first profound discovery was:

> … the force of gravity which pulls an apple from a tree is the same force, obeying the same law, as the force of gravity which holds the Moon in orbit around the Earth, and the planets in orbit around the Sun.[3]

Newton single-handedly destroyed the idea that 'the universe might be governed by capricious gods who could determine the fall of an apple or the motion of a star at their whim'.[4] Gravity was seen to affect every object in the universe – not gods.

Newton then tried to explain *light* in terms of laws that he said govern motion and planetary orbits. Because he was so esteemed by his peers, they accepted his untested theories about light. Light, Newton said, was composed of particles that bounced around between objects according to the laws of gravity.

Not until a century later were the light theories of Newton's contemporary, the Dutch physicist and astronomer Christian Huygens (1629–95), actually tested. Huygens believed that light slows down in water and travels as a wave. He declared that light moves slower in a denser medium – that is, more slowly in water than air. Light is waves, not particles, Huygens stated, and when a light wave hits a denser medium like water, it bends. These observations did not conform to Newton's more acceptable ideas, and so they were virtually ignored.

Finally in the 19th century, Hugyens' suppositions were tested and found to be correct. Another Englishman, the polymath and chief decoder of the Rosetta Stone, Thomas Young (1773–1829) created the key experiment proving Huygens was correct. He observed patterns created by light as it shone through two slits in a piece of card. His *double-slit* experiment has in it the heart of quantum mechanics, physicist Richard Feynman (1918–88) later claimed. Following Young, the French physicist Jean Foucault proved in 1850 that light does indeed slow down in water and travel as a wave.

This was the opposite of Newton's assumption that light moved faster through a denser medium like water. Was his assertion influenced by the fact that something strange had been noticed about light? Something rippled in light waves as they passed by in the air. Scientists termed it *aether*, not knowing what it was.

Not until the next generation of scientists was this explained. Michael Faraday (1791–1867) came up with the idea that a line of force was causing ripples in light waves as they passed through the air. He noticed that lines of force may be generated by a magnet or an electric current passing through a coil. This was one of the most important observations made by scientists of the 19th century. With force fields now observable, aether was unnecessary. The thing that rippled when light travelled was named the *electromagnetic field*.

Force fields

Now science was moving ever closer to technology, enabling man to create machines that used force fields invisible to the unaided human eye. Faraday discovered the secrets allowing the electric motor and electric generator to be invented. His observations lay the groundwork for our understanding of electromagnetism. Theoretical physicist James Clerk Maxwell (1831–79) took Faraday's ideas further, uniting magnetism with electricity to create the concept of *electromagnetism*. Before then, magnetism and electricity were thought to be separate phenomena. His basic premise was:

> If the intensity of an electric field varies in time, it will generate magnetic fields, and vice versa.[5]

According to Newton's laws of motion, if you run fast enough you can catch up with a departing beam of light. But according to Maxwell's laws of electromagnetism, you can't.

Science's next big discovery was that of *thermodynamics*, or rather the second law of thermodynamics. Considered to overtake even Newton's laws, thermodynamics is the branch of physics that deals with conversions of energy from one form to another, and in terms of temperature, pressure, volume, mechanical action and work or function. The second law of thermodynamics is defined, simply, as: total entropy always increases.

Thermodynamics explains how heat flows from hot to cooler objects, with excess heat lost to the outside air. The second law states that, in a closed system, disorder and decline inevitably increase. That is, if no energy enters an object, then it will eventually lose energy and fall apart. Excess energy is always being lost from a closed system, such as a refrigerator. This heat always moves outwards or expands and dissipates. Physicists reason from this that energy in the universe expands, and therefore that the universe is expanding.

Thermodynamic behaviour was the basis for the invention of the steam engine. The machine technology resulting from this discovery set off the 19th century's Industrial Revolution. Meanwhile, our feelings about the universe were being influenced by the ideas of people like German philosopher Immanuel Kant (1724–1804). He wrote in *The Critique Of Pure Reason* (1781):

> Space and time do not exist independently of our consciousness.

In other words, *we* exist first. Whatever we are aware of starts with us. We are at the bottom of whatever we perceive. Interestingly, this conception of a less concrete universe is closer to observations made by Einstein than by Newton. Time and space, Einstein said, are not stationary but malleable. How fast things appear to move depends on the perceiver's position and state of motion. No object, influence or disturbance can move faster than the speed of light. Through this *theory of special relativity*, Einstein resolved the conflict between Newton's and Maxwell's ideas about the speed of light.

Then Newton's *theory of gravitation*, stating that gravity was the same everywhere in space, was overturned. Einstein, with his *general relativity theory*, said that space and time are influenced by one's state of motion. They curve or warp in response to whatever matter or energy is present. This means that the pull of gravity varies from one place to another.

> Space and time can [no longer] be thought of as an inert backdrop on which the events of the universe play themselves out; [rather] they are intimate players in the events themselves.[6]

Problems subsequently came up in the 20th century when physicists tried to apply these laws to microscopic levels of matter. So they developed a new theory called *quantum mechanics*. Zukav, in *Dancing Wu Li Masters*, describes it thus:

> A 'quantum' is a quantity of something, a specific amount. 'Mechanics' is the study of motion. Therefore, 'quantum mechanics' is the study of the motion of quantities. [Quantum] mechanics resulted from the study of the subatomic realm, that invisible universe underlying, embedded in, and forming the fabric of everything around us.

Quantum mechanics actually differs more from Einstein's general relativity theory than Newtonian physics, which also deals with the material world that we see. Yet Richard Feynman (1918–88), alleged to be the greatest of American physicists, claimed not to understand quantum mechanics. Said to have developed the most complete and straightforward version of quantum physics in the 1940s, winning the Nobel Prize for his theory of quantum electrodynamics, he commented:

> I think I can safely say that nobody understands quantum mechanics ... Do not keep saying to yourself, if you can possibly

avoid it, 'But how can it be like that?' because you will go 'down the drain' into a blind alley from which nobody has yet escaped. Nobody knows how it can be like that.

Brian Greene in *The Elegant Universe* states:

[Scientists' vision of] the gently curving geometrical form of space emerging from general relativity [was] at loggerheads with the frantic, rolling, microscopic behaviour of the universe implied by quantum mechanics.

An attempt to reconcile quantum mechanics with general relativity was made in 1927 by Einstein and Niels Bohr of Copenhagen. The answer that Bohr came up with became known as the *Copenhagen interpretation of quantum mechanics*. Bohr claimed that quantum theory is about correlations in our experiences. That is, what we observe under specific conditions is all that we can comprehend about existence. Einstein argued against Bohr's interpretation until his death, but acknowledged that it had advantages in explaining subatomic phenomena, as the theory works in all possible experimental situations. Bohr said that whatever experiments human beings are capable of creating, they will find answers that go along with quantum theory – that is:

[Whether] something is true is not a matter of how closely it corresponds to the absolute truth, but of how consistent it is with our own experience.[7]

According to Gary Zukav, the Copenhagen interpretation rejects the idea that some kind of absolute reality exists. Bohr's view was that our rational minds are incapable of interpreting or understanding what is actually happening, so we deal with what we can on this human level as best we can. Einstein would not accept this. But he could not disprove Bohr's assertion.

Zukav says that, 'scientists attempting to formulate a consistent physics were forced by their own findings to acknowledge that a complete understanding of reality lies beyond the capabilities of rational thought'. Physicist Henry Pierce Stapp of Lawrence

Berkeley Laboratory said that the Copenhagen interpretation was a rejection of the presumption that nature could be understood in terms of elementary space-time realities.

Zukav adds that Newtonian physics deals with the world as we know it through our ordinary sense perceptions, describing things and their changes over time, predicting events according to what we know. Quantum mechanics is based on the notion that sub-atomic particles and systems exist that are not directly observable by our ordinary senses. We can predict what will probably happen regarding whole systems, but we cannot observe something without changing it. Quantum mechanics claims only to 'correlate experience'. Furthermore:

> A subatomic particle is not a 'particle' like a dust particle. ... A dust particle is a thing, an object. ... Quantum mechanics views subatomic particles as 'tendencies to exist'. A subatomic particle is a 'quantum', a quantity of something. What that something is, however, is a matter of speculation.

String theory provided a resolution to this in the 1980s. It made Einstein's theory of general relativity compatible with quantum mechanics, and offered the view that more than three spatial dimensions exist. It stated that there are many dimensions en-folded and 'tightly curled into the folded fabric of the cosmos' according to Greene in *The Elegant Universe*.

The universe is described as being entirely composed of strings of ultra-microscopic ingredients. Strings are said to make up the particles out of which atoms are made. They are so small that Greene writes they 'appear point-like even when examined with our most powerful equipment'. Scientists perceived these point-like particles as being like strands of string. Strings, not particles, are seen as being the fundamental ingredients of everything. They are one-dimensional and a bit like infinitely thin rubber bands which vibrate constantly.

Some physicists say that this resolves the conflict between general relativity and quantum mechanics, providing a single theory upon which we can base our understanding of what we are made of. In other words, as *The Elegant Universe* states, 'all matter and all forces ... arise from one basic ingredient: oscillating strings'. This radically changes our understanding of space and time, so that our universe may be conceived as composed of infinite Aeolian harp strings, not particles.

One might now imagine the universe as a moving, living, breathing, musical being, of which every human being is a part. Our universe may not only be influenced by what we do. It seems to actually breathe and undulate according to what we do – and to be as alive as we are.

Today some physicists are moving beyond quantum physics into even further uncharted territory. Russian physicist Lazar Mayants suggests that paradoxes simply contain questions for which we have not yet found answers. Certain paradoxes 'cannot be resolved without making use of proper new principles'. He says that no new principle of the natural sciences is helpful in settling the chicken-and-egg paradox (that is, which came first?).

> This paradox [arises from] the inadequacy of our conventional way of [thinking;] the new principle needed [must] be related to our perception of [reality]. A number of quantum mechanical paradoxes [and some] in classical statistical mechanics [and] probability theory are also of that kind.[8]

He notes that the *Schrödinger's cat paradox* is built upon an absurdity. This paradox states that an observation or measurement itself affects an outcome, so that the observed outcome as such does not exist unless the measurement is made. The name comes from an experiment involving a cat:

> [The] experimenter is free to postpone the examination of the cat's [dead or alive] state for an indefinite time interval, during which the cat must stay 'alive-dead' (neither alive nor dead!). Is this not absurd?

Mayants suggests that Schrödinger himself had a critical attitude about the conventional interpretation of quantum mechanics, citing the way he introduced his cat paradox argument with: 'one can construct also completely burlesque examples'. He concluded, 'the alive and dead cats (if I may say so) are in equal parts mixed or smeared (melded)'.

So the controversies continue raging. Once one gets into the fray by learning the basics of theoretical physics, it is infinitely fascinating. Groups like The Royal Society and the Scientific and Medical Network of Great Britain, the Institute of Noetic Sciences in the US, and the International Mind and Life Institute are investigating wide-ranging phenomena and extending the reach of science to those who are ignorant of its intrigue. Their aim is to educate and stimulate discussion.

As cross-pollination continues between disciplines, scientific experimentation will probably increase, with experimenters diversifying into ever more adventurous areas. It is estimated that over 65 per cent of the world's people have had experiences for which they cannot offer explanations, while theoretical physicists have moved beyond the Cartesian (Descartes') mind-body split of the 18th century, and more deeply into and possibly past the sub-atomic 'quantum' ideas of the 20th century. Physicists have entered the realm of what once was fantasy, seeking wormholes through which we may walk into other dimensions, exploring shifting-sand perceptions where time and space are more malleable than we could ever imagine.

We can just about grasp that we may be living in a kind of universal nervous system, and we are only beginning to ask questions of that nature. Is there truly a nervous system in the universe – one containing force fields and synapses? Perhaps an invisible something actually does connect us all, or a background force is moving us inexorably into some new psycho-spiritual state. If so, where are we going? Does it have consciousness? Is it a consciousness like ours – or is it an amalgamation of many consciousnesses, different from ours?

Are we part of a universal energy grid, while still having individualized mind-body consciousness, as Taoism suggests? How does this nervous system work? Perhaps it is a network through which impulses travel – an infinite nervous system. Are we part of something, or are we simply 'it'?

If human beings consist of ever-moving atoms, then we must be a kind of soluble mass, not solid at all. Some say that most of the human body is water; others say it is light, air or 'energy'. Other views exist, for instance, Tibetans perceive the body, and the Earth, as filled with other beings that comprise the natural elements. Water is *nagas* (water beings). Light is *salamanders* (fire beings).

Mind and matter

If thoughts arise from the body, a system of constantly moving particles held together by some kind of wave-like nervous energy, and manifest as energy themselves, thoughts could influence material things. Documented tests, like those carried out on meditators and with Random Event Generators (REGs) spread all over the world, seem to prove this is true.

REGs indicate changes that are on their way before disasters occur. They also react before the public does to dramatic events. The mechanical equivalent of flipping a coin continuously, these machines constantly generate random zeros and ones. They behave differently just before some big world event happens. Researchers think this occurs at times when masses of people are focused upon the same experience or idea. After the tsunami struck Asia in December 2004, 91 REG machines across the world recorded non-random patterns. The same thing happened during the funeral of Diana, Princess of Wales, and the 9/11 attacks on New York's World Trade Center.

These REG experiments seem to indicate that our thoughts are part of a universe composed of energy waves. Could it be that each and every object we see is no more than a *thought*? Could each of us be a mere thought of some vast, all-encompassing universal 'consciousness'? This brings into question the concept of free will and whether there are unperceived dimensions beyond our visible world. Many things unseen by the naked eye have already been proven by scientists to exist. Today they are busy manipulating them.

Soon our own Earth's 'invisible universe' could be peopled by minuscule man-made 'nanobots'. This is the new nanotechnology that worried Prince Charles enough to make him once again risk ridicule by speaking out against the mindless development of what he saw might create a new 'grey goo' kind of pollution. Although at present this is only science fiction, it may not be so for much longer. Already we have textiles and computers that contain these invisible nanobots.

Most of us are way behind regarding the ethical issues surrounding such technology. When I heard that some scientists are working to create a robot that looks like a human being, composed of billions of microscopic robots invisible to the human eye, I realized that I am living in quite a different world from the one that some scientists occupy. In this case, ignorance is not bliss, for humanity is fast moving into situations it is ill-fitted to handle.

Moral dilemmas

Science is something we must think about in order to be prepared for decisions we will soon have to make regarding health, ecology, energy resources; community, societal and building structures; the kind of morality these will express, and how long we will live, not to mention how or when we wish to die. To give one example, governments have not yet properly explored the ethical dimensions of forcing the world's farmers to buy genetically modified 'terminator' seeds that cannot self-reproduce, which are patented by multinational corporations bent on cornering global food markets and stopping farmers from using naturally self-reproducing seeds.

It is time to reconsider the connections that appear to exist between things. We can observe them without the aid of microscopes or computers. We may begin by learning how to perceive in a way that enables us to experience the forces beyond and behind the material realm. This may be crucial to our continued existence.

In the past, those who lived according to Earth's ways intuitively understood laws of the universe that today's powerful leaders must not ignore, except at their peril. Now so far from nature, we must return to it and again become husbandmen to the land, relearning the skills our industrialized world has pushed aside. As Fritjof Capra put it in 1982:

> [Most] academics subscribe to narrow perceptions of reality which are inadequate for dealing with the major problems of our time. These problems [are] closely connected and interdependent. They cannot be understood within the fragmented methodology characteristic of our academic disciplines and government agencies.[9]

Capra does not believe that this fragmented approach will ever resolve our difficulties. It will merely move them around within a complex web of social and ecological relations. Only if the web itself is changed will some kind of solution be found. He says this will involve profound transformations of our social institutions, values and ideas, that 'most of our leading thinkers use outdated conceptual models and irrelevant variables'.

Rather than dismissing as woolly-minded those who investigate these areas in a less intellectual manner, perhaps we should consider what they may be in the process of discovering. They normally work through trial and error, which of course is how scientists conduct their experiments.

Many non-scientists think along such lines, but they take different routes to influencing our world. Some work separately from governments – which they regard as inadequately protecting and conserving our landscapes, food, resources and wellbeing – to create new substructures through experiments such as cohousing and ecovillages. Others actively engage in destroying what they consider to be obsolete or unsatisfactory systems of rule. Today's global unrest may indicate that some new way of perceiving existence is being born.

As an indicator of how thought – hence, science – has influenced our societies in recent decades, note what Capra said, again in 1982:

> Our progress [has] been largely a rational and intellectual affair, and this one-sided evolution has now reached a highly alarming stage, a situation so paradoxical that it borders insanity. We can control the soft landings of spacecraft on distant planets, but we

are unable to control the polluting fumes emanating from our cars and factories.

Our high standard of living is based upon what magazines and businessmen tell us to believe, encouraging us to live glossy lifestyles with the latest fashions, hairstyles, cosmetics, automobiles and pet foods. Meanwhile, economists tell us we cannot 'afford' health care, education or public transport adequate to everyone's needs. Now, as in 1982:

> Medical science and pharmacology are endangering our health, and the Defence Department has become the greatest threat to our national security.

Capra noted that all of this – 'combined with the mechanistic model of the universe', which originated in the 17th century and emphasized linear thinking – produced 'a technology that is unhealthy and inhuman; a technology in which the natural, organic habitat of complex human beings is replaced by a simplified, synthetic and prefabricated environment'.

One approach to the Cartesian, mechanistic way of thinking would be to test how much our thoughts affect our surroundings. Do thoughts affect events and the movements of our phenomenal world – things like the weather and growing plants, not to mention our friends, pets, and relations? Certainly the founders of Scotland's Findhorn Community approached the world from this perspective.

The Findhorn Community has been working with invisible *elemental spirits* and so-called fairies, *devas* and angels since the 1970s to create a situation in which people may live in harmony with their environment without resorting to man-made chemical methods of control. Born in the harsh climate of Britain's northern coast, Findhorn has proven that human beings and plants can thrive without harming each other, in mutually sustaining cooperation. Their attempts to become sustainable include windmills to generate electricity and a plant-based waste-water purification system.

From waste-water purification to environmental biology, the world is awash with companies experimenting with ways to limit pollution and provide sustenance through utilizing plant life. It has all arisen from people simply being open to possibilities. Science is becoming so exciting and test results so unprecedented that physicists sometimes resort to using language that sounds religious because they are meeting phenomena for which they have no other words. No language has been invented for this new world they are discovering.

Improving our connection with the universe

Is the world becoming more complicated? Perhaps it is simply that, as Swami Chinmaya of the Chinmaya Mission says, 'the world is not complicated. It is man who is complicated.' He says:

> All the sorrows [in] the world, including the disturbances in ecology, are not because the world is bad, but because [too] much lawlessness, covetousness, hatred, jealousy, greed, passion and lust are in our minds. [We] disturb the equilibrium and balance of nature around us.

Most damaging to humans, Swami Chinmaya finds, is 'the practice of whipping up your desires. Each individual is trying to fulfil all his desires. [The] father wants his satisfaction; the mother equally wants it as well as the child.' The remedy, he claims, is selfless love, which is 'neither the privilege of the poor, nor the luxury of the rich. It is the choice of the wise man.' [10] In the Hindu epic The Mahabharata, it is written:

> One should never do that to another which one regards as injurious to one's own self.

A Buddhist aphorism is:

> He who for the sake of his own happiness hurts others who also want happiness, shall not hereafter find happiness. He who for the sake of happiness does not hurt others who also want happiness, shall hereafter find happiness. [11]

As Buddhists say, clinging to 'self' stops us from being effective in the world and prevents us from having clarity so that we can act appropriately. They say that if the mind is pure, you can do good with even the smallest act. Cultivating the wish to help all beings enables you to be skilful in your actions. Furthermore, if you calm your conflicting emotions and 'keep your sword sheathed' with others, you can live with them in harmony and bring greater happiness into the world.

Christianity's golden rule is:

Do unto others as you would have them do unto you.

Jesus, in the Gospel of Mark (13:33), exhorted his followers to:

Love your neighbour as yourself.

Muhammad is recorded by the Hadith as having said:

No man is a true believer unless he desires for his brother that which he desires for himself.[12]

All of these major religions show similar approaches to the universe. Thus, on some level it has to be true that they, and we, are linked.

How minds are connected

Random Event Generator experiments have shown that the mind can be altered by influences or thoughts from other minds, as have experiments conducted on remote viewers, notably those who have worked with the governments of the United States and the former USSR.

Remote viewers are clairvoyants employed to obtain answers to questions about people and places via visual hallucinations or other ways of sensing. During the 20th century, many were trained and used in top-secret labs by some governments to spy on enemies, locate missing objects and find secret laboratories. From them it was gleaned that the mind acts something like a television antenna that constantly receives information on subtle sensory levels, including telepathically.

Emotions seem to play a part regarding the clarity with which one person telepathically communicates with another, although sensitivity to stimuli varies greatly. Couples, especially long-term ones, can develop strong intuitive connections with each other. The sexual component of relationships sometimes plays a part in this. The closer people are to each other emotionally, the stronger their communicative bond. For instance, twins have great empathy for each other as well as strong telepathic links, according to research conducted by the British writer and paranormal investigator Guy Lyon Playfair (documented in *Twin Telepathy*).

Telepathy was not seen as something extraordinary or unusual in many parts of the world in the past, before machines took over. The 'sixth sense' was considered normal in Tibet, where physical life was hard and distances between people great. Lamas from there sometimes talk about mind-to-mind communication. The French explorer and spiritual occultist of the early 20th century, Alexandra David-Neel, observed telepathy many times in her travels in pre-Chinese Tibet. Her bestselling books, such as *My Journey to Lhasa*, describe it as accepted practice in that pre-technologized country.

Telepathy between pets and their human masters has been observed by British scientist Rupert Sheldrake. He has collected much anecdotal material about this phenomenon and also notes that animals are known to avoid disasters like earthquakes.

The world media was struck by how few animal carcasses were found after the tsunami hit Asia in December 2004. It was reported that, when the ground began shaking, one man saved himself from death by following the fleeing monkeys and birds. Alan Rabinowitz, director for science and exploration at New York City's Wildlife Conservation Society, says that at one time humans had the same sensory capacity that animals have. They could sense 'impending danger by detecting subtle or abrupt shifts in the environment', but lost this ability when it was no longer used or needed.

The indications are that our brains constantly make choices

about what information to pay attention to, and what to ignore. Research seems to point to our being linked on some infinitesimal level.

Although unseen, these links are very much present. In the following chapters, I will show more strands of this invisible web or network of 'strings' and the science behind new social, medical and environmental experiments that could catapult us into an entirely new way of living and thinking in the 21st century.

2

INVISIBLE INTERCONNECTIONS
BETWEEN US

It is no longer a choice ... between violence and non-violence.
It is either non-violence or non-existence.

MARTIN LUTHER KING JR, 'REMAINING AWAKE THROUGH A GREAT
REVOLUTION', 31 MARCH, 1968

The unleashed power of the atom has changed everything save
our modes of thinking, and we thus drift toward unparalleled
catastrophes. ... Time and space are modes by which we think
and not conditions in which we live.

ALBERT EINSTEIN

LOOKING AT THE EARTH from space, you see only swirls of colour
and cloud. Astronaut Edgar Mitchell had a kind of epiphany
as he gazed at our blue-green ball from the Apollo spacecraft,
meanwhile conducting secret telepathy experiments with people
back on Earth. It was home, yet somehow independently alive.
So transformative was this experience that, after he returned, he
pursued further studies in clairvoyance and telepathy. Despite
ostracism, he eventually established the Institute of Noetic Sciences
to 'explore the frontiers of consciousness to advance individual,
social and global transformation'.

Visionaries like Mitchell have chosen not to worry about the financial and national security pressures placed on them by financiers and governments. They focus instead upon the good that can be done for those now alive. Many of these humanitarians have formed groups whose members are conscious that things need to be done to avert catastrophe and steer humanity away from the cliff edge. Thinking of humans and animals as friends allows us to create a much better environment for everyone.

Visionaries and their organizations

In the UK, Forum for the Future wants to encourage an ecological approach to maintaining and improving what we already have without destroying natural resources. One of its aims is to educate the scientific and business communities about sustainability, and to get them to assess 'profit' in terms that include encouraging a healthy, non-polluted environment.

A US initiative called the Environic Foundation aims to bring about better environic (social, economic and environmental) conditions on a global scale by providing practical educational programmes that balance people, place and priorities. Its primary aim is to encourage movement away from a culture of self-interest and strife to one of improved quality of life, equity and stewardship. One aspect of its work is motivating people to protect groundwater, a vital resource susceptible to contamination.

Many ecological organizations exist in the UK whose members are conscious of the importance of seeing our Earth as a home we should look after. Of course dangers lurk in these ethical efforts, as extremism can cause overall aims to be lost. For instance, if it is decided that organic food must be imported by sea instead of air, there is a risk of discouraging the growth of the organic market since natural produce can deteriorate if transported by sea. This could defeat the primary aim of the organic movement: to encourage farmers worldwide to grow food naturally, without pesticides or genetic modification.

The UK's Soil Association is against pesticides, genetic modification and intensive monoculture. It promotes organic farming and biodiversity and has established standards for assessing organic quality. Literal stamps of its approval may be found on bread and other products sold in shops, although complaints sometimes surface that it has lowered its standards to gain wider acceptance.

The Friends of the Earth (FoE) covers the spectrum of ecological concerns. It promotes new, alternative energy like the controversial wind farms. The latter cause consternation among some environmentalists, who claim that wind farms are not the most economic or sustainable way of generating energy. They are also unsightly in beautiful country areas, particularly since they are normally placed on high ground and can be seen for miles around.

The international organization Greenpeace aims to protect the environment even more stridently than FoE. Greenpeace encourages environmentally sustainable agricultural and building practices while taking direct action to combat activities it perceives as detrimental to the health and safety of all living creatures.

The World Wide Fund for Nature (WWF) has identified six main areas of focus: climate change, forests, fresh water, marine and coastal areas, endangered species and toxic materials. Its UK branch concentrates on the conservation of plants in an effort to counteract the loss of biodiversity. Seven areas are its focus: 1. agriculture and rural development; 2. companies and finance; 3. ecological footprints; 4. economics, trade and investment; 5. international development policies; 6. oil, gas and mining; and 7. UK social change.

Then there are the more directly politically active organizations like the Nuclear Policy Research Institute (NPRI), based in the USA but international in scope. Its aim is to educate people about the nuclear industry, radiation and health and the availability of sustainable alternative resources. Established by a straightforward Australian paediatrician named Helen Caldicott, who founded Physicians for Social Responsibility in 1978 and Women's Action for Nuclear Disarmament in 1980, she is the author of many environmental and anti-nuclear books, such as *Nuclear Madness*.

At the Great Mystery Re-thinking Conference in Oxford in 2004, Caldicott told of the horrors she had observed, of children and babies dying of cancers like leukaemia as a result of nuclear radiation poisoning. She said we suffer from 'psychic numbing'. When we discover terrible things are being done that we cannot seem to stop, she says it is very important to let ourselves fully experience the grief we feel, and not to run away. Avoiding grief leads to numbness or various forms of socio- and psychopathology. This is happening to many people today because humanity is not addressing the problems it needs to face.

'The thing that is not being talked about by our leaders and our media is simply too awful to contemplate', she said. 'We are creating our own cancers, giving cancer to our children and creating a world that will be full of nuclear waste that will poison our soil and our food and, therefore, us. Nuclear waste does not deteriorate for thousands of years. America is now churning out hundreds of thousands of bombs and shows no sign of letting up, when only one of those bombs is capable of decimating our planet. Do we really want these nuclear bombs circling our planet in outer space, when a bomb can be triggered by the weather and any number of other false signals?'

Caldicott asked whether anyone had thought of what could be lost if anything went wrong with the nuclear reactor just outside Oxford. 'All that learning ... hundreds of years of history and the many great minds built there – minds that could come up with solutions for the problems of our world – could disappear.'

Greater responsibility is required of our leaders, Caldicott said. 'As a surgeon, I make a great mess in my surgery ... but I never clean up anything. The nurses do that.' This creates arrogance, she said. 'If a doctor, scientist or leader makes a mess, they should be expected to clean it up. We should make them accountable. Every leader should undergo psychiatric and psychological tests to make sure he is fit to run for office.'

'Human beings are not amenable to slavery and will eventually rebel, once they realize what is being done to them', Caldicott says. 'It is common sense to allow people the freedom to choose for themselves ... if we want to be happy and war-free.' Each of us has the ability to be endlessly creative. There are solutions to the problems we face. If we face them, we will find answers.

Many other nuclear watchdog groups exist, like the Campaign for Nuclear Disarmament (CND), the Nuclear Age Peace Foundation, the Institute for Energy and Environmental Research, the US Public Interest Research Group and the Committee to Bridge the Gap, which provides legal, technical and organizing assistance to communities near existing or proposed nuclear projects.

Some organizations approach the problems affecting our external world from the angle of how they arise within the realm of the mind. The Dalai Lama's Mind and Life Institute aims to investigate the mind and understand the nature of reality by establishing a working collaboration and research partnership between scientists and Buddhist scholars. It strives to strengthen a sense of ethics in the practice of science. Its aim is to promote the creation of 'a contemplative, compassionate and rigorous experimental and experiential science of the mind which could guide and inform medicine, neuroscience, psychology, education and human development'. It believes that notions such as designated identity, co-dependent origination and emptiness have no counterpart in the philosophical heritage of the West and that Buddhism may lead to answers for certain questions in modern physics.

This approach could help modern physicists identify a universal law that will, as the Institute's website attests, 'bridge the minute levels of quantum mechanics where observations regarding non-locality and the role of the observer in what happens in the universe have been found to diverge from the macrocosmic laws' behind gravitation and Einstein's theories.

As safeguards to creating a successful cross-cultural dialogue between scientists and the Dalai Lama, the organization's first conferences in the 1980s on the 'science' of religious contemplation were planned with the following guidelines as their foundation: 1. inviting open-minded, competent scientists, with some familiarity of contemplative traditions, to discussions; 2. ensuring that meetings encourage full participation; 3. engaging excellent translators who are comfortable with scientific vocabulary in Tibetan and English; and, 4. holding discussions in a private, protected space, away from the eye of the media.

As a result of annual discussions since 1984, collaborations have begun between scientists and religious scholars, in which controlled experiments are conducted on long-term meditators. Their brainwave patterns and reactions to stimuli of various kinds are being compared with those of new and non-meditators.

Fiction writers are encouraged to contact Sci Talk, a website set up to make connections between the book trade and scientists. Professors like Mark Brake of the University of Glamorgan in Wales, a representative at NASA, has joined a UK government-sponsored initiative that uses science fiction to make science accessible to children and non-scientists. Professor Brake is also setting up a network of community advice offices, similar to the UK's Citizens Advice Bureaux, for laypeople who need to find out scientific information for legal or health reasons. In 2006, he was awarded £1.5m to set up Science Shops in south-east Wales, to help the public learn about how science is being applied in their communities and to put people in touch with scientists and science students. Organizers hope that knowledgeable grass-roots constituencies will grow up from these small beginnings so that ethical questions surrounding science may come to the attention of lay-people, who will learn that they have choices about how technology, agriculture, businesses and governments apply and use science.

The historical background behind these frontier organizations

Rebellion against questionable technology has taken different forms. An example is the Arts and Crafts movement in England of the 1880s. Architects, artists and tradespeople joined forces to protest against the degradation caused in the cities by industrialization, homogenization and the consequent loss of craftsmanship. They were vehemently opposed to what machines were doing to their way of life. Not until the advent of machines could we produce identical copies and shapes cheaply. Mass production created an uglier world, obliterating the individual and his power over his environment. Britain's Arts and Crafts members were among those who sought ways to stop this. Its most militant proponent was William Morris, known for his textiles and hand-printed wallpapers. Building materials and craftwork made by individuals were valued by, and signatures of, the Arts and Crafts movement.

Its main inspiration was the art critic and artist John Ruskin. Associated with the Pre-Raphaelites and active in the early 1800s, his book *The Stones of Venice* inspired Arts and Crafts supporters. Ruskin wanted artisan-labourers to take part in intellectual activities, and the gentleman classes to learn to make things by hand. He rebelled against the use of men as if they were mere cogs inside factory machines. He wrote that, within every human's nature exists 'some tardy imagination, torpid capacity of emotion, tottering steps of thought' which 'cannot be strengthened unless we are content to take them in their feebleness, and unless we prize and honour them in their imperfection above the best and most perfect manual skill'.[1]

In other words, the unique constellation of each individual and his imperfections contains seeds of greatness. Our mistakes hold answers to coping with problems that arise in our lifetimes. We do not make useful errors as long as we remain mindless automatons doing others' work, thinking of ourselves as mere machines within societies and industries under someone else's control and management.

Letting money and profit decide building and environmental styles ensures the proliferation of soulless structures that the young, growing up amongst them, believe to be normal. Taking away the art and architecture of the past denudes the world of its history and human warmth. Without beauty in our surroundings, what chance have the young to appreciate the nobler qualities of humanity?

Against the tide: modern boat-rocking

Today, many of us respond positively to the Arts and Crafts movement's fight 'against ruthless commercial expansion, the cynical proliferation of the useless, the squalor and pollution carelessly created by industrial production, against monotony and [the] deadening of the human spirit'.[2] Technology and monocultural agriculture are today destroying our natural environment more quickly than ever before – because of their inattention to what is small, natural and health-giving.

Satish Kumar, the editor of England's *Resurgence* magazine and formerly a Jain monk, battles an ongoing war against thoughtless mass commercialism. He supports unique handicrafts made from natural materials, preaching that a holy trinity of soil, soul and ecology is the new religion for today's world. He 'worships the worms – for without them where would we be?' How would soil be fertile and grow plants for us to eat? How would waste be transformed? He says it was no coincidence that the Buddha became enlightened while sitting under a tree – if you want an answer to a problem, sit under a tree!

Kumar is part of a movement seeking to protect rural landscapes and help small farmers and businesses survive in the flood of a corporate wave washing over humanity today. Are the creations of our scientists destined to become uncontrollable monsters? Scientists do mention this, but not usually the ones paid by corporations, since they must sign gag orders to gain employment. Our backwardness was noticed back in 1982 by Fritjof Capra, who wrote in *The Turning Point*:

> We propose Utopian communities in gigantic space colonies, but cannot manage our cities.

More and more, we are living with and through technology. We are letting it use us instead of remembering to use it as a tool. Viewing situations from a distance on computer screens does not allow our senses to be part of the equation in decision-making. Errors are more frequent when our senses are not directly engaged with what surrounds us. Technology creates an unease of the sort that leads to impatience and poor judgement.

> With the mechanistic model of the universe, [which] originated in the 17th century, [we have] produced a technology that is unhealthy and inhuman; a technology in which the natural, organic habitat of complex human beings is replaced by a simplified, synthetic and prefabricated environment.[3]

This synthetic environment may partly be why many people suffer from sensory overload. It is happening to more of us than ever, especially with increasing international travel, transplantation of war-torn or disaster-ravaged populations, and information obtained in isolation via mechanisms like television and the internet. We easily become shell-shocked with information, which appears to make people either over-excited or dull and listless. Too much activity is exhausting, particularly in unnatural environments. Nowadays no one is immune to the world's intensely expanding population or the environmental crises caused by its inevitable over-consumption. Capra's decades-old observation still stands today, that the 'business world makes us believe that huge industries producing pet foods and cosmetics are a sign of our high standards of living'.

With the strains of living in an increasingly crowded, technology- and information-heavy world, it often seems that societal and ethical structures are collapsing around us alongside the environmental degradation we are causing. This is partly due to new scientific and technological developments. Whether these will be for good or ill depends on us, the people down here on the ground.

That is cause for optimism. Once we awaken to what is being done to us 'for our own good' – especially if the wheels of power spin out of control due to environmental disasters or economic meltdown – we will be forced to become aware of what we are capable of doing for ourselves.

Organizing forces working for a healthier world

Many grass-roots groups with a sense of our interconnections are funded by forward-thinking visionaries who understand how important it is to involve as many people as possible in counteracting global environmental problems, growing populations and shrinking resources. We need to create ways to funnel people into the kinds of organizations they wish to support, just as much as we need to channel funds towards groups that are actually doing something to improve the world.

Many organizations are not very helpful to enquirers. Laypeople quickly discover that they need qualifications and contacts even to begin to take part in the great works such organizations purport to be engaged in. That means a lot of positive energy is wasted. One useful thing such organizations could do is to find ways to train and channel into employment those inspired people who lack experience or credentials.

Groups and individuals are attempting to change the structure of our world on a grass-roots level, while some scientists and engineers are sidestepping industries and governments to directly introduce inventions to the public. An example is the electric town car, the G Whiz. Greater caution is being exercised in the area of patents, a fee for which must be paid annually by inventors – otherwise the patent for the invention may be bought by someone else. Often inventors cannot afford to pay for patents and corporations buy them to stamp out innovative competition in order to protect their less ecologically friendly systems.

The Indian activist, ecologist and physicist Vandana Shiva says that patents are a replay of the colonialization process of 500 years ago. Columbus and other adventurers carried 'letters patent' with them from their own governments. With these, they claimed as their property any territory they found that was not already ruled by European princes. In the same way, today's patents give corporations the chance to claim ownership of knowledge as well as plants, seeds and medicines not owned by other corporations.

The patenting of seeds and plants Shiva deems 'biopiracy'. One example is basmati rice. Grown in India for centuries, it is now being treated as a new invention by the company that bought its patent. Even the bark of the neem tree, which Indians have used for millennia as a medicine, pesticide, disinfectant and skin cream, was patented by the chemical company Grace.

Pharmaceutical and chemical-producing giants are taking out patents on natural substances that should be free to everyone. In India, allopathic medicine is promoted above its traditional Ayurvedic medicines, many of which are based on herbs and spices available to countryfolk, which they use as food. The old piracy we call colonization took over only land. Now piracy takes over life itself, Shiva says.

In 2004 at the Oxford Union, she joked that a plaque on the wall stated that the building was kept in good condition by a Japanese trading company. Behind her hung a curtain with a gaping hole in it: 'a perfect picture of why corporations should not be running our world'. They are not here, down on the ground, and they can't see the holes.

Shiva noted that some Indian farmers are now committing suicide because genetically modified seeds they have been sold by a large US corporation often do not grow. They say this is a curse from their gods, whom they think are indicating they have done something wrong. They *have* done something wrong, Shiva said, but they are not responsible for that wrong. Companies forcing them to use such seeds are the wrongdoers. Attempting to control the production and sale of food – especially by farmers who grow it by the sweat of their brow, on land they live upon – is wrong.

Shiva mentioned that the corporation has been advertising itself in India by using traditional imagery from Indian folklore and religion. This makes the uneducated believe it is a godly organization that is doing good for them. A great part of its advertising campaign has been about putting vitamin A in rice, but a natural rice already grows in India that is extremely high in that vitamin. Besides, every Indian housewife knows you do not eat rice for vitamin A, so the whole exercise has been pointless.

Shiva noted that India's people are being 'pushed' to speed up, with foreign corporations using people there as cheap labour. Indians do not refuse such work, because they cannot pass up good pay. However, roads are being built where giant, ancient trees once stood, and rivers are being re-routed according to the whims of corporate officials. Even the country's once sacred white cows are being slaughtered and sold to foreign countries to raise India's meat-production levels. India's sacred heart is being eroded, as is her culture, Shiva said. The same thing is happening all over the world today. India is not alone.

Ensuring our humanity endures

What can be done about all of this? How can it be made more obvious that we are functioning in outmoded structural models in business and government? It may be a slow process, but today we are seeing the beginning of a movement that could one day push movers and shakers to act according to people's true needs.

We can start by learning what is happening in science and taking back the power wrested from us by large businesses run by unaccountable individuals. We can make sure our countries' laws make leaders responsible to humanity, not just to big business, so that the ordinary kindnesses that help us all get along are not made irrelevant by those who want power over others. We are capable of radically changing our lifestyles and can build new social structures on a healthier, more nature-based ethic.

We do not have to follow the notion of Descartes – that mind is separate from body, both of which operate mechanically. This notion upon which science and the industrial and technological revolutions were based is now obsolete. Fledgling movements leading away from a Cartesian worldview include small free newspapers like England's *Positive News*, which has expanded into the US and is slowly stretching its international network to operate as an information tool for new environmental initiatives and activities that have an impact upon society's developmental direction. It depends for its survival on donations, volunteers, advertising and subscriptions. Similar ventures could be the start of a grassroots movement that might eventually become more influential than governments.

Much depends on whether we allow leaders to gain and keep control of communications systems, especially our international media. A new battle is developing over internet censorship and control. The first country to prosecute an internet blogger was Iran, in 2005. Already Google and Yahoo have bowed to demands made upon them by China – for instance, to block all computer searches in China for words like 'democracy' and 'freedom'. Small book publishers are being absorbed by larger publishers, sometimes in different countries. Newspapers generally report what their shareholders and owners tell them to report. It is interesting to international travellers how differently the same news is reported in different places.

Information should circulate as freely as the blood does in our bodies. When it doesn't, stagnation and sickness in the form of misunderstanding and war develop in the body of the world.

The world's circulatory system

Global pollution continues because its solutions are often held up by special interest groups. We can easily see the effects of our actions through observing the way pollution circulates within our planet. Industrial pollutants leach into the water, air and soil, transferring to insects and animals.

Too many bacteria cause sickness in the body and, in a sense, we humans are bacteria on the body of the Earth. The world will try to correct any imbalance in itself just as the body does, and we are beginning to experience the effects of our polluting activities through the appearance of new pestilences and the occurrence of increasingly powerful 'weather events'.

Native Indonesian islanders followed animals as they moved inland away from the tsunami of 2005. As a result, few were killed by it. Just before it struck, eyewitnesses claimed that elephants screamed and ran for higher ground, dogs refused to go outdoors, flamingos abandoned their low-lying breeding areas and zoo animals rushed into their shelters and couldn't be enticed to come back out.

The reports of Sri Lanka's elephants fleeing to higher ground didn't surprise Joyce Poole, who has worked with elephants in Kenya for 25 years and is director of the Savannah Elephant Vocalization Project (of Norway). Her research indicates that elephants could easily feel vibrations from the tsunami and earthquakes. This has been registered in seismic as well as acoustic arenas. She commented, 'I have been with elephants during two small tremors, and on both occasions the elephants ran in alarm several seconds before I felt the tremor'.

According to Alan Rabinowitz, director for science and exploration at New York City's Wildlife Conservation Society, earthquakes bring vibrational changes on land and in water while storms cause electromagnetic changes in the atmosphere. Some animals have acute senses of hearing and smell that allow them to determine something coming towards them long before humans know that something is there.

When weather patterns alter, so do food-growth, animal, fish and bird migratory patterns. Birds are said to 'orientate themselves to the compass points using the position of the Sun during the day and the stars at night. They can also sense magnetic north' and 'use other clues such as visual layout of the land, smell (of the sea), sound (waves on shores, winds through mountain passes)'.[4]

Normally pollution acts initially upon the senses of sight, smell, taste, hearing and touch, affecting emotions and therefore overall behaviour. Later, higher concentrations of pollutants alter one's perspective and mental processes and finally the physical body. Visible physical mutations usually occur only in second and subsequent generations, but for that to happen in a living organism, a change within the chemical and physical make-up of previous generations must have already occurred, even if those mutations do not show outwardly.

Patterns in nature may change for no obvious reason. Dowsers claim that when birds fly in discernable patterns for no reason that we can ascertain, they are responding to energy, not only to wind currents. Their annual migrations are affected by climate, temperature changes and ocean currents, as well as food supply. Habitat destruction may disturb them also, as they have certain stopping places along routes engrained in their memories. Losing these resting places hinders their ability to refuel. Forms of destruction that affect them include wetland drainage, forest cutting and pollution of the sea, water and air.

> Migrating birds are also distracted and killed by lit-up skyscrapers, lighthouses and other unnatural man-made formations that mislead them.[5]

Butterflies, locusts and other insects migrate according to weather and crop changes. Fish, animals and nomads have also migrated since time immemorial. Today global warming, pollution, over-consumption of natural resources and harmful agribusiness practices are affecting these migratory patterns.

Wind and rain have their own patterns, allowing meteorologists to make predictions about the weather. Seismologists watch the slow shifting of the Earth's crust and can often tell when a volcano is going to erupt because of patterns observed in exploding volcanoes of the past. Water currents flow in certain ways that we can chart. All of this is a kind of circulatory system in and around the Earth. The naturalist Lyall Watson says that, without the wind, most of the Earth would be dead, and certainly uninhabitable. Tropical areas would grow unbearably hot while the rest of the planet would freeze. Nothing could live anywhere but near moisture, which would probably only be near the oceans and the edges of the large continents along a narrow temperate belt. All the rest would be desert. The wind brings the Earth to life.

> Winds provide the circulatory and nervous systems of the planet, sharing out energy and information, distributing both warmth and awareness, making something out of nothing. ... We are the fruits of the wind – and have been seeded, irrigated and cultivated by its craft.[6]

Some Indian tribes call the Amazon rainforest 'the Earth's lungs'. To their minds, their forest breathes in and out the world's winds. Since we are part of the Earth, it seems logical that we must also have our part to play in the invisible circulatory system of this planet. Perhaps we need to find out what that role is, in order to be more effective in our attempts to right the balance that we have upset. But how?

Humans' role: rituals and rites

Perhaps answers may be found in the rituals of pre-industrialized tribes and societies. The Aborigines of Australia uphold spiritual practices involving travelling along 'invisible roads'. It once was normal to 'go on walkabout' as part of a coming-of-age ritual. American Indian tribes had their young men spend time alone in the wilderness for a few days, where they would meet the animal guardian spirit who would protect and work with them in life and in battle. They would perform seasonal ceremonies, engage in group pattern dancing (very like the dances of Peruvian Indians and Tibetans) and take part in sweat lodge rituals for healing and problem-solving. The rhythms of the day, the year and time of a person's life were all accommodated in these rituals. Like other pre-industrialized peoples, solitary and group rituals would take place at specially protected sites the Indians considered sacred. Battles did not happen in sacred places.

Evidence of similar rituals may be found in ancient stone circles and monuments scattered all over Britain and Ireland. Newgrange, Knowth, Dowth and the Hill of Tara in County Meath, Loughcrew and the Hill of Uisneach in County Westmeath, and Carrow-more in County Sligo are some of Ireland's better-known sacred sites, while Stonehenge and Avebury in Wiltshire, Boscawen-Un in Cornwall, and Callanish in the Outer Hebrides are some of Britain's.

Sacred sites are strategically placed all over the world. Perhaps some kind of link exists between them? The evidence for this possibility may be found in the networking rituals that folklorists have observed in certain countries. Ireland had a ritual on the eve of Beltane (1st May) in which a bonfire was lit on the Hill of Uisneach. In response, people on surrounding hills would also light a fire. This carried on from hilltop to hilltop, each bonfire figuratively lighting other fires, until the whole of the island was covered in golden burning eyelets. Then, from each hilltop fire, every householder in its surrounding community took a burning torch and lit their home hearth fires with it on May Day. Having part of this fire in their own homes would bring good health and safety to their animals, crops, and families.

They had no problem with seeing how one thing or event was related to another. For them, such connections were obvious. This fire ritual was a symbolic and literal linking up of a group mind and country, a ritual that made people feel part of something bigger than themselves. People from outside one's own tribe or village were therefore to be trusted to some degree, because they had the same beliefs and ways of life – evidence for which was their taking part in the same ritual.

Many initiatives in modern Britain have created their own rituals to encourage cohesiveness and instil structure in their new communities. While initially artificial, because they were created intentionally without natural evolution over a long period of time, some have proven to work well, so long as changes are periodically incorporated to go along with community members' views.

Invisible interconnections in a community

I visited the Findhorn Community near Forres in faraway northern Scotland to find out what ecovillages were and how to create an environmentally sustainable way of life. With frequent planes from the neighbouring British Royal Air Force base at Kinloss searing the wintry clouds just over our heads, I couldn't help feeling a sense of urgency about my task.

'Sustainable' meant using available local materials, and cleaning, rather than polluting, our environment, while keeping most of the comfortable aspects of 21st-century living. The idea was to recreate the good habits of our pre-industrialized ancestors. Far from Findhorn's New Age reputation – based upon its originators' belief that they were working with elemental spirits to grow vegetables, which grew extremely large in uncompromising coastal sand, and which gained them fame in the 1970s – this was a nuts-and-bolts approach to showing people how to survive with shrinking resources.

Findhorn's ecovillage course was carefully planned so that participants would begin to talk to each other about the profound issues that disturb and affect us all. We were part of a well disguised experiment in which we ourselves were its subjects. Its objective seemed to be to draw out our latent and submerged ideas so that we would pool them and begin to seek answers to the problems of our time. It became quite exciting as we began to realize that we had the power to garden our ideas just as we have the ability to remove weeds and plant seeds in the earth.

Gradually I began to understand the reasoning behind 'circle dancing', one of Findhorn's signatures, and playing games associated more with the children's nursery than with ordinary normal adults. Such jostlings wake up modern city-stiffened psyches to other perspectives, other ways of being with people. They also made us acutely aware of each other.

Group dances, music and games were used ritually in pre-industrialized communities until they started dying out in the 20th century. This kind of play created a cohesive glue for communities. It brought people closer together and ensured that they got to know each other. At Findhorn, through playing for no purpose but that of play, participants began to look at those with whom they were playing. By looking out from oneself, one begins to see who other people are beneath the surface reserve most of us hide behind.

Paramount in our modern everyday lives is the fear of losing or not getting things we need because of other people. When we overcome such fears and learn to reverse the competitive pressures put upon us, we start to work *with* instead of against one another. That week at Findhorn, we experienced work as fun because of our relationships, our conversations, our common humanity and a growing sense of having a special purpose in life. This secret may well be the way humanity will discover how to heal our world.

Findhorn is an active experiment that is constantly changing. My brief spell there made me see that what each individual does with what he has and knows really does matter in terms of his surrounding community. We are part of a pattern that we can observe, possibly uniquely among living creatures on this planet, while we are in it.

New quantum physics experiments are beginning to prove that a sort of mutuality exists between every material object. On minuscule, invisible levels we seem to influence and be influenced by our surroundings in ways that today's physicists are only beginning to glimpse.

Since the 1970s, Findhorn has attracted an international crowd of people who consciously experiment with societal, economic and agricultural structures they have grown to question, their aim being to create a lifestyle that is sustainable ecologically and satisfying spiritually. Now that Findhorn has reached maturity, having been started by three visionaries in 1962 – Peter and Eileen Caddy, with Dorothy Maclean – it has become apparent that autonomy and privacy need not be completely sacrificed in a community, that autonomy and privacy are part of what allows goodwill to blossom in a place where everyone knows everyone else. At the same time, the movement of new faces and ideas through the community is essential for its strength.

Experimentation is the key to Findhorn's success. This is something scientists would appreciate. Its main focus is as a non-denominational spiritual community, but if someone is upset, then everyone comes together to consider and address the problem. Anyone is free to come up with solutions, which everyone considers. Eventually a consensus is reached and a solution chosen to be applied to the problem. For instance, when those working in one department of the community are unhappy about their manager, they may replace him or her with one of their number, while the manager returns to being an ordinary working member of the department or goes elsewhere to a different job. This truly democratic way of operating its business efforts seems to work at Findhorn, although the same kinds of problems arise in communal settings as in other social environments. Power-plays occur there just as they do everywhere else.

However, Findhorn's seasoned leaders are wise to this aspect of

human behaviour and constantly work out new ways of counter-
ing the negative effects of the many-headed hydra of egotism, in
all its infinite expressions. The fact that Findhorn survives as one
of the Western world's oldest intentional spiritual communities,
despite having a variety of religious practitioners working together
in it, proves that some extra element is present.

I tried to find out what that element was, but I didn't stay long
enough to identify it. Could it be that the community's fluidity is
the reason for its outer stability? Or is its non-denominational
spiritual orientation the glue that holds it together? A longtime
Findhorn worker who moved there from New York City, Eva Ward,
says, 'The spirituality we practise has no name – it is all-inclusive.
The values of every major religion (and none!) are actually practised in everyday life here.'

Before and after every day's work activity, in which every community member must take part unless sick or excused, workers
engage in a ritual in which those involved recollect themselves and
why they are doing what they are doing. The focus is always on
what they consider to be a noble or positive action, and their own
personal ultimate aim or reason for doing the activity. Merely
doing a job because you have to survive is not good enough at
Findhorn. People go there because they choose to, and are constantly reminded of that fact. After the job is finished, workers
consciously allow themselves to feel thankful for what they have
accomplished and speak of their gratitude to the forces that have
allowed them to accomplish it. This ritual may be an additional
element in Findhorn's success.

Before meals in the common dining room, Findhorn members
even thank the creative forces (including gardeners and cooks)
that have produced the food, perhaps noting that the vegetables
have grown from seeds once planted by someone to whom they
should also be thankful. Every action is undertaken with gratitude
and some higher purpose in mind – essentially that of healing and
caring for our planet and those living here. In this kind of atmosphere, destructive human behaviours are somehow becalmed.
After all, when you feel comfortable, warm and well-fed, and

those around you are grateful for what you are doing and acknowledge your contribution to their happiness, what is there to be upset
about?

It may be possible to work with the dynamics of our planet and
our minds in some new way that will alleviate many of our social,
environmental and economic problems. Finding out how, by consciously investigating experimental communities like Findhorn,
and by observing how they continue operating relatively peacefully, may be useful in our quest to create more satisfactory and
sustainable ways of life in the 21st century.

3

THE INNER UNIVERSE OF THE HUMAN BEING: MIND SCIENCE

Reality isn't what it used to be.

DEAN RADIN, *ENTANGLED MINDS: EXTRASENSORY EXPERIENCES IN A QUANTUM REALITY*, 2006

WHAT IS CONSCIOUSNESS? According to the scientific rationalist, it is sensory and emotional experience. Yet we have vivid visual and emotional experiences when we sleep. The rationalist gets round this by further defining consciousness as a state of 'aroused wakefulness'.

Neuroscientists say that a network of centres in the brain controls wakefulness. Stimulation of the reticular formation – which is near the top of the brain stem at the base of the brain – increases wakefulness. Coma occurs when this reticular formation is destroyed. Just beneath the reticular formation are the *locus coeruleus* and the *pons* areas of the brain stem. These modulate the activity of the reticular formation and what is just beneath them, the Raphe nucleus. Lesions on this part of the brain stem can cause insomnia.

Is there more than one type of wakefulness? Certain activities performed by the body, speech and mind seem to induce different types of consciousness, as do different stimuli.

Long before the advent of modern neuroscience, 'spiritual' researchers all over the world spent centuries analysing and experimenting with various states of consciousness without recourse to surgical intervention. Consequently, these researchers view human consciousness altogether differently.

In Tibetan Buddhist teachings, the nature of consciousness is termed *dharmakaya*. It is a level of existence without form – with which our essence (termed *buddha mind*) is unified. It is defined and experienced as emptiness, or *shūnyatā*, and viewed as the 'fundamental truth' – the foundation and background of everything. That is, whatever arises, or appears to arise, in space has no concrete form or substance. In Zen Buddhism, consciousness is defined as the essence of all things, the unified existence that lies beyond all concepts. This is consciousness on a universal level, which we are all part of. It is also our essence. It is a place of repose as well as the source of all action or activity. It is the 'background' of thoughts, the place from which they arise.

According to this view, consciousness is the space *between* things – their relationship – yet without objects that are in relationship with each other. No objects actually exist, if you define an object as something that stays the same and does not change, because all things are moving and changing in every moment. Nothing is still or permanent, so how can we say that any one thing actually exists? Such is the logic of this approach.

In Hindu religions, existence is often described in a more poetic manner:

> At the dawning of the day, [all objects stream forth from the Unmanifest]. When evening falls, they are dissolved into It again. The same multitude of beings, which have lived on Earth so often, all are dissolved as the night of the universe approaches, to issue forth anew when morning breaks. Thus it is ordained.[1]

Consciousness is the 'unmanifest' background of things – pure perception, plain and simple. The East's 'science of the mind' may be conceived as philosophy or even a form of psychology, but it is also something more. It actually works to change the processes of the mind.

Meditation and brain wave technology

Meditation has been proven by scientists to act upon the electrical wave patterns the brain produces. The late Hindu guru Maharishi Mahesh Yogi made much of this in the 1960s and 70s, bringing these brain states to the attention of the media while promoting his Transcendental Meditation technique. Since then, Buddhists have moved to the forefront of such study, assisting scientists who have gone on to develop more precise testing methods.

One technology that has been around for a long time is EEG (electroencephalography) technology. With that, nodes are affixed to the surface of the scalp to measure the brain's electrical activity or wave pattern emanations. A pattern is conveyed via the EEG machine, showing frequency signs of four states, described below. Most frequencies emitted are below 30Hz.

State	Frequency range	State of mind
Delta	0.5–4.0Hz	Deep sleep
Theta	4.0–8.0Hz	Drowsiness (also first stage of sleep)
Alpha	8.0–14Hz	Relaxed but alert
Beta	14–30Hz	Highly alert and focused

All of these frequencies operate constantly in the brain, but only one is paramount at a particular time. The dominant frequency registers on an EEG machine. That is the level at which your brain is said to be functioning. If the amplitude of the Beta range of frequencies is highest, then your brain is said to be in the Beta stage, which means you are highly alert and focused. This is usually the state in which your brain operates during the day while you are working.

Learning is enhanced in the Theta state (4–7Hz) – where children dwell for longer periods than adults. Some claim that spending half an hour a day in the Theta state can replace up to four hours of sleep. New meditators often fall into the Theta level, whose main characteristic is drowsiness, something meditation teachers encourage them to overcome. Experienced meditators spend more time in or on the borderlines of Beta and Alpha frequencies. Good frequencies for meditation are said to occur in the Alpha range. A brain operating at this level is better able to absorb information. It is a frequency where subliminal messages are easily received.

The brain can be *entrained* to move from one frequency to another by applying an external electrical stimulus to it. The starting frequency of such a stimulus should be as close to your current brain state as possible. When your brain shifts to another level in response to the applied stimulus (called *entrainment*), you feel yourself relaxing.

The brain is most easily stimulated by sound, although visual stimuli also affect it. Often both sound (at auditory frequencies lower than our ears can hear) and visual stimuli are used at the same time to cause brain frequency changes.

One way of making this happen is to listen to different frequencies over headphones. If your right ear hears a frequency that is 10Hz different from the one heard by your left ear, the two frequencies do not mix until they are in your brain. Your brain hears this 10Hz of difference. This is called a *binaural* beat. Binaural beat frequencies are very helpful for brain entrainment, as long as tones below 1000Hz are used. However, just listening to binaural beats does not always alter your state of consciousness. To do this, you must relax and focus your attention on them. Some people use this technique to help them change their brain frequencies to particular desired states, or as an aid to meditation. The brain can learn to reproduce desired brainwave states at will when meditation is practised alongside machine-induced brainwave entrainment. Eventually the machine becomes unnecessary, once the brain learns what to do.

Meditation without machines

Meditators working without machines traditionally take several years to learn techniques that alter their brainwaves. Learning to meditate requires time and effort, so meditation teachers tend to focus first on creating positive mental habits in their students by encouraging repetitive actions which can be valuable in training the mind. They do not consider the mind to be merely the brain, but to also encompass the heart and body. By habitually reproducing specific thoughts and actions and following a well established protocol of mental training, the mind may eventually overcome its ordinary, unthinking responses to stimuli, its computer-like behaviour. At that point, it is no longer at the mercy of subconscious thoughts, emotions, pain or external stimuli, and awakens into a more conscious state. Practised correctly, certain meditation activities enable the mind and emotions to become more active or relaxed.

Like an elastic band, thoughts and emotions too often return to habitual negative states. British author Colin Wilson notes that 'intelligent people can usually cure themselves of a tendency to negativity'. The mind's power to focus upon detail can cause 'a flood of emotional negation', he says, suggesting that the mind needs to remain aware of other times and places in order to maintain good health. In his book *The Occult* he calls this 'Faculty X' – presumably an awareness of a larger universe and a wider consciousness than that of oneself alone. As a young man, Wilson observed that if he didn't allow his mind to collapse into a state of tiredness or boredom, everything went well for him. In *Dreaming to Some Purpose: An Autobiography*, our major problem, he said, 'is a tendency to allow our energies to leak. And as soon as they leak, consciousness is dimmed.' Then we may have accidents, lose control of situations or make mistakes.

He says that extreme emotions like jealousy or falling in love can produce a mild form of insanity. He writes of waking up in this condition every day while a teenager, apart from certain spring mornings when he experienced a sense of revelation, usually after contemplating experiences of heightened states of awareness. Most people, he says, brood too much on their ills, worries and resentments, which makes their vision shrink. While sitting listlessly in a room, he might feel stuck in a narrow reality, but when rain patters on the window, he feels a sudden delight at being reminded of the existence of another reality 'out there'.

Humans' habit of passivity is more dangerous than cigarette smoking or drugs, Wilson believes, because it produces an inner condition of boredom and stagnation that makes us long for crisis and excitement. He thinks this explains the steady rise in the crime rate, and the increasingly violent and motiveless nature of crimes. Were we to recognize that we have within us the power of an atom bomb, we wouldn't allow ourselves to remain in such a bored 'mono-conscious' state. However, we choose to suffer from this 'spiritual head cold' for a reason.

> A man who wants to think locks himself into a quiet room, and perhaps closes all the windows. [It] allows him to concentrate, but it cuts out the fresh air and the sound of the birds.[2]

Using positive mental powers

To illustrate what we are capable of, Wilson describes how a heart-broken lady went to the Irish playwright George Bernard Shaw for help. Shaw allowed a telepathic link to grow between them while they were walking together silently, so that she heard a disembodied voice speak to her comfortingly. By allowing his intuition to operate, Shaw was using 'the authentic magical method', defined as using one's powers for the expansion of the human faculties beyond the merely personal – the only correct use of occult powers, Wilson suggests. These are normal powers we all have, which we have merely neglected in our attempt to develop rational ones.

The problem of knowing how to use our intuitive powers correctly is an issue indirectly addressed by religion. The general religious view seems to be that the most profound thing people can do is to forget about individual personal desires and think only of others. Zen Buddhist Katagiri Roshi observes:

> *I have been reading your Descartes.*
> *Very interesting. 'I think, therefore I am.'*
> *He forgot to mention the other part.*
> *I'm sure he knew, he just forgot:*
> *I think, therefore I'm not.*

To Katagiri's Buddhist mind, while one is thinking, only thoughts exist. The self does not. His subtext is that scientists following Descartes' ideas are egocentric and therefore not really thinking properly at all. Longtime meditators discover it is possible to think without reference to themselves. This is helpful when selfless action is required.

Connections: East and West, right and left brain

The idea that one should stop thinking thoughts that are not useful has come to the West from Eastern teachers such as Tibetan lamas and Krishnamurti. The latter spent most of his life in England after being moved from India as a child by the Theosophists Charles Leadbeater and Annie Besant, to become 'the new world teacher' – a notion he rejected upon reaching adulthood. In lectures he often repeated the idea that the mind was much more than the concepts it held. For Krishnamurti, consciousness was perception, clear sight, experiencing a still and peaceful mind without emotional disturbance.

Near the end of the 19th century, a potent mix of Hindu, Buddhist, Jewish Kabbalist, Platonic and esoteric Christian thought, alongside the occult and scientific ideas of the time, was espoused by the Russian adventuress Helena Petrovna Blavatsky. She claimed to have travelled to Lhasa, the capital of Tibet and the Dalai Lama's official seat, during a period when foreigners were not allowed into the country. In Tibet, Blavatsky said she was contacted by 'secret masters' or 'adepts' (possibly Tibetan lamas, although allegedly one of them was Count Saint-Germain) who gave her information to send into the world. She presented this as a science, trying to make it convincing to Westerners, through her magnum opus, *The Secret Doctrine*, published in 1888. It was the basis for what she termed 'Theosophy' (meaning 'wisdom of the gods' or 'divine wisdom').

During the early 20th century, Theosophy influenced many respected artists, such as the Anglo-Irish poet Yeats, who wrote of conversing with a Hindu guru. Today's New Age movement arose from groups like the Theosophists, the Spiritualists and the Hermetic Order of the Golden Dawn, a group of esotericists of which Yeats was a prominent member.

Perhaps integration, like that of Eastern ideas in the West and Western ideas in the East, is what must happen to our consciousness, if we are to experience and create greater balance in ourselves and our world. Today the rational, left side of our brains overworks by asking too many questions of its sensory input. Ideally, the intuitive right side should function in a balanced way with the rational left.

> [Both] literature and mythology associate the right hand (the brain's left hemisphere) with rational, male and assertive characteristics, and the left hand (right hemisphere) with mystical, female and receptive characteristics. [The] advent of 'science' marks the beginning of the ascent of left hemispheric thinking into the dominant mode of western cognition.[3]

The creative mind

This has not gone unnoticed by an army of writers and scientists who have expressed their sense that humanity has been moving in the wrong direction. J R R Tolkien wrote about it in *The Hobbit* and his *Lord of the Rings* trilogy, while Aldous Huxley and George Orwell approached the same subject with their books *Brave New World*, *1984* and *Animal Farm*. People living close to the land were losing their Faculty X consciousness and their sense of power. The Irish visionary George Russell (Æ) intuited this in a poem he wrote about his countrymen called 'Exiles':

> *The gods have taken alien shapes upon them*
> *Wild peasants driving swine*
> *In a strange country. Through the swarthy faces*
> *The starry faces shine.*
> *Under grey tattered skies they strain and reel there:*
> *Yet cannot all disguise*

The majesty of fallen gods, the beauty,
The fire beneath their eyes.
They huddle at night within low clay-built cabins;
And, to themselves unknown,
They carry with them diadem and sceptre
And move from throne to throne.

A sense of lost nobility pervades our increasingly technological world. We also seem to have lost a healthy connection with nature. How do we get them back? Nature seemed to send the American poet Walt Whitman, a nurse during the American Civil War, into a heightened state of awareness. It is as if he experienced no separation between himself and what was outside him:

I celebrate myself, and sing myself,
And what I assume you shall assume,
For every atom belonging to me as good belongs to you.
I loafe and invite my soul,
I lean and loafe at my ease observing a spear of summer grass.
… A child said 'What is the grass?' fetching it to me with full hands,
How could I answer the child? I do not know what it is any more
    than he …
Or I guess the grass is itself a child, the produced babe of the
    vegetation.[4]

The poet is describing the kind of experience that physicists sometimes speak of having after contemplating the universe. It is similar to that felt by the few people who have seen our planet from outer space. Gary Zukav suggests our ability to have this type of experience has not atrophied but our skill in 'listening' to it has been dulled by neglect.

The next time you are awed by something, let the feeling flow freely through you and do not try to 'understand' it. You will find that you do understand, but in a way that you will not be able to put into words. You are perceiving intuitively through your right hemisphere.

The trouble is, we underestimate the power of our minds. The mind and heart are indivisible. They affect our bodily health as well as the people and the world around us. Worryingly, some people have a mind-body split, a condition that deadens both fear and enjoyment of life. It is a type of illness that has been encouraged by the hot-housing of intellectuals in academic environments and the demands of our economically driven business climate. The state of mind that we ordinarily adopt quite directly affects our surroundings and what happens to us. Thinking habitually about harming others will eventually lead to destructive behaviour, just as thinking of doing good things encourages creativity and health. A thought is like any other force. Human beings themselves act as forces.

Physicists are beginning to accommodate such ideas in their theories. It is no longer unusual for group meditation or 'thought experiments' to be taken seriously in scientific studies. In fact, long-term extrasensory perception (ESP) testing has already been funded by the governments of the US, Russia, China and Czechoslovakia.

Remote viewing

Psychic 'remote viewers' (clairvoyants) are known to have been used by the Russian and American governments in their spying activities. The CIA conducted a 24-year investigation of the potential use of extrasensory perception through the American Institutes for Research (AIR). Such a connection like this between governments and people with superpowers might be of some concern to most of us, but physicist Hal Puthoff, who set up the US government's first remote viewing programme in association with AIR, told me it didn't worry him. He had found that people develop greater understanding and compassion as a side effect of remote viewing.

That was the case with David Morehouse. After an injury in the 1980s he was shifted from the US Army to a government remote viewing spy programme after showing signs of psychic powers.

He believes that humanity is now undergoing a transformation. At a lecture he gave in London in April 2005, he said discovering his psychic ability was like suddenly having a new thumb. It was a difficult adjustment for him, but it was his calling and he had to follow it. 'Each of us must find our calling', he said. How do you find out what that is? You stand outside others' judgements, opinions, evaluations and assessments of you, and trust yourself. If you are asked to do something that doesn't honour what you feel is your 'path', stand aside and follow another track. 'You don't have to keep grinding away on one path if it doesn't suit you', he said. 'What's the story of your life and how are you going to write it?'

If you try to work with the gifts you have been given, you will be given the knowledge you need to work with them. You will be part of the positive transformation that humanity is undergoing. Morehouse defines remote viewing as 'seeing distant' in space and time. He describes it as a learned ability to detect wave-form data in one dimension of time and three dimensions of space. The brain reads this data and transforms it into the three-D thought-form called language. Remote viewers stand outside our three-dimensional world. He has seen that humanity stands on the brink of a destructive phase that could expand or contract in the coming decades. He says:

> Frequencies of fear and hatred dominate the human condition now, so don't involve yourself in the framework of fear and upset. If you do so, you feed that frequency of fear.

Morehouse quoted the author Istak Benav, who said in his book *Stalking the Wild Pendulum* that the Earth carries a negative ionic charge and the ionosphere a positive charge. Together they create an electrical charge storage capacitor around this planet. Morehouse likens this capacitor to jello and human beings to raisins in the jello. When the jello is vibrated, you can't avoid vibrating the raisins in it. Only, we are raisins that can move and think. We can do things that uplift us, and can stop others from limiting our capacity to do them.

When the dominant frequency in the electrostatic field around you is that of fear and hatred, don't allow yourself to resonate with it, he cautions. Catch yourself when you're falling into that frequency and consciously reverse the negative feelings and thoughts you're having. He says there are enclaves of negativity all over this planet. You can't beat them. You have to create alternatives and, if you do, you'll be part of the tide of creativity that is also happening. Quoting the physicist David McCallum, who said that 11 per cent of the world's population (around 700 million people) could cause a 'critical mass' surge of energy that can change the world for the better, he comments:

> Forgiveness must precede all things, but that requires us to give up the need to be right and to even the score with others. If we can do that, we will be able to give something positive back.[5]

The US government's first remote viewers included Morehouse and Joseph McMoneagle who trained at the same place as Morehouse, Israeli spoon-bender Uri Geller, and American artist Ingo Swann. The scientists who set up the first remote viewer training program at Stanford Research Institute (SRI) were the physicists Hal Puthoff and Russell Targ. The latter had been a pioneer in the development of the laser and worked for Lockheed Martin. Targ claims that the years he spent doing remote-viewing experiments in a dark room at SRI helped him to become more aware of his own 'interior landscape'. He learned that God does not have to be a matter of belief but may actually be experienced.

> I have sat in a darkened room with hundreds of remote viewers and shared their mental picture with them. It is a fact that people can experience a mind-to-mind connection with each other. Fifty years of published data from all over the world attest to this.

He described the experience as being like meditation – a kind of oceanic connection with all other living things. A quiet mind, he claimed, is the key for both psi and other experiences of the mystical domain. Remote viewers at SRI learned that time-space distance makes no difference to accuracy. Something that will happen tomorrow is no less viewable than something happening today. British physicist Dr Brian Josephson states:

The CIA's Stargate Project provided clear evidence that people can intermittently pick up with their minds images of distant objects such as military installations, sometimes with striking accuracy. The research arm of the project found that under controlled conditions the extent to which this ability exceeded chance guessing was statistically highly significant.[6]

The mind's powers

Not just remote viewing is being used by military agencies, but also remote *influencing*. The power of the mind could become a tremendous instrument for good, were it turned towards healing and regeneration rather than warfare and money-making. Some psychics claim to be able to sprout seeds, which could bring great benefit in times of famine. Others experience *telekinesis*, where things move around spontaneously without anyone's intervention or conscious involvement. Uri Geller claims to have both abilities and allowed himself to be tested by academics and researchers. He worked with the remote viewing programme he helped set up with Dr Puthoff and Ingo Swann, until about 30 years ago when someone asked him to kill a pig with his mind, to stop its heart in a laboratory. This was requested because the heart of a pig is the closest to a human being, he told me, with its horrific implications still in his eyes.

Nowadays he prefers to encourage the positive uses of 'mind power'. He maintains that he used it once in negotiating an agreement between the Palestinians and the Israeli equivalent of the Red Cross. 'I told them, come on guys, let's think positive, let's make this work, let's come to an amicable agreement', after bending a spoon for them to help them realize that they had the power to do what seemed impossible.

British author and filmmaker Jon Ronson claims that Geller, an ex-paratrooper for the Israeli Army, was re-drafted into the US remote viewing programme after 9/11, but Geller does not speak of this. However, he did hint at meeting American leaders, mentioning how he hoped to turn their minds towards ways of finding peace. Officially, Geller uses his 'mind power' to locate oil for money and to help the Red Cross and sick children in hospitals. He hopes to get millions of people worldwide to focus their wills at the same time on environmental healing and world peace, perhaps via satellite and television. He thinks this might turn around things now happening on our planet. Recently he has been in Israel, hosting a television programme searching for psychic showmen. Is its purpose to find young people who can be trained as remote viewers? Could it be that Geller hopes to train more people to do what he does? In 1973 he felt that 'unknown energies were being transferred to others' after so many people watching his television demonstrations also began bending metals. At that time he said:

> There is no question in my mind that the Earth is on the verge of discovering a whole new power [that] goes far beyond me. ... I am convinced that there are people here on Earth with incredible power, and many of them are not aware of it.

One Russian psychic who did know her psychokinetic powers and often demonstrated them physically by literally moving things with only the power of her mind was Nina Kulgarina. She was extensively tested during the Cold War for the last 20 years of her life. Known to move objects on a table without touching them, in 1970 she slowed, sped up and finally stopped a frog's heart that had been beating while floating in solution. Before attempting such things, Kulagina required some time to clear her mind. She knew she had achieved the focus needed the moment her vision blurred and she felt a sharp pain in her spine. Her heartbeat would become irregular, her blood sugar would rise and her endocrine system would show signs of disturbance – all reactions consistent with extreme stress. She would lose her sense of taste, suffer from pains in her arms and legs, feel dizzy and become uncoordinated. After her psychokinesis sessions, she usually felt exhausted. Once she was found to have almost no pulse and to have lost almost 4 lbs (1.8 kg) in half an hour. This was thought to be because her body matter was being converted into energy for her mental exertions.

Monitors of mental phenomena

These kinds of mental phenomena are monitored by the Cognitive Sciences Laboratory (CSL). Its stance is to assume that all such phenomena will eventually be understood within the context of physical science, so it downplays a more mystical approach. Scenes perceived clairvoyantly are described as targets transmitting information through space and time to a human receiver. The CSL also monitors and classifies parapsychological phenomena in particular descriptive terms, including that of 'applied research' – that is, research aiming to increase the effects of something.

Technologies arising from new material science developments and theoretical physics ideas are dovetailing with many organizations and universities now studying psi and the paranormal. Physicists can no longer tell the public that their scientific theories are based on concrete facts. Transpersonal psychology professor David Fontana says:

> In the world of microphysics, it [has] never proved possible to make a direct observation of subatomic entities. We simply infer their existence from circumstantial evidence (such as traces in a cloud chamber, produced when they interact with certain measuring devices).[7]

Could thoughts be the subatomic entities to which Professor Fontana refers? The eminent Oxford University zoologist Richard Dawkins in *Unweaving the Rainbow* describes how the American neurobiologist William Calvin believes that thoughts do not come from particular places in the brain. Rather, they behave like shifting patterns of activity over its surface or 'units which recruit neighbouring units into populations becoming the same thought'. These unit populations compete 'in Darwinian fashion with rival populations' that think other thoughts. 'We don't see these shifting patterns, but presumably we would if neurones lit up' when thoughts became active.

If thoughts do behave in this fashion, then it is no wonder that certain meditation practices seem to work. One practice is to collect a supply of black and white stones, then simply to note when negative and positive thoughts arise in your mind. When a negative thought arises, set down a black stone. When a positive thought comes, place a white stone in a different spot. Continue doing this until eventually you have two separate piles of stones. At the end of your first meditation, your pile of black stones is usually largest. But, over time, this usually changes. When you make your mind aware of what it is doing, it naturally changes its behaviour.

Teachers of meditation emphasize that you must actually do the practice for it to work. By meditating, somehow the 'habitual' mind is tricked into changing itself. This can be done without stones, of course, but they make obvious what is actually going on in the mind at the time it is happening.

Similarly, higher states of consciousness arise from other types of practices. However, the mind must be trained gradually before it is able to profit from doing them, just as one must study facts and mathematics in a steady progression before becoming a physicist. Sometimes perceptive states of mind arise spontaneously, as poets, scientists and other creative people experience, but it is said that the highest kind of awareness is inexpressible.

Invisible interconnections in telepathy and higher consciousness

The Hindu teacher Sri Ramana Maharshi (1879–1950) spent nearly his whole life sitting in silence on Arunachala Hill in Tiruvanna-malai, Southern India. With no interest in the life the rest of us enjoy or hate – a life that Maharshi saw as illusory – he is quoted as having said:

> [What] is called the 'world' is only thought. When the world dis-appears, [that is] when there is no thought, the mind experiences happiness; and when the world appears, it goes through misery. [Telepathy,] knowing past, present and future happenings, and clairvoyance do not constitute wisdom-insight.[8]

Maharshi implies here that telepathy and clairvoyance are a kind of technology of the mind. They are simply part of what happens in our ordinary material world.

In pre-Chinese Tibet, telepathy was seen as a useful technology of the mind, but not particularly significant. It was observed to happen all the time, occurring spontaneously between people. Those who were strong mentally and secure emotionally were more astute telepathic senders and receivers. Usually telepathy occurs more precisely and frequently between those who are in some way close for a long period, as between husband and wife, genetic twins, or teacher and student.

In *Magic and Mystery in Tibet,* Alexandra David-Neel wrote about a lama who conveyed a request to his servant telepathically. She described the servant as more like a disciple than a servant, which it turned out he was, since part of a student's discipline in Tibetan spiritual training is to help a lama. David-Neel, seated some way from the lama, was having trouble eating some dry roasted barley called *tsampa* that he had given her. So she whispered to her companion, asking him to buy curd for her from a nearby farm after the lama went away.

The lama appeared to have heard her but said nothing. He merely stared fixedly at his servant some distance away, who was bringing a horse to them. The servant suddenly stopped in his tracks and turned away to walk towards the farm. Later he returned with some curd, looking at the lama as if to say, 'Was that what you wanted? What am I to do with this curd?' To the unspoken question the lama answered with an affirmative nod and told the servant to give the curd to David-Neel.

Professor Arthur Ellison states that:

> Hindu philosophers believe that our observations through our awareness of the physical world lead to *maya* or illusion and not to reality – that things are not at all as they seem. The American psychologist Charles Tart calls this the 'consensus trance' which we nearly all share almost all the time.

Ellison, a British researcher into the paranormal, suggests that the practices of meditation are designed to awaken us to reality so that we are no longer entranced or 'in trance'. He adds that the founders of the world's great religions had paranormal experiences, which they interpreted in different ways. Meditators often experience heightened states of consciousness or super-sensitivity (extremely good hearing or 'night-sight', for instance), the ability to perform superhuman feats, and telepathy.

During the early 20th century, telepathy became synonymous with stage trickery. It recovered as the result of enthusiastic research by members of the Society for Psychical Research, especially after J B Rhine and his colleagues at Duke University in the US developed reliable ways of testing for it.

More recently, the British parapsychologist Guy Lyon Playfair underwent telepathy tests and discovered that images would arise in his mind of whatever picture someone he focused upon was seeing, as well as that person's thoughts about it. He had two clearly telepathic experiences on the same day that left him in no doubt that images could be transmitted between minds over long distances. In the first, he saw a 'dark animal standing on a rock and a blue background' when the picture being looked at by the telepathic sender was of a donkey being led past a large rock 'with a moon-like landscape in the distance'. But what really surprised Playfair was that, at the very minute that he announced he was seeing a desolate moon-like landscape, the telepathic sender in a different room wrote, 'rather like the surface of the Moon'.

In the second test, he saw a dark statue of Mao Tse Tung on a pedestal with a bright light shining behind it. His telepathic sender was looking at Blake's painting entitled *Glad Day*, in which an angel stands 'on a pedestal-like rock with a brilliant light behind it'.

Zukav noted that some physics theories suggest that telepathy occurs. In *Dancing Wu Li Masters*, 1979, he wrote, 'one of the implications of Bell's Theorem is that, at a deep and fundamental level, the "separate parts" of the universe are connected in an intimate and immediate way'. He suggests that *Bell's theorem*, indecipherable to the non-mathematician, opened the door to the 're-cognition' of the psychic aspect of our thinking by scientists, who until then had ignored it.

Physicists have observed that subatomic particles that are split and set far apart behave in exactly the same fashion when a stimulus is applied to only one of them. So how do they communicate? Physicists say that particles are not particles but waves, and yet at times they are also particles. Something invisible seems to connect them to each other. Their behaviour implies that telepathy happens, a notion that most scientists reject.

The British physicist Brian Josephson of Cavendish Labs at Cambridge University has come under fire for believing that telepathy is a real phenomenon. While a graduate student, Josephson studied superconductivity, and extended to superconductors the idea that electrons can 'tunnel' through an insulating layer between metals. He showed that the organized behaviour that makes such metals perfect conductors of electricity can extend across such insulating barriers, with a number of important consequences, such as the ability to detect very weak magnetic fields for medical purposes. This was termed the 'Josephson effect'. Experiments subsequently confirmed the truth of the Josephson effect on superconductors. For this, at the age of 33, he won half of the 1973 Nobel Prize for Physics.

This recognition enabled him to espouse less orthodox beliefs in subjects such as telepathy. In 2001, he noted how physicists had tried to explain nature's complexities with a single 'theory of everything', saying that quantum physics was the closest they had come to such a theory. Josephson said that after Max Planck tried to determine the exact amount of energy that hot bodies radiate, physicists began to describe our universe with mathematics that accommodated the concept of 'spooky interactions at a distance'. This led to inventions such as the laser and transistor.

Dr Josephson says that: 'Quantum theory is now being fruitfully combined with theories of information and computation. These developments may lead to an explanation of processes still not understood within conventional science, such as telepathy.'

Scientists, he says, keep quiet about their thoughts on such things when in scientific company, despite the fact that surveys show a considerable proportion believe that paranormal phenomena take place. Yet they do not apply their intelligence to the paranormal as they do to matters concerning the material universe.

Before winning the Nobel award, Josephson grew interested in the possible relevance of Eastern mysticism to scientific understanding. An avowed supporter of David Bohm's notion of 'implicate order', which Bohm defined as 'undivided wholeness in flowing movement', where entities such as atoms or subatomic particles are not seen as autonomous. This must have drawn him towards a more mystical approach to the universe. In 1978 he and V S Ramachandran organized an interdisciplinary symposium on consciousness in Cambridge and published the proceedings under the title 'Consciousness and the Physical World'. Josephson wrote that 'if scientists as a whole denounce an idea this should not necessarily be taken as proof that the said idea is absurd; rather, one should examine carefully the alleged grounds for such opinions and judge how well these stand up to detailed scrutiny'.

This is a refreshing attitude to encounter when so many neuro-scientists maintain that dreams and supernormal experiences are the results of no more than chemical changes in the brain and body. What is consciousness? Perhaps the only certainty is still Descartes' observation: 'I think, therefore I am'. However, it is still a matter for conjecture what that 'I' actually *is*.

Meditation

Perhaps meditators like Ramana Maharshi experience something on subatomic levels that scientists cannot yet comprehend. Some theoretical physicists say that waves of energy can turn into particles, which is how matter comes into existence. The notion that everything is illusory relates very well to this hypothesis. Nothing is separate from anything else when everything is in the form of waves of energy. 'This is that' and vice versa, a Vedantist would say.

Directing his questioners to their own 'true self', Maharshi recommended a form of self-enquiry starting with the question: 'Who am I?' Descriptions of 'non-duality' in the Vedas – the ancient religious teachings of India – seem close to modern physics. The Vedas state that no division exists between the Absolute or 'background' of everything, known as *Brahman*, and the individual's 'true Self' or *Atman*. Brahman is omniscient, all that exists – material and non-material – including all concepts – good, bad and indifferent. The individual self or ego is linked to this higher or background Self, which is Atman *and* Brahman at the same time – they are one ocean of consciousness. If individuals are part of that 'background', they are not separate from that background. Therefore whatever one does to others, one does to oneself.

Ramana Maharshi spent most of his life sitting still and silent in the experience and contemplation of that background. He is said to have had the power to affect people and the world, while silent and unmoving. He taught:

> Desirelessness is wisdom. The two are not different; they are the same. Desirelessness is refraining from driving the mind towards any object. Wisdom means the appearance of no object. In other words, not seeking what is other than the Self is detachment or desirelessness, [not] leaving the Self is wisdom.[9]

Perhaps we can express the qualities we wish to have – by simply contemplating them. Qualities are of course invisible. They are not like body cells or bacteria, visible if enough are present. Cells and bacteria capture visible light and in that way become visible. Micro-organisms are invisible to the naked eye, but become visible when viewed with a microscope. Things that are invisible to us affect matter, so perhaps human beings radiate qualities that act upon their material surroundings. Those qualities may be forces that our states of mind emit.

> A kind of fixed determination [shows in Westerners'] minds, which makes their movements and gestures stiff and awkward. [People in the East move] not from the conscious mind but from the unconscious [which makes them have] the natural spontaneous beauty of flowers and animals.

The English Benedictine monk Bede Griffiths noticed this in the 1980s. He thought that Indians were beginning to behave like Westerners – from the masculine half of the soul that is conscious and rational, which ignores the feminine unconscious, intuitive dimension. In *The Marriage of East and West* he writes:

> The future of the world depends on the 'marriage' of these two minds [but] often the impact of the West on the East is that of a violent aggression, whether by armed power [or] by the much more subtle aggression of science and technology exploiting man and nature.

Observing that the West had almost lost the contemplative dimension of human existence and the East was losing it, he described a visit to a poor Hindu family that emanated a quality missing from many modern homes.

One little boy was lying ill on a mat on the floor while his two brothers gave Griffiths and his Western companions a concert of Indian classical music. Another boy played a stringed instrument, as both sang together, beating the time with their hands and completely absorbed in the music. Griffiths commented that 'sitting on the floor in this little cottage with no modern conveniences', he felt he was 'brought face to face with one of the most profound religious cultures of the world'.

If the world's increasingly aggressive freneticism was felt by Ramana Maharshi, perhaps he chose to balance it by going into silence. At times it is useful to allow your mind to lie fallow, in the way that farmers let fields rest between plantings. Both meditation and daydreaming are ways of doing this. They are a necessary part of the creative process.

The novelist Raja Rao often said his books arose from daily morning meditations, and from silence. To his mind, the point of any artistic effort was to take him back to his real, deeper nature.

For this purpose, traditional Indian dance and theatre performances begin with a prayer to a god. Similarly, North American Indians conducted rituals before decision-making meetings, beginning with a prayer and perhaps a 'smudging' ceremony in which everyone would be anointed with sacred smoke from burning aromatic plants like cedar, sage and sweetgrass.

Indians communed with nature by going away from their tribes to chant, sing, conduct rituals or sit alone in deserted areas. As a rite of passage into manhood, adolescent boys would undergo certain wilderness hardships. In a vision or dream, they would meet their totem animal, who would be their mentor, protector and guide in the spirit realm and the ordinary world. Dreaming while sleeping, daydreaming, praying or meditating, and visions during rituals are not always distinguished in American Indian folklore.

However, advanced meditators quite definitely distinguish meditation from daydreaming. Daydreaming allows the mind to ramble over all sorts of territory, going off on tangents, leading to all kinds of intricate stories you may imagine, which has value as a form of lateral thinking. But meditation is described as a state of watchfulness in which you don't follow or elaborate upon thoughts. You just notice whatever thoughts come up and let them float away or dissipate like momentary clouds in empty sky.

In an effort to induce higher states of consciousness, rituals have long been used in India. The priestly class, the Brahmins, spoke Sanskrit as a magical mantra for this purpose. The observation that sound and word have an effect upon their hearers is probably how poetry was invented. The earliest Vedantic text, the Rig-Veda (The Veda of Poetry) starts off with *Agni*, the fire to which sacrifices are offered. Agni symbolizes the principle of a universal level of fire, perception and light – or higher consciousness. For Hindus, it appears in the heavens as the Sun, in the air as lightning, on Earth as fire. Yogis offer this fire of consciousness their speech, *prana* (breath) and minds in a Vedic fire ritual called *Vagna*, in an effort to attain heightened perception.

Ireland's bards chanted elegiac poems in Irish Gaelic for similar purposes. Sometimes the poetry acted as a magic spell so that the chanter could enter the Otherworld or the land of faery immortals – where higher beings and higher consciousness are – often to effect changes such as the healing of some animal or person. Poetry is said to have been the vehicle by which humans were transported to Tír na n'Óg, the goddess/fairy-inhabited island of eternal youth – symbolic of 'poetic realization' – off the west coast of Ireland. Human access to Tír na n'Óg depended on the poet, whose words were needed to carry adventurers to it.

Irish bards, the tradition-bearers of pre-Christian Ireland, trained to become poets for at least 20 years, dwelling in dark underground chambers where they memorized histories, poetry and songs and learned rules of oral composition, since they did not write. It is said that they would enter Tír na n'Óg through certain caves in the west of Ireland. The English poet Edmund Spenser visited Ireland in the 16th century and observed how:

> [Even] when poets emerged to hear their works sung by bards at social events, out of respect for the divine source of inspiration, they lay in darkness (facing Tír na n'Óg) as they had been taught to do while students of the art.[10]

Also known as 'the many-coloured land', Tír na n'Óg sounds very like the place that yogis describe seeing after spending years in darkness. Tibetan Buddhist yogis who have stayed in caves for long periods say that eventually the eyes become capable of seeing in the dark. Some claim to enter a world more crystalline and colourful than this one, but very real. Alexandra David-Neel wrote of speaking with men in Tibet who had undergone training in dark, secluded grave-like dwellings. She was told that, after a while, hermits in these conditions begin to see their surroundings and 'enjoy, at times, wonderful illuminations. [Their] cell becomes bright with light or, in the darkness, every object is drawn with luminous outlines [or] a phantasmagoria of shining flowers, landscapes and personages arises before them.'

David-Neel goes on to say that optical phenomena of this kind are well known and Tibetans believe this to be a kaleidoscopic mirage caused by the uncontrolled agitation of the mind because the phantasmagoria vanishes when the mind nears stillness. Only a moving spot remains in the vision at that point, either dark-coloured or like a small globe of light. The meditator aims to fix it in space. Once it becomes immobile, without changing in size or colour, the meditator is able to focus his attention on anything without breaking concentration. A further stage occurs when the spot disappears altogether but, David-Neel notes, many 'proudly enjoy the fairy-scene thinking that they have obtained a glimpse of paradise'.

Intuition and development of higher consciousness

The early 20th-century Austrian visionary, scientist and educator Rudolf Steiner said that the mind is a powerful tool once one contains its negative aspects. If we experience a problem, we can find its solution through the intuition, if not the intellect.

What is intuition? The famous 20th-century Irish psychic Eileen Garrett, who used scientific methods to study her own clairvoyant gifts, likens it to an urgent inner voice that impels and inspires one to act spontaneously. It cannot be mistaken for imagination, but is close to inspiration. In *Adventures in the Supernormal*, she writes:

> The compelling stimulus and the experience which allows for growth arrive without any inner search or known subjective belabouring. The nature, therefore, of such inspiration would appear to be wholly spontaneous and … of external origin. It impels one beyond the field of [one's] experience.

Steiner agreed with Garrett that spiritual truths were in danger of being stifled since humanity had advanced too rapidly in commanding the forces of nature, leaving little time for reflection. Although the intellect helps us analyse difficulties and deal with the everyday world, he predicted it might become overactive and lead humanity into the problems we currently experience. He sought to keep the onslaughts of technology away from children as long as possible by creating an educational system meant to keep their imaginations alive, and through inspiring teachers to use their intuition in teaching their charges.

Interestingly, children have been noticed to have greater psychic abilities than adults, as Uri Geller showed as a youngster. Geller believes that children may be better at showing such powers because they haven't yet taken on the negative attitudes that adults pick up in life. In 1975, he wrote that the powers he has may be hidden in all of us. He felt that some kind of cosmic connection must be tuned into for psychism to work in us as it does in him. In *My Story* he wrote:

> The main key, I think, is believing. It works like an ignition key to open up these energies in the body. Seeing or hearing about these unusual possibilities can establish [a] direct channel to this cosmic connection.

Steiner sought not to break this connection, which he perceived that children have at birth. Partly in order to avoid a sharp break with the spiritual dimension, where he believed everyone dwells before being born, children in Steiner (Waldorf) primary schools are not given computers or technological devices. The whole curriculum is geared towards allowing their bodies and minds to grow in rhythm with the seasons and the natural world. Steiner teachers aim to provide a structure and foundation for children so that, when they grow up, they don't feel overwhelmed. The best consciously enchant their students, tricking them into learning through play.

One trick used for teaching children emotional-intelligence and social skills is a dance form called eurythmy. This aims to sensitize children to each other and their surroundings so that they learn to move and interact harmoniously with the visible and invisible forces around them.

Another subtle trick arises in drawing lessons. Children are encouraged to draw the ground first and then something on top of it. This teaches them that all properly built things must have foundations or something to stand on. Children from state schools who came into my Steiner classes often drew foundation-less objects and it did seem that they felt suspended mid-air, unaware of the Earth that supported them or their surroundings.

Waldorf teachers tend to feel that children in state schools are forced to do things they are not yet physically or emotionally equipped to do. Teachers rush them to learn in a hurry, without considering that children must learn to coordinate their limbs, emotions and minds – often in alien, inorganic city environments. Damage caused by harmful education may not show until many years afterward, but usually shows in one way or another during the developmental years, manifesting perhaps as dyslexia or a mental or emotional imbalance.

Steiner observed that there is a link between the processes of the brain and the motor functions of the hands. So in his school curriculum, knitting, drawing, painting, sculpting and playing a musical instrument were as important as writing. Rhythm is considered so important that, after kindergarten, a three-day rhythm is used to teach children new concepts. The idea is to engage children's hearts first, then their minds, and last of all their bodies. Around the age of five or six, they cannot stop themselves copying whatever someone in front of them is doing in a rhythmical manner.

Steiner believed a person develops just as human history developed, moving through the same stages. Knowledge was orally transmitted before writing was invented, therefore oral teaching is most important to young children, not least because of the warmth thus developed between students and teachers. Singing songs, chanting poems, and telling stories come naturally to youngsters, so Steiner teachers consciously use them to encourage the development of memory, communication and imaginative skills.

Rudolf Steiner proposed a scientific method for learning to meditate in the only book that he actually wrote, *Knowledge of Higher Worlds and Its Attainment*. In meditation, 'higher knowing' or 'intuition' may arise, through which we can find solutions to every problem we encounter. Everyone has access to a higher intuition and may find his or her own way there, he believed.

One of man's chief problems is to remember that intellect is telling him only half the truth.[11]

The foundations of consciousness

Dr Julian Jaynes, author of *The Origin of Consciousness in the Breakdown of the Bicameral Mind*, states that:

> [Even] as recently as 1000 BC, human beings did not yet possess consciousness – [consciousness being] what goes on behind [Man's] eyes. [Homer's] heroes do not have free will in the sense that we do … the gods make them do things.

Concluding that ancient Man experienced auditory hallucinations, Jaynes believed that the voices people sometimes hear 'originate in the right hemisphere of the brain, and make their way across to the left hemisphere which, in human beings, controls speech'.

> [The] right hemisphere of your brain is 'dumb', irrational, incapable of speech [but knows] a great deal more than the 'verbal you' knows. [In] the days before he developed human speech, man must have lived in an 'unconscious' way, altogether closer to nature, responding with his intuitions.[12]

It could be that ancient peoples externalized their emotions and thoughts, seeing them as personified gods, angels and demons. Tibetan Buddhists tell a story of how their mythical yogi saint, Milarepa, while sitting alone meditating in a cave, suddenly found demons inside it. No matter what he tried, he couldn't get rid of them. Finally he gave up and welcomed them. Then they disappeared! The demons may be perceived as his own projections, personifications of Milarepa's negative characteristics or fears.

However, Tibetan teacher Lama Samten says spirit beings are all around us and that the weather and elements around and inside us are beings. That is how he senses the world. Lama Samten says that some countries have more of one kind of spirit than another. He noticed that England has more earth and water beings than any others, while Australia and North America have more fire beings.

Western mysticism and the intuitive mind

This kind of perception seems to be like that of all mystics everywhere, including the late Irish visionary Æ and the very much alive Canadian Dorothy Maclean, one of the founders of Scotland's Findhorn Community. George Russell (Æ) described seeing 'over-souls' of landscapes, as does Maclean, who claims to perceive *devas* who oversee plant life – by 'sensing' rather than actual physical sight. In deep meditation, she meets 'intelligent energy' rather than something three-dimensional and material. I was delighted when this self-contained, quiet lady consented to consider her experience in the spotlight of my questions. She told me:

> To me, faeries, devas and so on are beings living in dimensions beyond normal human vision. I do not see them. I sense them, become one with them, and have to use my own words to describe my experiences. I do not know how this sensing can be scientifically proven, though science is becoming more aware that there are realms beyond our known ones.

When asked how one communicates with other intelligences, she replied, 'by getting onto the same wavelength as other intelligences'. She wants to encourage the idea that people may 'co-create' with nature.

> The Findhorn Garden was a successful experiment in applying this idea, and I believe was a major example for the world to see, understand and apply elsewhere. That nature has an intelligence needs to be accepted everywhere for the continuing health of our planetary life. The intelligence of nature wants to help humanity to counteract the negative effects that our unintelligent behaviour has foisted on the world, wants to help us deal with the pollution we have thereby caused. But to get this help we humans have to have enough humility to ask.

In her book *To Hear the Angels Sing*, she speaks of how we are able to enlarge our awareness through attuning to the divinity inside us, thus going beyond the polarities with which we experience life.

She says that we normally do not focus on our 'soul' level and judge most things as good or bad, whereas our souls, and the souls of nature, are above opposites. For example, the Angel of Joy and the Angel of Sorrow are the same angel. We have no words for such beings, which are 'formless energy fields'. To her, the words 'angel' and 'deva', as we know them, are inaccurate. The first time she communicated with one of these higher beings – 'an aspect of the soul or intelligence of the species called garden pea', which holds the archetypal pattern for that species – she sensed the Pea Deva was 'speaking from a remote distance, remote in that humans and angels are separated because their ways are different and they didn't particularly care to come close to a mankind bent on spoiling a planet'.

Her most urgent message from the plant kingdom came from a cedar tree in 1967. It spoke for all trees, she said, and begged for more trees to be planted, as the spirit beings behind them were worried that the Earth did not have enough of them covering it. Today that is still their most pressing concern.

One of Maclean's Findhorn cohorts was the late Robert Ogilvie Crombie (ROC), a Merlin-like figure in the early Findhorn Community, known in the 1970s for his clairvoyant communications with the flute-playing nature spirit Pan, whom he met in Edinburgh Gardens. It was in ROC's company, in those same gardens, that the Findhorn Community artist and potter Brian Nobbs had his first vision of fairies.

Nobbs arrived at Findhorn in 1970 after spending five years as a monk with the Benedictine order and another five as a teacher. Initially he helped out with the cooking. Even now he speaks with awe about the giant vegetables growing at Findhorn at that time, mentioning the particularly exquisitely flavoured, enormous parsnips he cooked – parsnips of a quality that he has never eaten anywhere since.

Since 1971, he has managed the Findhorn pottery studio, where he draws, paints and writes when he isn't making pottery. It is all part of his dream of working with the 'nature forces' and 'the inner voice' inside him to find new forms of communication through the universal language of art.

I visited the inviting little studio that served as his pottery just as the bare northern light of winter was arriving. The bearded Nobbs, whom one could easily imagine in the brown habit of a medieval monk, told me the fairies and elves he sees are elementals or nature spirits, some of whom have individual consciousnesses, while others may be connected to a kind of group mind. He doesn't see fairies as some people do: they aren't exactly solid and yet he senses them quite strongly when they are present. They manifest to him in the way that figures sometimes do in that twilight state you fall into between dreaming and being awake – when something, maybe an insect, quickly flits past the corner of your eye but is gone before you can look at it. He says most people begin to see the fairies at the periphery of their vision, when their eyes are not quite focused.

Nobbs told me that the actual sight is a part of the mind or brain that registers a vivid image which has not come via the eyes but rather seems almost implanted in the mind. 'It is not only as clear as normal vision, but more powerful and capable of blocking out other realities.' The occasion when he first saw fairies (in fact Pan and some elves), he described as a sort of initiation that occurred spontaneously in ROC's company. The experience was similar to undergoing a perceptual shift after staring at a three-D computer-generated stereogram for a long time and suddenly seeing the image that was there all along. In the *Findhorn Community Newsletter* he writes:

> What happened immediately was that I found myself with a vivid feeling, as physical and undeniable as any sense impression ever is, of wading through a medium as resistant as flowing water but carrying a tingling electrical charge that flowed around my ankles and through my whole body. [The] seeing was enabled by the elemental beings themselves, which is normally the way it works.

ROC told him that it seems necessary to have reached some level of cosmic consciousness before you can experience nature spirits directly. Brian's other Findhorn mentor Dorothy Maclean frequently stressed that 'sensitivity in these realms is a natural outcome of being centred on the inner divinity, and must be approached in this way, rather than with curiosity and a desire for novelty alone'.

Nobbs feels that humans have for too long thought of themselves as the only creatures on this planet who are self-aware and capable of rational thought. By removing a Creator or God from our reality, we have created a situation in which there is no need to consider anything except what might be expedient for our immediate purposes. Out of this has come the systematic abuse of the planet and all life on it. He believes that Eden was a symbolic paradise garden, lost by an act of arrogance and Findhorn is a restoration of lost innocence and lost connections that we once had in that paradisiacal place. He writes:

> In the microcosm ... particles that are also waves can be in more than one place at a time, interchange instantly with other particles across light years, may or may not be where you think they are and even travel backwards in time. [Every] solid thing we experience is actually only an energy field that is experienced as a solid because [our] bodies [are] a mesh of energy fields. [The] phenomena of faeries, elves, devas and all the angelic and elemental creatures of myth and legend are a human overlay of a reality [which] is simply another normal part of the universe. We mythologize everything. It is how we understand our existence. [Mythology is] a different category of truth than, for example, that water boils at sea level at 100° Celsius. [Increasingly] quantum physics is finding it hard to leave consciousness out of the laboratory. The observer's gaze affects the outcome of the experiment. Mind plays a part in the most fundamental aspects of the interactions of matter. Mind seems less and less like a remarkable accident of evolution and more like the directive force behind it.[13]

The so-called 'fairy faith' was common in Scotland until quite recently. You will still find ordinary people there and in Ireland who accept the 'Otherworld' as a probable reality. In the early 20th century, the Irish literary renaissance was in great part funded by the Anglo-Irish aristocrat Lady Gregory, who said in *Visions and Beliefs in the West of Ireland*:

[Faeryland] exists as a supernormal state of consciousness into which men and women may enter temporarily in dreams, trances or various ecstatic conditions [or] at death. [Though] it seems to surround [and] interpenetrate this planet ... it can have no other limits than those of the universe itself.

Each of us has an interior universe that can be explored. It is as deep, vast and full of secrets as outer space. We don't need expensive machines or the intellect of a genius to explore it. But we do need to give ourselves time and quiet to find out how our minds work and how our hopes and visions relate to what surrounds us. Even when we can't do that, we can experience our own strength and power. Jesus was not joking when he said that if we have faith as small as a mustard seed, we can move mountains, nor that his followers would be able to heal others more than he could, if they had but faith. People have been known to lift a whole automobile under which an injured loved one lies.

The way we think itself has great power over what happens to us. When playing in a filthy dive in Hamburg, several young boys in a pop group used to encourage each other by replying to John Lennon's 'Where are we going, boys?' with 'Straight to the top, Johnny!' and of course that is precisely where they went. Interestingly, the Beatle who was fired just before they hit the big time confirmed in an interview many years later that they had always said that, but had never really believed it. Perhaps he was the only one who hadn't!

Extraordinary unexplored territories are within us. The Irish psychic Eileen Garrett (*Adventures in the Supernormal*) said psychical research may reveal answers to problems that cannot be solved until man's reason permits him to understand that, through his intuitive self, he can reach beyond the conditioning of his environment. 'The doorway to the soul of man is through intuition, and it is through knowledge of his soul that all his conceptual understanding must stem.'

Garrett believed that paranormal abilities are generally distributed throughout the human race and need only be developed in order to give great benefits to the world.

[In] the hurry of life we live in constant unawareness of the fact that we are natural creatures. [We] have become so absorbed in the formulae of living that we look to these and not to nature for [our] sustenance.

Garrett said her clairvoyant knowledge was revealed sometimes by pictures and sometimes by sound or feeling. She described it as coming to her during waking and sleeping in a 'flow of mobile symbols ... of every conceivable kind ... a constant flow of images that move steadily, like a river, under the bridge of one's active interest'. She said that this flow appears to be different because it takes place at unnoticed levels of consciousness 'and is related to the field of association and imagination in which all images – mental, emotional, and physical – are received'. At some point she focuses on something and then suddenly she knows what it means. This knowing comes 'like a reflection of one's image in clear water', where 'perception, sensation and knowledge are not differentiated but united'. Garrett found it difficult to describe because this fusion of faculties is so different from what one experiences on ordinary levels, where these faculties are so definitely different-iated. The loss of this kind of consciousness in today's world has been observed by shamanic practitioner and author on Celtic subjects Caitlin Matthews, who says:

> Recently we have begun to live in only one side of reality – the side that we call 'the real world' – never realising that we are making our-selves prisoners of an ever shrinking and fearful place that craves the assurance of pre-shrunk knowledge and scientifically verifiable answers ... the consequence is that we live much less fully.[14]

In *The Faery Faith: An Integration of Science with Spirit*, the para-psychologist Serena Roney-Dougal agrees:

> [As] our culture gets progressively more and more material, as we become [more] divorced from nature, as the wild places disappear and our lives are lit by bright lights and there is no darkness, no bog, no wild wood, no moorland, so this aspect of our being fades away.

Roney-Dougal believes that the fairy faith is derived from a philosophy that 'underlies the world's religions, from animism and shamanism to the present-day pagan revival'. When she first started studying parapsychology, she felt she was exploring the foundations of religion.

> Originally religion came out of people's actual experience of the sacred. And psychic phenomena are part of that sacred reality. [When] we deal with faery, we are dealing with the world of the psyche, with the world of glamour and illusion.

In Scotland the ability to see the fairies was called 'second sight', which only later came to mean 'precognition'. British and Irish fairytales are 'pre-Celtic, pre-patriarchal, from the goddess worshipping, Neolithic, shamanic people, of which the witchcraft of Britain was a remnant'. Roney-Dougal describes parapsychology as the science of magic.

> Throughout time, people of many different cultures have consciously entered at will this reality, this mode of thought, for spiritual purposes. These people are called shamanic and they use many different techniques to enter the Otherworld.

The kind of reality to which she refers seems to be available to us via heightened activity in the right side of the brain. Colin Wilson, in *Mysteries*, says this non-verbal, intuitive right side understands complicated definitions, performs complex reasoning, perhaps explaining the prowess of mathematical prodigies, and may be a gateway to the unconscious, giving access to higher levels of consciousness.

Overcoming the robot mind

Colin Wilson's stance is that our 'robot mind' stops us from being creative and 'whole'. 'Creativity demands effort', he says. Habit robs us of experiences that will pay us for our effort by giving us the experience of more intensity.

When life ceases to excite much response from us, we say we are 'disillusioned', the implication being that the moments of delight were a lie, and boredom is the ultimate reality.

Dr Augustin M de la Pena of the University of Texas Medical School inferred that this state was possibly responsible for cancer. This disillusioned, bored state of mind could have something do with humans' propensity for creating disasters and wars, Wilson suggests.

Were human beings able to stimulate their ability to be interested in things, inspiring their own creativity, then would they cause fewer problems and experience better health? Were we to encourage a spirit of enquiry and the study of ideas that our establishment science and religious leaders consider irrelevant, would we create a healthier world?

British engineer-turned-physicist Ronald D Pearson in *Origin of Mind*, says there is a core of truth in every religion if the paranormal is seen as part of an extended physics. But the established Church helps to prop up physics by joining forces with it to discredit the paranormal, thus helping materialistic science 'to maintain a kind of equilibrium despite their obvious incompatibilities'. Together they 'block the path to the vista of delight which lies beyond'. They are supported by parapsychologists who help discredit the paranormal by looking for rational explanations for effects not easily explained by physics. Consequently:

[The] majority of the population then shy away and refuse to believe in anything. [Youngsters] feel deprived and see no need for moral inhibition. If this life is all there is [why] balk at crime if you can get away with it?

Pearson accedes that giving too much attention to the paranormal and religion can cause mental problems. Mental illness with developmental or traumatic roots can lead to psychosis. However, folk tradition attributes psychic ability to some people after they emerge from what seem to be acute psychotic breakdowns. Roney-Dougal is now exploring this from a neurochemical perspective and says the pineal gland produces a neurohormone called melatonin, which regulates the circadian (seasonal) rhythms of the body and produces an inhibitor chemical called pinoline. The latter's chemical structure is virtually identical with the key ingredients of the *ayahuasca* drink used by Amazonians to induce clairvoyance and out-of-body states of consciousness.

Pinoline inhibits the breakdown of serotonin, which causes the accumulation of amines – including dimethyltryptamine (DMT), a main active ingredient of *ayahuasca* – within the neuronal synapses. This can lead to hallucinations, depression or mania. Other chemical links seem to explain why psychedelics such as LSD, psilocybin and MDMA may trigger psychotic episodes and induce a state of consciousness that is similar to both an acute psychotic breakdown and that which shamans experience while in trance. Roney-Dougal suggests that the ordinary dream state is associated with the same neurochemical pathways in the brain as psychosis and shamanistic experience. This all goes along with anthropological reports of shamans exhibiting psychism and the ability to 'walk between the worlds'.

People who seek this kind of super-experience risk developing too great a dependence on the paranormal, Pearson believes. Young people especially need to learn to relate to the material, relative world rather than to what lies beyond it. Overemphasizing non-material or otherworldly states could affect them psychologically, not to mention materially. Of course it is also true that materialism does not fulfil the emotional and psychological needs of humans. In fact, Pearson's attitude toward this world and the 'otherworld' of the paranormal reflects a common misunderstanding that is partly the result of Cartesian ideas, in particular its concept that objects are mechanistic in nature with a material or physical cause behind every action.

Exploring the invisible universe through the structure of religion

One of Hinduism's core practices is yoga. Over time, yogis gradually begin to interact with their surroundings and the universe at a more sensitized level. Yoga means 'to yoke together mind, spirit and body'. The ideal in life is to have those three aspects cooperating, so that we do not suffer from a split in our thinking, feeling and physical activities.

Some Buddhist visualization practices are said to enable practitioners to know reality directly, which can only be understood through experience, not description. Certain meditation practices may affect the mind so strongly that they become dangerous to some, especially when undertaken without a well-trained guide. In Hindu tradition, spiritual training is handed down orally, often through members of the same family. Respect towards teachers of yoga and meditation is considered necessary if you are to actually learn anything. A *guru*, a spiritual teacher in Hinduism, is a 'remover of darkness' or ignorance. In the Tibetan Mahayana Buddhist tradition, a lama is 'mother to all beings of the universe'.

Respect is very much part of most religions and an important aspect of humanity's conception of God. No one can be happy without the cooperation and collusion of the world and without respect for others, which is not possible without self-respect. Steiner said that respect for something higher than oneself is necessary to ensure that the intellect remains humble. Intellectual arrogance will lead humanity into terrible mistakes, he declared, predicting many of those we are currently making in society, technology and science. The knowledge that there is always something or someone greater than oneself is very helpful in keeping one, as the late Lama Chögyam Trungpa said, on the razor's edge of awareness.

Religions have always spoken of a consciousness, or a personification of consciousness, that is higher than ordinary human consciousness. Christians call it 'God'. The more academic may consider God to be a concept created by the human mind, but today physicists are beginning to explore regions where religious concepts no longer seem so far-fetched. Physicists are now talking about 'the God particle', the most fundamental particle in space.

F David Peat observes in *Blackfoot Physics*:

> [The] mystical traditions of the East stress the employment of
> instrumentation, experimentation, and observation in their med-
> itative and spiritual practices. These are considered scientific ...

because they are disciplined and reproducible. There is a codified body of practices that will lead to predictable and well-defined results.

Buddhism is possibly the world's most scientific religion. Buddhist practices seem particularly suited to modern scientific study. One of their by-products is an improvement in thinking processes and greater clarity of mind. Buddhist meditation teachers first make students familiar with their many different mental states, then offer techniques or experiments for studying the mind.

And yet, what is the mind? The Tibetan teacher Ringu Tulku, in *Mind Training,* says that what we call 'mind' does not really exist. It is merely a passing awareness, activated when an object outside us attracts one of our senses. We mistake 'continual mental interaction with sense objects' for the mind, but what we are actually experiencing is a stream of temporary states of mind changing from one instant to the next. Ringu Tulku reasons: 'We have created the illusion of a unique and unchanging self, an individual "I" that we believe remains fixed somewhere within us.' But our feelings and thoughts come and go all the time, so how can there be an individual self? The 'pure enlightened mind', on the other hand, is limitless. It has the potential to be anything, anywhere, anytime. Buddhists equate this individual 'I' with the 'ego' of the West. Ringu Tulku adds, 'Our assumed identity leads to discrimination and splits the natural oneness of our mind'.

Tibetan teachings seem very close to modern physics. In both, the observer is seen as part of what is observed, affecting whatever reality is encountered. Subatomic physics experiments show that a particle becomes a wave or a wave a particle according to whether there is an observer and what the observer expects to see. Vajrayana teachings (a sect under the umbrella of Tibetan Buddhism) suggest that the material world is malleable. Thoughts are said to have a profound effect upon the world we experience. Through meditation practices, this is experienced directly. They say: 'I am that which I see.' However you treat others is how you are treating yourself. What you believe is possible makes it possible.

When meditators use Vajrayana visualization techniques for a while, they begin to notice the mind battling with imaginary notions and generally wasting time tormenting itself. Therefore much emphasis is placed on what they term 'calm abiding' meditation, where you watch your thoughts without elaborating upon them or following any particular train of thought. Eventually practitioners find out what they are really thinking beneath the surface mind. This happens naturally as they learn to notice how they feel while meditating. Meditation practices lead them on a merry (sometimes not so merry) dance through different mental states, eventually helping them learn to calm disturbing feelings. Vajrayanas aim to transform negative thoughts and emotions into positive thoughts and helpful actions by encouraging the subconscious and the conscious, or heart and mind, emotions and intellect to work *with* instead of against each other. Sometimes male and female symbolism is used to depict these, or opposite qualities of the same mental state or impulse. For instance, compassion is symbolized by the calmly active male god called Chenrezi and his energetically active female equivalent, Tara.

Such symbolism refers to different aspects or energies within and outside the human being. They are forces in the universe, just as fairies are perceived as nature spirits connected with the elements (hence 'elementals'). Hindu gods are also perceived as different forces operating in the universe. Brahma is the creator force – his four heads indicate omniscience, from each of which the four Vedas (or scriptures) came. Brahma's consort is Saraswati, the goddess of learning, who rides upon a white swan and plays a stringed instrument called the *veena* (perhaps hinting at the musical, 'string-theory' universe we inhabit).

Interdependence of mind and nature

The forces of nature and nature-centred ideas are woven into the world's major religions and folklore, although often relegated to the realm of mythology or storytelling. A constant battle has raged worldwide for centuries between those who embrace nature and those who wish to control it.

In the 5th century BC in what is now Southern Nepal, someone who simply 'woke up' from the illusions of our world to see the way things really are was called the Buddha. This is said to have happened while he sat meditating under a bodhi tree.

Colin Wilson in *The Occult* notes that this tree produces figs which have an exceptionally high serotonin content. Serotonin is produced by the pineal 'eye'. It is known to inhibit sexual development and increase intelligence. Primates, men and apes have far more serotonin in their brains than any other species.

Buddhists refer to 'buddha nature' as residing within every sentient being. They say we are essentially no different from the Buddha, except we don't realize we are 'awake'. Occasionally in meditation, an awareness arises of a peace so deep and profound that it feels almost boring, at other times absolutely riveting, energizing, inspiring, yet calming – all at the same time. You may feel you are moving in a kind of river, as if you are only the tiniest particle in a universal movement. Then you realize that what you know of the universe is so very little. The universe is a vast, vast space that you could fall into eternally, infinitely, not knowing where you are within it, foundationless, your feet forever in mid-air. Buddhists call this infinite space 'the ocean'. Like them, Hinduism's Vedantists see it as an ocean of consciousness or pure perception that is devoid of a personal 'I'.

British ecologist Stephan Harding brings this ocean of consciousness down to the level of our own Earth. William Golding and James Lovelock gave it the ancient Greek name *Gaia* in the 1960s, to represent a great, intelligent living being. Harding says:

> [We should] develop a deep sense that we are embedded in the life of the great planetary being that has given birth to us and to every other creature that has ever oozed, crawled or sent its roots into our planet's soil [and which] we walk, talk and live our whole lives inside.

We are in a symbiotic relationship with our world, 'just as the mitochondria live in an intimate relationship with their larger, unseen host' and are 'utterly part of Gaia, biologically, psychologically and spiritually'. Our bodies, dreams, creativity and imagination come from her.

> Once you allow yourself to feel this deep belonging to Gaia, there is no question that what we are doing to her now is wrong, and that we have to do something about it.[15]

All the world's 'primitive' cultures were aware of being interdependent with their surroundings. They also were aware that without a group protecting them, individuals could die in the wild. Babies, for instance, do not develop properly without someone's constant care and attention. My American cousin who worked in Vladivostok told me that she saw babies in a large Russian orphanage who did not even bother to cry. They were sluggish about learning to walk and, when old enough to stand, just sat in the playground, not knowing how to play and exhibiting no interest in it. My cousin thought this was because they had had little physical contact with people as babies and so had become autistic. The orphanage was understaffed, with too few nurses around to cuddle the children. The babies lay in their individual cots day in, day out, untouched except when fed or their diapers were changed. They didn't learn to speak until very late and, after they grew up, displayed hearing and other health problems.

A mother's physical touch is crucial for the healthy biological development of a baby's brain and body, the Dalai Lama says. Our existence depends upon others. We are social animals. Insects and other animals also depend on the group they're part of. Their very existence depends on working together. That, the Dalai Lama said, is the nature of the human animal: cooperation. In a talk at London's Westminster Cathedral in 2003 he described how both the turtle and the moth have no contact with their mothers. Their subsequent behaviour appears to indicate that they have no capacity for affection and, even if they do, they may be eaten by their mothers. But for human beings, recognition from the mother is very important. Without it, babies do not develop their mental faculties properly and even their health becomes poor. Some even die.

The compelling evidence from neuroscience and medical science of the crucial role of simple physical touch for even the physical enlargement of an infant's brain during the first few weeks [of life] powerfully brings home the intimate connection between compassion and human happiness.[16]

The Dalai Lama stated that it is quite clear that compassion arises not through religion but through our biological nature, linked as it is with our initial contact with our mother. Our basic instinct is to feel gentle towards her, not hostile, since she is the one who gave us life. When we grow up, we think gentleness is not so important, yet we are happier when surrounded by friendly people and genuine smiles. Even the dying who are given compassion are happier than those who are not. Gentleness is our basic nature, he claimed, adding that the majority of people have goodwill towards each other. This is proven by the fact that otherwise we would have all killed each other long ago.

Psychologists have observed that, in early childhood, healthy people pass through egocentric stages before they develop maturity, which they define as being able to defer gratification – the ability to wait for satisfaction of desires. People who do not move through certain stages in their emotional and intellectual development become unbalanced in their behaviour with others. The problems we encounter while we're growing up determine the balance or imbalance we have in these areas. Those who do not pass the egocentric stage of their development may become narcissistic, autistic or, in worst case scenarios, psychotic and unable to deal appropriately with what they encounter in their surroundings.

Maturity has always been the aim of religious leaders. They have for centuries sought to devise methods to enhance the mind's processes in order to help people experience clarity and happiness.

In the East, they call these methods 'meditation', but meditation may be defined in many different ways. The Dalai Lama says that Buddhism has long argued for the tremendous potential for transformation that exists naturally in the human mind. The main purpose of Buddhist meditation techniques is to cultivate compassion alongside insight into the nature of reality. The aim is to unify compassion with wisdom. This means that we learn to minimize our foolishness and mistakes so that we begin to act appropriately, in context with whatever situation we encounter. Two key techniques are used to unify compassion and wisdom: the sustained application of a refinement of attention and the regulation and transformation of the emotions – in short, practising meditation correctly.

Defining meditation techniques for scientific study

[The] term 'meditation' is often employed in a highly imprecise sense [because] it refers generically to an extremely wide range of practices [as] diverse as the ritual dances of some African tribes, the spiritual exercises of the desert fathers and the tantric practices of a Tibetan adept ... all forms of 'meditation'.[17]

Neuroscientists find defining such a wide variety of techniques problematic because the common element in them all is mystical experience. This is difficult to test because it transcends thought, language, reason and ordinary perception, which are necessary for reliable brain studies. Using meditation as a generic term for so many types of practices trivializes them.

[To] make zikr and t'ai ch'i describable with the same term, one must ignore a good deal of what makes them radically different from each other. This would be akin to the use of the word 'sport' to refer to all sports as if they were essentially the same.[18]

Dr Antoine Lutz, Dr John D Dunne and Dr Richard J Davidson say that every meditation practice is particular to a specific culture and linked inextricably with a unique set of traditions, with its own kinds of boundaries. Literature on meditation tends to ignore the boundaries of culture and tradition in an effort to emphasize the universality of human experience.

However, for scientific reasons, it is important to note the differences in contemplative traditions. Specific practices should be linked with the parts of the brain affected by them. How they affect attention should be noted. Techniques that target specific underlying processes are likely to engage different neural circuitry.

From the standpoint of the researcher, it is therefore important to separate the transcendental claims that form the metaphysical or theological context of the meditation experience from what actually occurs in the brain neurologically. In Buddhism, meditation is taught as a science. This is particularly true of Tibetan Buddhism, which hints at pre-Buddhist and shamanic techniques for moving into different mind-states. Lutz, Dunne and Davidson state that:

> Most Buddhist traditions use a term for meditation that correlates with the Sanskrit term *bhāvanā*, literally 'causing to become'. In Tibetan traditions, the usual translation for *bhāvanā* is *gôm* (*sgom*), which roughly means 'to become habituated to' or 'to become familiar with'.

In Tibetan Buddhism, the meditator becomes familiar with a wide range of contemplative practices. He may visualize a deity or 'energy' flowing in the body, recite a mantra, focus his attention on his breathing, undertake various types of objectless contemplative practices or analyse and review arguments or narrative discourses.

The Dalai Lama says that the Sanskrit term for meditation refers to cultivating a particular habit or way of being, while the Tibetan term connotes cultivating familiarity. Therefore, meditation is a deliberate activity involving becoming familiar with something – such as an object, fact, theme, habit, outlook or way of being.

Two basic categories of meditation exist. Stabilizing meditation focuses on stilling the mind. Discursive meditation focuses on the processes surrounding the acquisition of knowledge and understanding. In both categories, meditation can take many forms. You might meditate on your transient nature, or upon developing a specific mental state, such as the desire to alleviate others' suffering, or on developing ideas, imagery, and the imagination to cultivate wellbeing.

The states induced by meditation practices are said to be predictable and to have expected effects on mind and body that are positive in nature. A meditator who induces such states repeatedly learns to enhance positive experiences or conditions and to inhibit undesirable traits. This improves, the more the activity is performed. Experiences then may be analysed and classified in repeatable experiments. The Dalai Lama suggests that the scientific research method used should match in sophistication the complexity level of the meditation practice it is investigating.

One monk's opinions about the effects of meditation

Frenchman Matthieu Ricard, a respected microbiologist who gave up his career to become a Tibetan Buddhist monk, has great respect for the 'science of meditation'. He spent 35 years in the Himalayas learning from Tibetan lamas. In *The Quantum and the Lotus*, he writes about the interface between science and meditation, and has taken a scientific approach to achieving happiness in his book entitled *Happiness*. During experiments to prove the effects of meditation, his brainwaves showed a happiness quotient higher than any other meditator then being tested.

Ricard says disturbing emotions distort your perceptions so you cannot see reality as it truly is. When you are emotionally attached to something, you idealize it. When you dislike something, you demonize it. When you experience selfless love, you reflect an understanding that all things are intimately interwoven and interdependent. You experience that your happiness is linked with and inspired by others' happiness. Ricard says this notion is attuned to reality. Selfishness opens an abyss between you and others. One aim of meditation is to identify the types of mental processes that lead to wellbeing and those that lead to suffering, because aggression and jealousy represent a setback in our quest for serenity and happiness.

In 2005, Ricard spoke in London at the French Institute about new experiments being conducted upon advanced meditators entitled 'Mind Training and Brain Plasticity'. He described one experiment in which they and a non-meditating control group were hooked up to monitors that measured their physical reactions to a series of photographs projected before them on a screen. Results showed that meditators responded more quickly on an emotional level to images that showed people in distress.

Other experiments showed that brainwave patterns were different in advanced meditators, in comparison to beginners and those who didn't meditate at all. One significant side-effect of meditation seems to be that effective and appropriate compassionate action is undertaken more quickly in emergencies by people who meditate. Ricard's view is that meditation increases compassion and shortens the time-delay between receiving an impression of need and experiencing the impulse to act. Meditators' responses are more immediate and in many cases more appropriate.

Everyone's control of the outer world is limited but our ability to influence it depends on how well we deal with our 'inner conditions'. If we feel alright inside ourselves, we have inspiration, enthusiasm and enough contentment to carry on living and doing things.

How do you change the way the mind works? First, consider what inner conditions or attitudes might hamper or favour a genuine sense of wellbeing. You quickly find out that selfishness makes you sad and compassion for others makes you happy. Other people experience the same feelings. Ricard asked: 'Aren't you more attuned to your real nature when you give something to a child with no one knowing, as if you were Father Christmas?'

After continual observation of your emotions for some time, it becomes easier to tell what your positive and negative qualities are. It is normal to have qualities of shadow and light inside you, so you mustn't insult yourself for having negative ones. After all, unending happiness would be boring because it's always the same. Suffering is so much more *interesting*, Goethe once said.

If you look at the source of your thoughts, you will notice the 'luminous mind'. It is called that because you sense it as a quality of luminosity. It has no communicative faculty whatsoever but is rather like a mirror. Thoughts and feelings are transitory and can be changed, as they are not part of that luminosity. You can get rid of negative thoughts by using what Buddhists call 'antidotes'. There is no way you can wish good *and* harm upon others in the same instant, so the more you cultivate generous and compassionate thoughts, the more you lessen negative ones.

Cultivate your inner freedom, and you gradually modify your inner landscape. Changes do not happen immediately, for habits are like rolled parchment that must be pressed flat over and over again to stay flat. The idea is not to let emotions run wild, and also not to suppress them so that they later explode like a bomb. If you gradually apply antidotes to negative emotions, their afflictive aspects are gradually neutralized.

Simply consider the processes that lead to anger or obsessive desire. Look at emotion as a phenomenon – part of the illusory world. Gaze at it, watch it and keep seeing it in your mind. When you do this, the emotion is defused. It melts away over time and vanishes if you simply look at it over and over again. However, don't look at the *cause* of the thought or feeling, as that draws you into obsession. The mind is like a boat and we should sail it the way we want it to go. We are like the pauper who has a treasure under his hat but doesn't know it.

For a long time, it was thought that the brain didn't produce new neurons in adults, but new experiments have proven this untrue. Physical activity can increase changes in some areas of the brain. So what happens to the meditator and his mind? Matthieu Ricard and other monks are studying this with scientists and theologians, partly through the Mind and Life Institute, which he helped the Dalai Lama set up in 1990 to study science and how inner and outer phenomena operate.

The wisdom mind and physics

The Nepal-born teacher Mingyur Rinpoche, like other Buddhist teachers, says that we all have buddha-nature or 'wisdom mind'. This is a state of higher awareness where we are free from suffering.

At his lectures at Marpa House, Essex, in 2006, Lama Mingyur says that the Buddha described it as being like a bird's nest.

> When the mother bird leaves her eggs and flies far away, her mind is always returning to her nest. Why is this? Because her real place is to be on the nest. This is why we long to see our natural nature. It's like being homesick.

As mentioned before, Tibetan Buddhist teachings wander very close to modern physics. Consider the Vajrayana Buddhists' view of 'this illusory realm'. The sensible thing to do, they reason, is to be good to everyone and everything around you, because it helps you. The interesting thing is that your subconscious isn't always thinking the same way that your ordinary, everyday mind is. The subconscious is the realm of feelings and the heart, while the conscious mind deals with everyday matters and concepts. When these do not work together, you don't accomplish much. In people who are disturbed, thoughts and feelings work against each other.

One of the aims of meditation is to bring together these two aspects. Meditators in traditions influenced by Hinduism slow down, relax and observe the chatter of their minds. Eventually their awareness spreads to include others' thoughts and feelings, so that they may relate to and even help them. In Western parlance, this is emotional intelligence. Religions that teach contemplative practices may be viewed as a type of psychology (or perhaps psychology is a type of religion?). Highly developed techniques of all kinds may lead to similar, and measurable, outcomes, according to Lutz, Dunne and Davidson in 'Meditation and the Neuroscience of Consciousness'. They say:

> [Similarities] between traditions tend to appear primarily in claims about the ultimate meaning or nature of the state attained (for example, 'pure consciousness') or in metaphysically charged phenomenological descriptions (for example, ineffability) that do not lend themselves to easy measurement or interpretation.

The question of how meditation should be defined in the context of neuroscientific study is not easily answered, they say, because of the many kinds of activities to which the term might be applied. In Buddhism, meditation refers to a wide range of contemplative practices:

> [The] visualization of a deity, the recitation of a mantra, the visualization of 'energy' flowing in the body, the focusing of attention on the breath, the analytical review of arguments or narratives, and various forms of objectless meditations.

Each practice is assumed to induce a predictable and distinctive state noticeable to the practitioner. By repeatedly inducing such a state, the practitioner may produce a predictable effect to enhance desirable traits and inhibit undesirable ones. Over time, this state improves. Improvement is marked 'by the acquisition of certain traits (cognitive, emotional or physical), and/or the occurrence of certain events (cognitive, emotional or physical)'. The last factor required is that the meditation practice must be learned from someone who is a virtuoso. As Matthieu Ricard said:

> Everyone is like a wounded deer. The meditation teacher is present only to help us heal ourselves.

Lutz, Dunne and Davidson suggest that diverse forms of Buddhist meditation practices may be used as a foundation for:

1. the claimed production of a distinctive and reproducible state that is phenomenally reportable;

2. the claimed relationship between that state and the development of specific traits; and,

3. the claimed progression in the practice from the novice to the virtuoso.

These factors, they say, may form the basis of a neuroscientific approach for testing the kinds of mental and physical states induced by meditative practices.

Consciousness

Parapsychologists offer a slightly different perspective to the neuroscientific one, which bases everything upon processes of the physical brain and body. Some parapsychologists suggest that an individual mind is not limited to the physical brain. Consciousness spreads beyond the individual and the mind is somehow overlapped by other minds it encounters, in this world as well as other dimensions. Some we cannot see and therefore we think of them as 'dead'.

British mathematician and parapsychologist Julie Rousseau suggested, in a lecture given in a seminar on the afterlife by the Society for Psychical Research in 2006, that reality may be something like this. Imagine yourself as a bubble or concentric circle, and each person you meet as another bubble or circle. Each relationship you have with someone makes a part of your bubble mix with part of the other person's bubble. The bubble we are is not only visible and material. It is also invisible and non-material, and that non-material part of us is in contact with a realm that disembodied beings inhabit.

Spiritualists say that these disembodied beings also influence people, sometimes without our knowledge. They may not always be on our side, as some are mischievous and like to cause trouble, just as some human beings do. It is important to pay attention to conscience and common sense in dealing with any information received from spirits. What they tell you, especially about the future, must always be taken with a pinch of salt, not as *absolutely* true, but rather as comments from people who may see a little more than you do. What they say is, of course, their own opinion.

Furthermore, the medium who delivers the information colours whatever news they bring. He or she may have opinions that influence how the information is conveyed to you, or they may not see something clearly or completely. It is like hearing gossip from the 'other side'. Some spirits may be who they say they are, and some may not be. Some may tell you truth. Some may be creating confusion on purpose, or unintentionally because the spirit has limited consciousness or that of a psychotic who can't assess things accurately. So, spiritualists say, you have to use common sense when dealing with non-material worlds, of which there seem to be many.

Dr Gary Schwartz of the University of Arizona suggests that some kind of circular feedback action operates in the body as well as in outer space, where feedback occurs between galaxies. He contends that information seems to be endlessly circulating in the universe. Brains can learn from feedback and therefore so can hearts. If our bodies are a storehouse of information, then part of the organ transplant rejection process is a body's rejection of the memory held in the donor organ.

Only a tiny percentage of a material object is solid or 'concentrated energy'. The majority is empty. This emptiness is a vacuum that is infinite, and merely punctuated by forms. So this circulating information remains in space. Consciousness and memories don't disappear just because your body does. Anything that has feed-back has a memory.

Schwartz maintains that atoms have memory. This means that places contain embedded memories, which makes some sites sacred. Objects interact with their owners (for instance, Schwartz's watch interacts with him) and so psychometry works. Water has a memory, so homeopathy works. If everything has a memory and interacts with everything else, then everything is alive.

Some sort of overlap seems to exist between the non-material and material realms that we do not yet understand. Numerous transplant cases have been documented to show that when someone receives someone else's organs, characteristics of the donor are experienced by the receiver. Immediately after her operation, the first heart-lung transplant patient, Claire Sylvia, a well-educated, health-conscious vegetarian and teetotaller at Yale University, experienced extreme cravings for junk food called 'Chicken McNuggets' and beer. Later she discovered that the lung and heart she had received had come from a young man who loved them. He had died while riding his motorcycle with some he had just bought in his coat pocket. Not knowing anything about her donor, she started dreaming of him, to the extent of discovering his name in a dream. Eventually she tracked down his family and they corroborated every aspect of his character and the strange new habits she had suddenly acquired.

Cases like this have been studied by Paul Pearsall, who writes (in *The Heart's Code*) about what is termed 'systemic memory'. He proposes that the body's system as a whole has memory, not merely the brain. The implication is that memory can also be located in the body's organs. So it seems that consciousness is multifaceted. It is not even located solely in the brain.

4

THE UNIVERSE OF THE HUMAN BODY

*I have observed that people frequently need to develop
a basic sensitivity to the life force.*

LESLIE AND TERRY PATTEN *BIOCIRCUITS: AMAZING NEW TOOLS
FOR ENERGY HEALTH*

The water can carry a boat, but it can sink a boat too.

TRADITIONAL CHINESE SAYING

IF EVERYTHING IS 'undivided wholeness in flowing movement', as
Bohm said, then the body may be conceived of as another form
of consciousness, an indivisible extension of the mind. The body
reacts to, and cannot be separated from, the mind. One flows into
the other like water.

Your physical 'consciousness' becomes fully awake when you are
drawn to someone emotionally. Could the 'something extra' you
feel be in a non-physical dimension? If invisible subtle bodies exist,
their interaction could be the factor that determines how deep a
relationship becomes – and what makes love a mystery.

Rudolf Steiner declared that human beings are composed of
several bodies. Humans, plants and animals have an etheric body,
which affects the shape of the physical body. Senses, impulses and
emotions arise from the astral body, which humans and animals
possess. But only humans have an 'ego' and are conscious of having

a 'self'. These 'bodies' influence each other. Illness can occur in one of them and cause disturbances in the others.

Our having non-physical bodies could explain why people often experience sensations, even pain, in places where they are missing limbs. This is something that the English inventor, healer and energy-medicine researcher Harry Oldfield observed in many of his patients. He invented a machine that seems to prove this so-called 'phantom limb' phenomenon is not merely psychological.

Paranormalists say the physical body is surrounded by an etheric shield. This is constantly in touch with the etheric aspects of other material things. Vestiges of material objects that have died or been ingested may linger in space, their invisible shells remaining long after they have gone, which partly explains 'ghosts'.

Epigenetics and how to be healthy

The substances and material objects that surround us, the water we drink, the people we spend time with, even the music we listen to, may influence us far more than we imagine. The notion that these kinds of things affect health through genes is termed *epigenetics*. Its core premise is that genes have a memory.

> The conventional view is that DNA carries all our heritable information and that nothing an individual does in their lifetime will be biologically passed to their children.[1]

Epigenetics suggests that a control system of switches inside the body turns specific genes on or off, depending on what kinds of things we experience and absorb, from food to the air we breathe. According to this theory, the things we do and see, how much stress we feel, and so on, affect the body's control system. The lives of our grandparents – the air they breathed, the food they ate, even the things they saw – have an impact upon us, albeit decades later, when we might never have experienced them ourselves. In other words, what we do in our lifetimes could affect our grandchildren.

Professor Wolf Reik, at the Babraham Institute in Cambridge, found that manipulating mice embryos or an environmental change may set off the switches that turn genes on or off. He also found that switch settings can be inherited – that is, a 'memory' of an event may be passed down through generations. Epigenetics implies that changes in the mind affect the body's health and therefore the mind has control over the body.

Believing in the absolute control of mind over body holds inherent dangers, however. A genuine illness could be declaimed as being 'all in the mind' by physicians unable to identify a particular disease or dysfunction. British sufferers of ME (Chronic Fatigue Syndrome) are most unhappy about being sent for Cognitive Behavioural Therapy (CBT), when many medical practitioners and scientists say that ME may well have a number of different undiagnosed causes.

A better balance must be struck in our perception of what creates good health so that people with chronic medical problems are not sent for CBT simply because no doctor has discovered the reason and solution for their malady, or because governments don't want to spend the money required to diagnose and treat such patients. The most important factor for good health may well be your emotional-mental state, but we should be aware that the body is also influenced by the ideas and emotions of people around it. What people think and communicate to each other are extremely important to good health. American Indians talk about 'good medicine', by which they mean anything that is good for one's psychological, emotional, spiritual and physical wellbeing. Similarly, Tibetan Buddhist teachers sometimes speak of 'mind medicine'. One important aspect of this mind medicine – and what city-dwellers need – is quiet. We are constantly surrounded by machine noise.

An American 'sound therapy' practitioner once told me that he had helped many pop musicians overcome drug addictions by putting them in quiet surroundings for an extended period of time. The loud amplified music they produced, he believed, over-stimulated them, giving them an adrenaline high to which they became addicted. This often led to the excesses of the rock star lifestyle, from promiscuity to drug abuse. Their bodies became used to adrenalin, demanding more and more. This was caused by the high decibel levels that pop musicians heard night after night.

Light pollution is another disturbance to which 'townies' have grown accustomed. Natural darkness is absent from most densely populated areas. There is nothing like sleeping in silent, naturally dark countryside and being awakened in the morning by the twittering of birds or mooing cows. You can rest deeply in such a place, in a way that you never can in cities and towns.

The body and mind need what the Earth offers, minus our many inventions. Yet we cut ourselves off from it. We are at the mercy of every kind of pollutant due to the growing activity of our vastly multiplying machines. Persistent noisy extremes make adults agitated and nervous, so their effect upon children must be enormous. Young children from an age of three to five are especially sensitive to loud noises. You often notice them covering their ears when accosted by unexpectedly loud bangs.

Children who watch television and use computers a lot have been observed to suffer more often from short-sightedness, obesity, premature puberty and autism. A new report analysing 35 studies on the effects of television-watching by children by Dr Aric Sigman, published in the science journal *The Biologist*, identified 15 effects that excessive TV watching can have on youngsters. Watching television, Sigman says, suppresses the production of the hormone melatonin, said to affect the immune system, sleep cycle, onset of puberty and cell DNA, causing possible mutations that could later produce cancer. With such influences, it is no wonder that so many children today show signs of one disorder or another, including hyperactivity. The latter has been proven to be connected with chemical additives in food and drink.

The types of art we encounter also have a profound effect upon us. People often have one sense that is more highly developed than the others and therefore are sensitized to one particular art form. Painters respond strongly to things they see, while gourmet cooks respond to their sense of taste and raise food to the level of art. However, all the senses affect the emotions and processes of the mind, and both mind and body respond to music's rhythms and tones on sensory levels.

The musical quality of the body

Classical music has been proven to quicken children's thinking processes. Gorgi Lazanoff, a Bulgarian psychiatrist, played 18th-century music (Bach, Telemann, Vivaldi, Handel) to his students and noticed they showed an increased capacity for learning after he had taught them to breathe to the rhythm of the music. Rhythmical movement seems to be necessary for learning, growth, healing and a healthy, happy life.

> Failing to understand the musical quality of nature, which fulfils itself in an eternal present, we live for a tomorrow that never comes – like an orchestra racing to attain the finale of a symphony.[2]

The body's cells breathe just as a person breathes. Good health results from keeping the body flexible and rhythmic, with its fluids circulating. Being inseparable from the body, the mind must be kept flexible too by loosening its fixed ideas. Psychological problems often arise due to stagnant notions that a person cannot release, usually because of fear of the unknown, or fear of loss. If things are not moving in our bodies, we are dead.

Futurist biologist Elizabet Sahtouris, in a lecture for the Scientific and Medical Network, London, 2006, pointed out that if cells in a body think only of themselves, they are called cancer. When a body's cells cooperate with and share information and nutrients with each other in a rhythmic fashion, then the body is healthy. Sahtouris believes that how the body functions can show us how to operate in the world, and how to set up healthy societal structures. Just as the rhythms of the body must function as harmoniously as an orchestra for it to be healthy, so must we learn to behave like players in an orchestra, if our world is to be a peaceful, healthy one.

Rudolf Steiner once observed that movement and rhythm were important for a child thought retarded by his family. That child grew up to become a physician. Later Steiner used rhythm in every aspect of the Waldorf School curriculum he created.

The importance of rhythm to growth and healing should not be surprising to physicists, who know that matter is energy. Einstein stated this in his $E=MC^2$ formula – a theory confirmed by recent decades' atom smasher experiments. Energy speeds up or slows down, moving between speeds and different states of matter and non-matter. Scientists have observed that the universe pulsates rhythmically. Since energy is constantly moving, no steady, stable state seems to exist anywhere – except, perhaps, in rhythm.

A pulse reflects this rhythm. Nearly all the world's traditional medical systems test the body's condition by means of its pulses. Only a single pulse is tested in modern Western medicine but, in many of the world's traditional systems, subtler pulses are used in diagnosis.

Chakras and the life force

In India thousands of years ago, points in the body where pulse or bodily activities intensified were noted. These were called *chakras*. When the body is healthy, these energy vortexes are open and spin quickly, but when it is sick, they turn slowly or close.

Hindus accept that the body contains chakras through which the basic life force moves. They call this life force *kundalini*. They describe it as behaving like a serpent. When dormant, it lies coiled at the base of the spine between the reproductive and eliminative centres. When awakened, it uncoils and rises along the spine and through the chakra centres to the crown, called the cosmic chakra because it links the body with a higher consciousness or 'God' outside itself. Sometimes when the body is recovering from illness, the kundalini force may be felt as warmth or movement along the spine.

Colin Wilson explains that the chakras are points where the physical and subtle bodies connect. Hundreds of such points are utilized in traditional medical practices such as acupuncture. However, seven major chakras are said to be in front of or along the spine.

This kundalini force is treated with great respect in the East. Described as being like fire, it has the capacity to harm or heal, to heighten consciousness and increase psychic powers, or to depress consciousness and cause insanity. Hindus insist that people who undertake yogic practices to awaken the serpent from slumber should do so only under the guidance of experienced teachers who are able to help them avoid the dangers, for the kundalini may destroy as well as give life.

Three channels for this energy run vertically along the spine. It is imperative that kundalini energy rises through the central channel, otherwise problems occur. Gopi Krishna thinks that kundalini may be some strange form of energy whose source does not lie in the physical body.

> Anything that makes us stiff can also break us. [Only] if we are supple, will we never break.[3]

Through the body you gain the flexibility and strength necessary for keeping the mind and kundalini balanced so that you may experience deeper states of awareness. Yoga encourages the healthy flow of pranic (breath) life-energies through the physical and spiritual bodies and the chakras. The word 'yoga' actually means 'union'. One of hatha yoga's main purposes is to establish and maintain flexibility in the body and its functions as part of an overall spiritual discipline. Yoga unifies the physical and psycho-spiritual (non-material) bodies. Its aim is essentially spiritual, to help you experience serenity, think clearly and conduct yourself with calmer sanity and greater humanity. In *Mysteries* Colin Wilson states that:

> [Life] comes from beyond the body – our individuality sustained by a greater individuality. Man gets his life by turning towards the source of greater life, as a sunflower turns towards the Sun.

How people once saw the world

Traditional medical and philosophical systems are built upon the notion of unseen energies and an invisible world that influences us. Modern people do not always sense these. Many things can make us unable to engage with nature – drugs, pesticides, chemicals and radiation we are not even aware of, not to mention technology which can isolate and desensitize us.

One thing that changed perceptions in the West soon after Europe's Enlightenment was scientists' rejection of the idea that things we cannot see are present, and that they have a material impact upon us. What was also thrown out was the possibility of perceiving something new, should one 'look' in a way that scientists did not. Imagining that things exist that you cannot see opens you to everything around you, so that you can find solutions for seemingly insurmountable problems. Without this perspective, rationalist materialism tends to encourage isolation and alienation. It points people towards thinking mainly of themselves, pursuing careers and mates and operating businesses without thinking about their impact on others.

Wealth makes this even more possible, often increasing isolation and alienation. The more isolated a person becomes, the sicklier and more fearful he becomes. Unchecked, this leads to madness. Near the end of his life, Howard Hughes would not even step on carpets without a protective covering between him and what he felt were germ-laden objects – which were everywhere.

Interestingly, India's traditional medical system, Ayurveda, views imbalances, not germs, as the cause of illness. Good health arises naturally when the mind, body and spiritual nature are in balance. Your thoughts are as important as the food you eat and the exercise you take. How you see the world makes it what it becomes for you.

American Indians of the past perceived the world in a way that is unfamiliar to most people today. Animals, plants, stones and the sky were as full of complexity and information for Native Americans as our newspapers, television and books are for us. These natural phenomena knitted them together in a way that we do not know is possible. 'From stars and leaves they read signs that correlated with the stirrings in their bodies and souls, and they grasped the integrity of the whole from a perspective that is not comprehensible to the intellect alone.'[4] American Indians told the writer F David Peat that a non-native had missed the point of their shamanic initiations. They could tell because he had made so much of having hallucinations after ingesting several plants that produced them. In his book *Blackfoot Physics*, he says, 'The non-native seeker had focused on plants and roots', not the ceremonial ritual, nor 'the way a person came into relationship with energies and powers of another world'.

This coming into relationship with other energies or worlds is what Indian tribes appreciate occurs when they take natural psychoactive substances. Amazonian Indians use medicinal mushrooms they call *reishi* (meaning 'very old beings') in their rituals. They believe these *reishi* have a calming, wisdom-inducing effect on people who ingest them because *reishi* have lived inside the Earth for thousands of years.

Using a plant entails communicating with its essence, Indians say, and helps you 'weave back into a synchronous interplay with that complex web within which it is embedded'. After contemplating a plant for a while, Stephen Buhner, an American herbalist immersed in American Indian ways, claims to slip into a kind of half-waking, half-dreaming state, during which the spirit of the plant communicates its purpose to him.

This way of communicating with plants was also known in Europe. Manuscripts in Ireland dating from AD 800 indicate that the Celts communicated with plants, animals and stones to discover their healing gifts. The Celts originated in Germany and moved outwards to Brittany in NW France, Cornwall in SW England, Scotland and Ireland, so such practices must have been widespread. Baths, sweat-houses, herbs, prayers, chants, charms and surgery of various kinds were employed by Celtic physicians, who based healing treatments on cleanliness, fresh air and pure water.

Traditional medical systems perceive that balance, rhythm and harmony with nature are paramount for good health. Defined by the World Health Organization as health practices, approaches, knowledge and beliefs incorporating plant, animal and mineral-based medicines, spiritual therapies, manual techniques and exercises, applied singularly or in combination to treat, diagnose, and prevent illnesses or maintain wellbeing, these systems sprouted all over the Earth as naturally as plants do.

Around 25 per cent of modern allopathic pharmaceuticals are made from plants classified as traditional medicines. Developed through centuries of trial-and-error observation, they comprise herbs and natural products like bones, precious gems, minerals and chalk.

Interweaving world traditional medical systems

The world's traditional medical systems found their own way of conceptualizing the individual in terms of the universe. The themes of circulation, fluidity, seeking balance and attempting to make sense of invisible unknowns recur throughout their histories. Humans strove to have some kind of deeper relationship with the universe, through which they could find health.

No clear distinction exists between the physical world and the supernatural realm for indigenous traditional African healers, more of whom exist in Africa today than allopathic medical doctors. African medicines come from everything, but mainly plants and animals. Life forces or spirits are seen to manifest in every event and object in creation. These life forces have their own personalities and place in the cosmos, and health cannot be maintained or restored without their and God's cooperation. A healer looks for the cause of a patient's illness in her natural, social and spiritual environment.

For medicine men of American Indian tribes, no separation exists between religion and healing. Medicine ceremonies are part of community life. Humans are viewed as one of many inter-dependent beings and forces. Harmonious relationships with the whole of existence are viewed as more important than one single individual. Relationships exist between all things, so events in the weather and nature are seen to reflect the drama of one's inner life, speaking about what is happening within. A mountain could respond to someone's distress with fire, and the sky could rain to quench that fire, to ease distress.

[Tribal] cultures interpret disease and human suffering as disharmony.

The medicine man is believed to control the forces of nature and can make it rain. He perpetuates tribal lore, establishing harmony by conducting birth, death and magical rituals, acting as prophet, priest or chief of his tribe. Famous American Indian chiefs were medicine men, including Sitting Bull, Geronimo and Cochise. The medicine given takes many forms, not only herbal. A medicine man is also an artist – healing and the arts are not separate. Music and dance arose from people's desire to be in harmony with the universe. According to Jamake Highwater in *The Primal Mind*, the Indian rain-dance is a group's prayer for the regeneration of their *spiritual bodies*, not merely a call for rain.

> [Dance is worship and a cure for] an ailment of the 'spiritual body' that has mysteriously lost touch with the cosmos. [Dancing] is the 'breath of life' made visible. [All of its] symbolic images and gestures are associated with the wind and with the breathing of the living cosmos.

An old Navajo belief is that the wind gave life to the first people. Through dance and song, American Indians 'imitate and transform themselves into things of the natural world that invest them with vision and strength'. Because motion is contagious, Indians believe that it can affect animals and the natural world as a kind of sympathetic magic. They sense unknown, unseen, uncontrollable forces through dancing and feel they receive power through singing. Chants and songs are valued for the response they produce within the singer, not the audience. In *The Primal Mind* Highwater says:

> The first stage of ritual is almost always the rise of the singer [to] a plane of power – a place of contact with the forces that move the cosmos.

These can be utilized as healing forces, American Indians know. This same view has been promulgated in India for many centuries, where:

> Ayurveda is deeply rooted in the mythology of India and in its religious beliefs. Myth, legend, religion and daily living are interrelated,

and the mantras used in Ayurvedic healing are part of the normal, unconscious routine in many orthodox Hindu households.

So says Gopi Warrier (in *The Complete Illustrated Guide to Ayurveda*), who comes from a family of Ayurvedic doctors and has promoted Ayurveda in London for many years. He has a habit of giving away medicines and treatments to the sick for free, in keeping with the spiritual principles behind Ayurveda. The sick are often poor due to their illnesses, and so should be cared for, according to the tenets promulgated by India's most ancient texts, the Vedas – the original source of Indian traditional medicine.

Ayurvedic practitioners accept that the body will encounter things that are not good for it. They aim to strengthen the body so that it will be strong in any environment. Paramount in any healing method is how the mind thinks, how the heart feels. 'Wellbeing is the harmonious interaction of body and mind, and disease is caused by a deficient interaction between them', according to Gopi Warrier and Dr Deepika Gunawant.

Ayurvedic hospitals create enjoyable conditions for patients, with foods and treatments tailored to balance individual personalities. Techniques like massage are utilized to induce feelings of comfort and activate dormant glands. Rhythmic discipline in lifestyle and behaviour is encouraged, alongside meditation, yoga and deep relaxation, seen as one of the most important aspects of healing. An Ayurvedic physician will make an initial diagnosis by examining a patient's pulse, tongue, voice, skin, eyes, general appearance, urine and stools.

Ayurveda teaches that the universe is composed of five elements that combine to create three vital energies – *pitta*, *vata* and *kapha* – which determine what kind of body you have, and three psychic forces – *sattva*, *rajas* and *tamas* – which determine mental health, from which springs physical health.

According to the Balinese, disorders in the body can arise in realms invisible to us, beyond our senses. Sound vibrations utilized for healing are created by chanting mantras led by a spiritual healer who must prepare for healing others through meditation, purification and making offerings, so that he does not also become sick. The elements of fire, water, earth, air and space are located in precise areas of the body, which mirrors the universal macrocosm. Everything constantly strives for equilibrium between poles of natural opposites – creation and destruction, male and female, light and dark, positive and negative.

Two equal, opposite forces interact constantly in traditional Chinese medicine. About 400 BC, Lao Tzu set down its principles, describing a dark, static, moon-like, negative force he termed *yin* and a radiant, active, sun-like, positive force called *yang*. Neither force can exist without the other and must be in balance. Their dynamic interaction is reflected in the cycles of the seasons, an individual's life cycle and other natural phenomena.

Early Taoist teachers believed that the Tao produces a third force, a primordial energy or life force called *ch'i* (*qi*). When it flows freely, a body is healthy, but when weakened or blocked, it falls sick. Doctors examine a patient's tongue and 12 different pulses on both wrists, which indicate the condition of the body's 12 vital organs.

It is thought that around 3500 BC, tribal shamans and holy men practised the earliest Chinese medicine while living as hermits in the mountains. Their 'long life' regimen consisted of doing kung-fu style exercises, special breathing techniques to improve vitality and prolong life, and eating herbs and plants.

Five Taoist axioms form the foundation for several schools of Chinese medicine under the umbrellas of Buddhism, Confucianism and Taoism:

- Natural laws govern the universe and all beings in it, including humans.

- The universe is harmonious and well organized. When we live according to its laws, we live in harmony with it and nature.

- Change is the only constant in our dynamic universe. Stagnation within it causes illness.

- All things within our universe are connected and therefore interdependent.

- Human beings are intimately connected with and affected by all facets of our environment.

In connection with this interrelationship, dissection of the body was originally forbidden and patients are charged for the services of a doctor only when they are healthy, not when sick. Today, in true yin-yang fashion, almost all of China's medical schools contain traditional medicine departments while schools of traditional Chinese medicine have modern medicine departments.

Ho'okahi ka la'au e Mihi - the first medicine is forgiveness.

Traditional Hawaiian healers, the *kahuna*, view sickness as an imbalance of *mana* (life-energy on a non-material level), which may be rebalanced by forgiveness. Being sick is not only physical, but an imbalance of spiritual and/or psychological wellbeing. In order to replenish the body's *mana*, Hawaiian healers see prayer and chanting to be as important as herbal medicine.

Amazonian Indians view plants as having personalities, and believe we take on the energy of plants when we eat or use them. The Kallawayas (shaman healers) of Bolivia are said to view health in terms of a cycle of fluids and semi-fluids. Air is a fluid that unifies and provides breath to people, plants and animals. Everything in the body but fat must be eliminated regularly, as fluids become toxic if they are left to accumulate. Disease, they believe, is synonymous with an interruption in the circulation of blood-distilling fluids and recycling wastes.

Incan plant-based medicine was considered superior by the Spanish Conquistadors who conquered Peru. Since then, Peruvian medicine has absorbed medieval European, African and Chinese medical ideas.

Tibetan kings from the 7th to 10th centuries invited physicians from China, Greece, India, Nepal and Persia to teach their doctors, until then steeped in shamanic and Ayurvedic lore. Very similar to India's Ayurvedic system, yantra yoga, meditation and elements of traditional Chinese medicine combine to create traditional Tibetan medicine. So much medical information is in Sanskrit and Tibetan that traditional doctors find it helpful to know both languages, although they consider the tantric text known as the *rGyu-shi* to be their most important medical book. The Tibetan system is tripartite, based on Ayurveda's three *doshas* (*Vata*, *Pitta* and *Kapha*), as opposed to China's completely different, dualistic yin-yang system.

Tibetan medicine practitioners do not separate psychospiritual or religious matters from physical ones. At an early age, they are steeped in a monastic environment where they study the Buddhist science of healing for at least 13 years. Their most central training method is a meditation practice involving visualizations and mantra chants related to a non-material healer-teacher they call 'the Medicine Buddha'.

> [One] visualizes that the teachings of the Medicine Buddha come pouring into one in the form of colours, sounds and impressions. [While] engaged in visualization and reciting the [Medicine Buddha] mantra, one may consider some health issue for oneself or someone else. Whatever one needs to know flows into one in a similar manner.[5]

Thus the trainee doctor learns to use his intuition. Several different pulses in the body, some so subtle as to be unnoticeable by the untrained, are used by Tibetan doctors to make their diagnoses. They do not look for a patient's heart rate but for the breath. Five beats per breath is healthy. More or less is not.

Tibetan medicine is good for dealing with energy imbalances, but perhaps not for viruses. Diagnosis is very much based on a physician's skill, 75 per cent of which is determined by pulse reading – similar to Chinese pulse reading, although the placing and pressure applied may be different. Part of a patient's cure might involve chanting certain mantras and taking herbal pills. This past century the Tibetan system has focused most on herbal medicine and a little acupuncture, but most important for healing are Buddhist practices like meditation.

Similar to Tibetan medicine, students of *Unani* traditional medicine are trained to have a clear state of awareness so that they can discern the pulse's subtle qualities. Particular visualizations are used, and exercises practised to control breathing and the voice (especially emphasized in the Sufi lineage of the Chishtiyyah order, who use music as meditation). *Unani* (an Arabic spelling of 'Ionian', or 'Greek'), or *Hikmat*, does not separate mind from body. Its central tenet is that spiritual peace is essential for good health.

Like the Greek medical system from which it comes, Unani is based on the concept of balancing four bodily humours. A power in the body adjusts these humours. If this power weakens, an imbalance occurs and causes disease. Diagnosis is through the pulse and sometimes bodily excretions. Natural medicines (herbal, and those of animal and mineral origin), correct diet and good digestion strengthen this power.

Developed within the Muslim world over 13 centuries, *Unani* flourished in Persia but originated with the Greek physician Hippocrates (*c*.460–377 BC), who gleaned it from the medicine and traditions of ancient Mesopotamia and Egypt. Later, when the Mongols swarmed into Persia and Central Asia, many *Unani* practitioners fled to India, where brain surgery, laparotomy and plastic surgery were developed. India today is a world leader in *Unani* medicine.

Other traditional healing methods

Respect for the Earth is linked with respect for ourselves, and both are significant aspects of the 'good medicine' that American Indian healers practise. Medicine men use herbs as medicines, but they define 'medicine' as something more all-encompassing. First and foremost, they say that healing takes time and time is healing. Giving your time to a sick person is an act of healing – and healing always occurs in the context of a relationship. Focused intentions make the effect of your touch stronger. Your thoughts affect everything you touch.

Second, they say, the same principles that guide the movement of the stars and the Sun work within the body. Biological systems behave similarly at all levels. Catalysts for change behave the same inside the body as outside.

Third, they say that modern culture systematically teaches us to ignore emotions and to maintain a low level of emotional awareness. Civilization, as it is now constructed, requires a level of emotional unawareness for smooth functioning. Schoolchildren are taught to ignore their bodily needs for elimination until it is convenient for the teacher and to ignore their wish to play until their scheduled recess.

Medicine men find it strange that a secretary is not allowed to take time off work if overcome by sadness in response to a case history she is typing – that emotions are considered secondary to efficiency. The ways of less hurried hunting-and-gathering societies are more realistic, they feel. Hunters must be prepared on many levels before hunting together. They make a final point: lowered alertness from the mental or physical exhaustion of any member of the hunting group could endanger the hunt and the tribe.

In modern society, no natural breaks or allowances are made for the body's rhythms. Putting a client to bed is the most important therapy, for it breaks old habits. The body's resources for healing itself are not usually available while we're active and running around. Excessive busyness and exhaustion stop someone from engaging in the self-contemplation necessary for gaining a level of emotional awareness at which change and healing can occur.

Ceremonies and rituals are important as a means of accessing help from the spiritual dimension for healing. Fasting and other purification methods like the sweat lodge are used to prepare someone to go to the top of a mountain, where they wait for a vision during up to four days of solitary prayer and meditation. Medicine men say that people need to rest face-to-face with themselves. Their healing treatment includes being expressive in some artistic manner and doing something to care for the Earth. Healing takes place on many levels according to American Indians. Most traditional medical systems take a similar approach.

One Ayurvedic therapy is called *Panchakarma* ('five actions'), used for detoxification and rejuvenation purposes. Treatment may include refraining from exposure to unwholesome stimuli, such as polluted, filthy or noisy environments, alcohol, drugs and cigarettes, tense or violent films, and anything that increases addictive responses and/or desire. The sick are told to replace these with meditation, yoga, self-observation, prayer, uplifting companionship, inspiring reading and visiting holy places.

Most traditional medical systems use water, sunlight and massage therapies. Traditional Chinese medicine also offers philosophy, lifestyle and dietary changes, and various treatments. These include acupuncture, which has been scientifically proven to relieve postoperative pain, nausea during pregnancy and chemotherapy, anxiety, insomnia and dental pain, with very few side effects. Added to this, moxibustion is used, sending heat to the body's *chi* points, and t'ai chi, which helps people move through space more sensitively – one side-effect being that the elderly become less fearful of falling.

Complementary and integrated medicine

Newer therapies are now termed 'complementary medicine' by the World Health Organization, which defines it as adaptations of traditional medicine in industrialized countries. Treatments deal with the whole body and attempt to stimulate its natural self-regulating, self-healing abilities. These include naturopathy, traditional medicines and bodywork. Complementary medicine use rose in 1990–97 from $13 billion to $38 billion a year in the United States, where twice as many consultations were made with complementary medicine practitioners as with allopathic doctors. The same thing is happening elsewhere.

Higher quality research in complementary medicines is needed, as are training guidelines for licensed healthcare professionals. Government research funds are rarely made available for herbal and traditional medicines, and only giant pharmaceutical corporations normally have the money to pursue the study required to prove their efficacy.

Integrated medicine means incorporating elements of complementary and alternative medicine into treatment plans, while using allopathic methods of diagnosis and treatment. Both patient and doctor are involved in maintaining the patient's health.

Diet, rest, sleep quality, exercise, the patient's emotional state and relationships are as important in creating and maintaining health as pills and potions. Rather than drugs or surgery, a simple dietary adjustment or relaxation training may be all a patient needs. HRH Prince Charles created the Foundation for Integrated Health (FIH) in England to encourage better research and regulation. As he stated in his address to the World Health Assembly in Geneva (May 2006):

> [The] world has for too long maintained a dangerously fragmented and abstracted view that has led to our abandoning much valuable traditional knowledge. [Now] we are beginning to reap the harvest we have sown through living off nature's capital rather than from her income.

FIH offers an awards scheme for projects that integrate complementary medicine with other treatments, and has created an association of clinicians developing integrated approaches.

Homeopathy

Britain's royal family have been strong adherents of homeopathy since Queen Adelaide was first treated with it in 1835. King George VI granted the title 'Royal' to the London Homeopathic Hospital, of which Queen Elizabeth II is now patron. The late Queen Mother used it, and lived to the ripe old age of 101.

Homeopathy was developed in Germany by doctor and chemist Samuel Hahnemann (1755–1897). Hahnemann based his theory on *The Canon of Medicine* (*Qunun*), the most important medical work of Avicenna (980–1037), which was the foundation for *Unani* medicine. He thought that disease meant imbalance, which could be put right by the principle of 'like cures like'.

Hahnemann believed that no matter how diluted a solution is, a remedy leaves an imprint of its properties in water molecules. Most remedies are derived from plants, but minerals, metals and even some poisons are also used. Very young children and animals seem to respond best to them, which believers say proves homeo-pathy cannot be placebo.

Most scientists were as sceptical as Professor of Immuno-pharmacology Madeleine Ennis of Queen's University, Belfast, was, until, that is, she failed to disprove the claims of the late French biologist Dr Jacques Benveniste (a specialist in allergy and inflammation and Research Director at the French National Insti-tute for Medical Research). In 1988, while studying how allergies affect the body, he diluted an allergic substance and noted that even when diluted to a point where the final solution contained only water molecules, it still caused an allergic reaction in a subject. Dr Benveniste concluded that a trace of the substance's molecules remained in the solution and proposed that water has the power to 'remember' substances it has once contained. The scientific establishment subsequently pilloried him.

To finally disprove Benveniste's findings, Madeleine Ennis devised a stringent experiment with a consortium of four inde-pendent research laboratories in France, Italy, Belgium and Holland. To her chagrin, they found that homeopathic solutions of histamine worked just like histamine itself, even though they were so diluted that they probably didn't contain a single molecule of it.

The universe of healing

Healing is part of every religious practice, and may include psychologically-influential rituals as well as faith or distant heal-ing. These are especially helpful sometimes to suffering caused by illnesses that are difficult to diagnose or treat.

Conventional medical doctors often ascribe psychological or psychosomatic causes to sicknesses without a specific pathology, or to those they are incapable of diagnosing. Some healers seem to have an ability to heal other people in some inexplicable way, often without knowing how it happens. They even specialize in particular ailments. In Ireland, 'bone-setters' reset broken bones, sometimes without touching them.

Faith healing is the systematic, purposeful intervention by one or more persons aiming to improve the condition of someone by hand contact or passes above their body, or focused intention alone, without conventional energetic, mechanical or chemical interventions. Distant healing means that the healer and the recipient of healing are physically separated by distance. A majority of scientific research projects undertaken over the past 30 years or more, studying how it affects disease and recovery, indicate that it enhances the healing process when used with other therapies.

Most scientists do not accept that distant healing works. However, experiments undertaken since Einstein's time have demonstrated that reactions to particles that are far away do occur. Distant healing intention effects have been replicated under controlled, randomized and blinded laboratory conditions on living non-human life forms. Quantum theorists take seriously the notion that observation and consciousness play a role in the physical world and that at some fundamental level, mind and matter may be inseparable.

In 2007, Lynne McTaggart ran the first of a series of web-based experiments with what she called an 'intention experiment' with 400 people in London. A web link-up enabled them to focus their attention on two plant leaves in a laboratory 5,000 miles away at the University of Arizona in the USA with Professor Gary Schwartz. Their aim was to use their thoughts to make one of the leaves glow. Light-sensitive cameras were trained on the leaf in Arizona, to watch for changes. Results were said to be immediate and surprising, as the leaf started to emit more light, noticeably even to the naked eye, only 48 hours later.

Some healers find it easier to focus on healing animals than plants or human beings, and significant results have been reported. I once watched a healer in County Wicklow, Ireland, give a laying-on-of-hands healing to a calf whose owner was concerned because the newborn had never stood up and could not reach high enough to feed from its mother. He didn't want to kill the calf – normal practice when calves can't fend for themselves. The calf's worried mother hovered nearby but stayed away throughout the healing procedure, as if she understood that the healer was trying to help. After about 20 minutes, the calf suddenly lurched upright. His mother snorted appreciatively, to my eyes looking pleased and genuinely surprised, and eagerly ambled over and sniffed him. Then he followed her out into the farmyard to suckle. The healer was delighted, because normally she worked with humans and had found it so much easier healing a cow. Animals put up no intellectual barriers to healing forces.

Animals as healers

Animals are known to heal humans also. Cats often choose to sit on people at the precise spot where they are feeling pain or suffering from some ailment. Many cat-lovers swear that the combination of their vibrating purring and bodily warmth is healing to them. Some people think that cats purr when they're injured, to make themselves feel better. But when bodies are traumatized, they shut down non-essential activity. Cats purr when they are severely injured or dying, so purring must be survival-related.

Cats apparently purr during both inhalation and exhalation with a consistent pattern and frequency between 25 and 150 hertz. These sound frequencies have been observed to improve bone density and promote healing, and are thought to have some effect upon humans. Cats do not display as many muscle and bone abnormalities as other domesticated animals, such as dogs.

New Yorker Judy Audevard's mother had a stroke and lost the ability to speak and use her right arm, so Audevard placed her pet dog Kizzy on her mother's lap. Suddenly her mother began patting the dog with her right arm. When Audevard exclaimed, 'Do you know what you're doing?' her mother replied, 'Oh, I'm petting Kizzy.' That was the beginning of Audevard's exploration of pet therapy.

This kind of interaction between humans and animals, particularly dogs, would be no surprise to British biologist Rupert Sheldrake, who has written about the empathy between humans and animals. In his book *Dogs That Know When Their Owners Are*

Coming Home, he talks about the telepathy and mutual healing that occurs between pets and their masters.

'A 1999 study in New York, Missouri and Texas found that medication costs dropped in nursing homes that allowed pets.'[6] At Quantum Leap in Odessa, Texas, horses are used to help military veterans who have lost limbs in action. Apart from the obvious health and pain-relieving benefits of exercise while riding a horse, riding offers a distraction to the disabled, who suddenly are able to move around without the aid of contraptions or machines. Horse-riding turns their focus from their disability to their abilities, improves their balance and memory skills, and rebuilds their confidence. A horse's gait closely mimics the human stride, so riding a horse helps to re-educate the brain about where a missing leg has been. This simulation helps to ease the sufferer's adjustment to using a prosthetic limb.

The wild dolphin Fungi, who lives in Dingle Bay in southwest Ireland, is said by local people to have healing abilities. The sick often go there specifically to swim with him. The dolphin's sonar system is thought to be so sophisticated that it can tell where scar tissue exists in the human body, which it tends to avoid touching. Its 'sonar can penetrate up to 3 ft (1 m) through sand and mud with resolution significant enough to distinguish between a dime and a penny'.

Some scientists who have studied this believe that dolphins can view the inside of our bodies. They seem to focus on an individual's specific area of impairment, or any spot containing a tumour. People who swim with dolphins often say they sense themselves being scanned by them. The sound a dolphin makes seems to resonate in the bones, bypassing the ears and travelling up the spine – similar to a sonogram. A dolphin navigates through the water by emitting a focused blast of ultrasound vibration that bounces off objects. Thus, the dolphin can tell what surrounds it – it 'sees' via sound. American veterinarian Gregory Bossart is convinced that this echo-location ability is responsible for the healing that humans often experience around dolphins.

Some scientists suggest that the dolphin heals human cells with its sonar. The sound waves it produces cause alternating regions of compression and expansion that create small bubbles in cell membranes. This makes it easy for certain neurological molecules to move from outer to inner neurons. American neuroscientist Dr David Cole, of Acqua Thought Foundation, US, thinks this enables the dolphin to change the cellular metabolism of humans.

> The Atlantic Bottlenose dolphin can produce [enough sound energy] to cause cavitation [the formation of cavities in a structure, or gas bubbles in a liquid]. The energy can actually rip holes in the molecular structure of fluids and soft tissues.[7]

He also believes that sonar-induced cavitation alters human brainwaves. After a human meets a dolphin, they shift from beta waves (high frequency) to low-frequency theta waves. Sharper concentration, memory and alertness arise with beta waves, while theta waves bring altered states of consciousness alongside better creativity and sensory integration (something people exhibit as they drift from consciousness into sleep). According to research, this change in brainwave patterns improves the immune system and synchronizes the two halves of the brain, inducing a transcendental, otherworldly sense of euphoria. This seems to last longer than the 'high' produced by endorphins and apparently enables long-term positive changes to occur in those who suffer from serious illness and depression. After dolphin-assisted therapy, children with developmental disabilities have shown remarkable improvements in learning and cognitive abilities, concentration and ability to communicate with others.

Dolphin sonar is four times stronger than the ultrasound therapeutically used in hospitals to destroy cataracts, kidney stones and gallstones, and is similar to the drumming, chanting and music used by ancient cultures to promote good health. Such sounds influence heart rate, breathing, muscle contractions, memory and immune function.

What makes the dolphin's sonar even more effective is the fact that it is delivered through water, said to be 60 times more efficient than air for sound transference, and it enters a human body that is already 80–90 per cent fluid. Ultrasound resonance is thought to be especially powerful within cerebrospinal fluid due to its influence on the brain and spinal cord.

Interestingly, 13 of the dolphin's 22 chromosomes are identical to human chromosomes, according to researchers at Texas A&M University. The nine remaining chromosomes are combinations or rearrangements of their human counterparts. 'The dolphin's anatomy is strikingly similar to our own, in spite of the obvious differences. Bones of the hands and feet are almost identical, only theirs are housed in their fins.'[8]

Is it possible that the dolphin is our closest relation in the animal kingdom? Humans are said to have a diving reflex that apes don't have. We also have a fatty layer beneath the skin, as dolphins and other ocean-dwelling mammals do. The neocortex area of our brains is supposed to be nearly identical to the cetacean brain, which the latest research indicates may be superior to ours. Tear glands are found in sea mammals and we cry and perspire, while apes do not. One Australian Aborigine tribe known as the Dolphin People believe their ancestors were souls of dolphins who were slaughtered by sharks and reborn as the first humans. Other primitive peoples tell stories that also link us to dolphins.

Subtle energy or vibrational medicine

'Sound waves are the most familiar form of vibration people think about when they use the term "vibrational".' But sound waves are just one form of what British MD Richard Gerber terms 'vibrational medicine'. It does not treat the body as if it is a 'sophisticated machine, animated only by electrochemical reactions', but as 'a complex, integrated life-energy system that provides a vehicle for human consciousness as well as a temporary housing for the creative expression of the human soul'.[9]

> [Illness] is thought to be caused not only by germs, chemical toxins and physical trauma but also by chronic dysfunctional emotional-energy patterns and unhealthy ways of relating to ourselves and to other people.

Both electromagnetic and subtle life-energy are utilized in vibrational medicine to bring about healing changes in the body, mind and spirit. This implies that the physical body may be cured by addressing its subtle body. One thing that does this is sound.

Sound healing

'In the beginning was the Word.' The sound! [Everything] is in a state of vibration. Everything is frequency. Sound can change molecular structure. It can create form … [We] can change our vibrational rate through our own self-generating sounds.[10]

American sound healer Jonathan Goldman believes our connection to good health is through sound. Music and the kinds of sounds we are surrounded by may harm or heal us, and can change molecular structures.

'The ancient mystery schools of Greece, India, Tibet and Egypt had a vast understanding of the relationship between music and healing.' For them, sound was the basic creative force of the universe. In ancient Greece, healing temples used music to effect cures by harmonizing body and spirit. Their god Apollo was the god of music as well as medicine. This idea came in part from Pythagoras of Samos, alive around 2,600 years ago. The father of geometry, he was the first person in the West to correlate the relationship between musical intervals by using a single-string instrument called the monochord to find the ratios between sounds. Pythagoras taught that the universe is an immense monochord whose single string stretches between spirit and matter, or the heavens and the Earth.

His aim was to help people to hear the 'Music of the Spheres', the sounds the movements of the heavenly bodies make while travelling through the universe. These he trained his students on the island of Crotona to hear. Unfortunately his school burned to the ground and his teachings were lost, apart from those imparted to his students.

By creating your own harmonics or overtones, you can heal your body, environment, and world. Harmonics can initiate changes on physical, mental, emotional and etheric levels, Goldman believes. 'The ripples and waves created by the pebble grow in size and strength until they reach the farthest ends of the lake.'

While learning overtone singing, first your hearing changes. You begin to perceive things that you couldn't previously. Then your voice changes and you begin to create new sounds. Finally, you become aware of a wider reality, and of consciousnesses apart from your own. Singer Jenni Roditi describes her experience of overtone singing as follows:

> Each note is like a rainbow of sound. When you shoot a light beam through a prism, you get a rainbow. You think of a rainbow of sounds when you sing one note. If you can use your throat as a prism, you can expose the rainbow – through positioning the throat in a certain physical way, which will reveal the harmonic series note by note. It's a physical thing that happens due to the way you control the muscles and the tongue, but a state of mind as well. It works much better if you're very, very relaxed, because then the overtone series begins to happen on its own.
>
> It's sort of mysterious. To growl a note, which is what the (Buddhist) monks do, you use your diaphragm, and when you move your lips forward while singing 'oo', and then out and back with other vowel sounds, it creates harmonics. The chakras are illuminated as you sing through the different pitches.
>
> Going through the harmonic scale is like going through the chakra spectrum. By overtone singing, you're activating the chakras and clearing out your whole energetic system. You're cleaning the chakras and getting them to spin without any mud or clutter around. It's all about moving energy. When this happens, you feel peace and insight into the nature of reality – insight into the nature of interdependent origination.

Could this be a state akin to what the American Indians experience when chanting or singing during their rituals? It is meant to put participants in touch with a mystery far greater than themselves, beneath and beyond speech.

'The universe is alive with sound. Every sound has overtones.'

French physician and specialist in otolaryngology Alfred Tomatis believes chants from the world's religious traditions are rich in high-frequency harmonics and have a neurophysiological effect which charges the brain. He discovered this when called upon to treat Benedictine monks for depression and exhaustion. Another physician had prescribed a meat-and-potatoes diet for these monks, who were vegetarian, but the monks had grown only worse. Tomatis discovered that a new abbot had made some changes to their normal routine. This abbot felt that the monks' daily 6–8 hours of chanting served no useful purpose, so he stopped it. Dr Tomatis reinstated their daily practice of Gregorian chanting and, all at once, the monks returned to their previous twenty-hour workdays with no problem. This, he felt, proved that high-frequency chanting has a strong therapeutic effect upon the body.

The brain is said by some to be a complex tone generator, and to command the body through frequencies it emits. It produces waveform patterns that can be measured, which indicate physical and emotional health levels. Are these waveforms our thoughts, or feelings beneath thoughts?

When the body is deprived of certain light frequencies, it can become sick. Sound behaves as light behaves. Both act upon the body like vitamins and minerals. Sound healers identify health problems and vitamins your body needs through analysing the sound waves your voice produces. Most people's voices lack some tones or frequencies. Sound healers heal people by playing back to them whatever tones they are missing, but at a low octave that corresponds to brainwave frequencies. These have even been used to alleviate pain. The body is helped to heal itself by activating the control centre in the brain that looks after healing.

> We are a dancing wave form; we are sound. We are not separate from the world we're part of … we operate the same way it does, as frequency wave forms configuring themselves in a certain way.[11]

Dr Shabna, an Indian doctor who combines Ayurveda with sound in her US healing practice, says the body is a chemical factory and its chemicals move around inside us at different frequencies.

Our voice-box amplifies these sounds, which repeat and resonate. The body resonates in sympathy with sounds that are played, so anything in the body that is not balanced will simply readjust itself to be in synchrony with them.

Dr Neff once used what she calls the 'oxygen frequency' for a neighbour who had congestive heart failure. After several minutes of hearing this frequency, his grey pallor turned pink and he began talking normally. Later when she got him to hospital, they discovered that he had an occluded artery and needed surgery, and was having a major undiscovered problem with oxygen intake. Sound therapy, she felt, had saved his life.

Dr Peter Moscow, a sound healer from Dublin, Ireland, working in America, offers his patients a musical bed that incorporates music, light and sound boxes that play tones for specific problems. He immerses people so that 'they're inside the sound box, inside the music'. Their problem usually goes away after 30 minutes or an hour of this treatment.

Sound healers claim that even addictions can be surmounted by making your own sound frequencies strong, so that you eventually realize you don't need the substance you're addicted to. One interesting observation they have made at Biowaves (US) is that some people stay in bad relationships with their partners because they need a particular frequency their partner gives them. Once they are able to maintain the sound frequency they need, they gain the strength to leave their abusive partner.

Toning harmonically has been observed to enable the normally stationary bones of the cranium to move. You can do this for yourself or to someone else, according to Dr Harlan Sparer, who has observed that toning affects the entire brain, the primary respiratory rate and the flow of cerebral spinal fluid through the cranium. Goldman thinks that cerebral spinal fluid may be equivalent to the kundalini energy of Eastern mystical traditions, as toning seems to affect a person's overall health.

London's best-known sound healer and overtone chanting trainer Jill Purce says that, when you do overtone chanting, you differentiate mental and physiological processes that are not normally differentiated. You use parts of the brain you don't normally use, which makes something else happen so that you enter 'the world of spirit'.

Religious and esoteric groups use sound today in their rituals and ceremonies. A magician called Israel Regardie used to chant various 'God names' of what his fellow Golden Dawn members thought of as different levels of existence. Stressing the harmonics in the elongated vowels of the names of God was thought to create 'a magical sonic formula for manifesting different aspects of divine energy'.

The Sufis attribute different divine qualities to vowels. The *muezzin* of Islam intones the Holy Koran from a minaret, placing both his hands on his temples and calling to Allah by singing in an unnaturally high tone with his head-voice, the falsetto. The notes, which in quiet areas can be heard miles away, sound in the distance like a soft woman's voice. Tremendous effort and exertion are required on the part of the singer to force and strain his voice to make this sound.

The Sufis, an esoteric branch of Islam, use vowels in their healing work. The three basic sounds Sufis use in healing are the long vowels 'a' (as in 'father'), which vibrates downward and slightly to the left from the heart until it centres in the heart, 'i' (as in 'machine'), which moves in the opposite direction up the nasal passageway to the pineal gland, and 'u' (as in 'hut') which, uttered correctly at the point on the pursed lips, arrives at the point of connection between the in- and out-breaths. The word 'Allah' is an elongation of the long vowel 'a', which 'activates the heart'. Another prayer that uses this sound is the Christian 'Lord's Prayer', said to open the heart chakra.

Tibetan monks from Gyuto Monastery use the fourth overtone, two octaves and a major third above the fundamental, in their tantric chanting. Once you become conscious of this fourth overtone, you can begin to heal yourself through sound since this brings one's whole being into tune and raises consciousness to a high pitch. Most importantly, if you sing very softly while being conscious of this fourth overtone, and send this sound into an area where energy is blocked or tensed, you can release the tension.

This so-called One Voice Chord or tantric voice is said to embody both the masculine and feminine aspects of divine energy.

Folktales tell of how Tibetan monks learned this way of singing – with one high (pure and sweet, like a child) and one extremely low voice (a very bass growl) at the same time from a 15th-century lama who discovered it in a dream. In Mongolia, this style of throat-singing, possibly the most developed in the world, is called *hoomi* and found in the Tuvic region, where shamans are said to have learned it by listening to a waterfall.

Goldman claims to have been given the ability to sing by monks he met in a dream, who told him never to misuse the voice for attention or ego. Professor of Indo-Tibetan studies, Robert Thurman attests that this form of multi-phonic singing is possible only when someone has reached a certain selfless stage of meditation, where they become open enough to be vessels of this sound. It is produced, he says, by people who are aware on a level in which they are not present; the sound comes *through*, but not from, them.

It is thought that shamans used overtone singing or harmonics to communicate with spiritual realms, or even with creatures and elements of nature. Padmasambhava, a tantrist from Udyana (now Pakistan) who brought Buddhism into Tibet in the 9th century, described the chanting style of the Bön, the pre-Buddhist religion of Tibet, as 'the clear high voice that is produced in a low place, like the black dog's barking'. He adjured his followers to use this voice only when chanting sacred Buddhist scriptures, otherwise they would invoke 'the voice of the Bön'. Mongolian shamans, like Bön practitioners, create wordless harmonics.

In Southern Siberia and Mongolia, among the Khakassy and the Tuvans, throat-singing techniques are found that scholars think were imitations of the jew's harp or the singing bow, used ritually for supernatural communication. Herders sang in this throat-singing style for the grasslands, mountains and steppe around them.

Other cultures use harmonics for various purposes, some explicit and some secret. Goldman speaks of how he helped to create light in a completely dark room through using harmonics with Mayan Indians in Mexico. He believes that harmonics may open a gateway between different realms of existence or create interdimensional windows through which the shaman can travel or through which an invoked spirit may enter this domain.

Native American shamans use vowels in their rituals but tend not to talk about them, professing ignorance to enquirers about their effects. However, it is known that certain of their rituals are meant to bring spirits into this world. One purpose of their Ghost Dance religion, popular in the 19th century, was to revive the spirits of their ancestors and reunite with them.

To create harmonics, Australia's Aborigines use an instrument made of a hollowed-out tree limb called a didgeridoo, which requires a circular form of breathing where you blow out as you breathe in – a style also developed in Tibet. The Aborigines say it creates a sonic field for healing, and an interdimensional window through which they can travel to the Wandjina, supernatural beings who brought the Aborigines to this planet and then withdrew back to their dimension. As Goldman states:

> Vocal harmonics create changes in the heartbeat, respiration and brainwaves of the reciter.

Even Gregorian chants, with elongated vowel sounds, are thought to be rich in high-frequency harmonics and to have a neurophysiological effect which charges the brain. Such sounds are produced in the bones, which vibrate the whole body. Sound resonates from cranium and skull throughout the body via the bones. Nearly all our cranial nerves lead to the ear, which is neurologically linked to the optic and oculomotor nerves, or vision and movement, and to the nerve that affects our larynx, the bronchi, heart and gastrointestinal tract. This means that our voice, breathing, heart rate and digestion are affected by what we hear.

Legends describe how, before human beings spoke languages composed of words, we used a harmonic language, with which to communicate with all the creations of nature. Thoughts and information were sent on the soundwave, in the way that dolphins (which can send and perceive sounds up to nearly 200,000Hz) communicate. They do this 'by transmitting three-dimensional holographic thought-forms of sound'. Later the consonants and tones we used separated into language and music. *Healing Sounds* says:

> Becoming one with the sound is a key to meditation with sound.

An English osteopath and MD called Dr Peter Guy Manners has been conducting research since 1961 on how sound affects the structure and chemistry of the human body, after discovering Dr Jenny's cymatic experiments. He believes that disease is an 'out of tuneness' somewhere in the body. The molecules of a healthy body work harmoniously together, he says. If different, foreign sound frequencies enter the body and overwhelm its native patterns, establishing disharmonious frequencies, then it creates disease. The cure is to send a harmonic frequency towards the body, so that intruding vibrations are neutralized, with a cymatic instrument consisting of a portable, briefcase-size computer and a sound generator resembling a hammer-like vibrator. It contains thousands of different combinations of harmonics for emotional and mental problems as well as physical diseases.

Goldman thinks that anything that can be done by a machine can be done by the human voice, and probably better, particularly if the healer's intention has anything to do with healing. The results of many studies, in which psychics attempt to influence other people with thoughts alone, indicate that our intentions do have an effect upon others. Therefore, sound and music must have an even more powerful effect when used with intention.

Inside the mind of a music and sound healer

Sound is used rather differently by music therapists, who utilize sound healing with other techniques. The Sufi musician Hazrat Inayat Khan spoke of how, after he had sung and played the *veena* for a long time, to him every soul became a musical note. His focus shifted to tuning souls instead of instruments – 'to harmonize people instead of notes'. A musician's work is to make himself harmonious so that the harmony of his soul will appeal to other souls and help them be harmonious too.

I have found in every word a certain musical value, a melody in every thought, harmony in every feeling. [The musician] should develop music in his personality [and] become musical in …

thoughts, words and actions. One should be able to give the
harmony for which the soul yearns and longs every moment.[12]

Perhaps this is the foundation for all music therapies, although
different systems take different approaches. Some music therapists work from the standpoint of music performance, as Jenni
Roditi does. She aims to encourage her clients to go beyond their
imagined limits. She thinks of working with someone on their
voice 'as creating a kind of instant composition that resonates with
the person and their movements'. In doing anything creative or
therapeutic, she says, she follows her inner sense.

> When you have an inner sense of something, if it's a clear sense,
> then it has an innocence about it – a truthfulness. When I com-
> pose, it has always been through that inner sense.

People who come to her for voice therapy often have multiple
layers of blockages that stop them from feeling their inner sense,
she says. 'What I try to do is clear away the layers so that they come
to the innocent innocence, in a sense … you know, "in a sense" –
inner sense!' She laughs at her word-play, saying she has tacked
up on her wall the phrase: 'my inner sense is my innocence'. She
tries to bring someone into a primordial state where anything is
possible creatively.

Roditi says this kind of therapy isn't like rebirthing, which takes
you into a hyperventilated altered state, and from there into a
primordial place. Her method is more conscious and playful. It's
about making noise with your voice rather than lying on a floor
with a blanket and breathing.

So how does she do this with a client? First she makes the room
quiet so the person can relax. Then she observes the person's
posture and breathing, listens to their voice and checks its range –
how high and low they can sing and what happens in the middle
when they go through the natural break in the voice – all things a
singing teacher might do at the start of a lesson. A person's vocal
range represents their psychic range. Their whole vocal spectrum
is like a rainbow with different tone colours. When working with
a particularly tearful person, she finds that suggesting the person

do something with their tears gives them a tremendous amount of creative energy. She says:

> I often think of the water in teardrops as 'blessed' water. One could collect teardrops and put them on a flower and the flower would grow very beautifully. For me, there's no boundary between crying and singing.

Singing is in many cultures just a formalized version of crying or laughing. The Mediterranean and Bulgarian cultures, and most indigenous cultures, have used singing as a way to weep and wail through the grief of bereavement. In their singing, you often hear a mingling of joy and sadness that's very potent. Experienced artists can mingle joy and sadness in a way that becomes almost non-dual, so that you're moving between emotional states very freely. The best singers can shine a light on the human condition with very few notes, [moving] from ecstasy to melancholy to joy to excitement.

But when you're working with your average person who hasn't got that, you can still practise, as I did just the other day with a client whom I asked to sing just three notes. I said to her: 'imagine you're in ecstasy as you sing these'.

'Why have you given me just three notes?' she asked me. 'It's just doh-ray-me.'

So I said: 'Fill the transition' between the vowels being sung 'with your imagination, your experience of life. You're making a transformation from one state or vowel to another. Ecstasy is that place where you don't know quite what's going to happen next, but you're very happy and excited. You can fill sounds with imagination and intensity.'

Doing that brought her alive, and she said to me, 'It's not an exercise anymore; it's a whole exciting drama'.

Allowing [pain] to be there actually begins the process of healing. [Resistance] is worse than the pain itself. Resisting pain is like building up another layer of suffering. You've got your original suffering, then you've got your resistance to it on top of that, so it's twice as bad. I always remember this image that Trungpa uses about the deer …

(Chögyam Trungpa Rinpoche was a notoriously wild Tibetan lama who first taught in Britain in the 1960s and later set up the Naropa Institute in Boulder, Colorado, during the 1970s.)

> Before it grows horns, it has two little pokey things and they're so soft. It's as if you've got to be a deer without your horns and these two little growths on the top of your head – very vulnerable and very raw, but full of potential. They're going to turn into fantastic antlers. But you come to the place where they're just these wobbly growths and that's where you're very alive. As you go into that, it starts to grow all on its own and the stream will do it for you.[13]
>
> It's a trusting thing. So much is belief. At the moment when you stop resisting, the connection starts to happen and you feel more in yourself. You feel you've come home on some level. You've come home to the truth – whatever it is.

Presumably you relax when that happens, and the voice opens. Returning to a primordial place means directly experiencing life as normal healthy children do. That implies an emotional healing of some sort occurs for people in this kind of therapy, which is fundamental to every other sort of healing.

If music be the food of love ... and health

Sufferers of Parkinson's Disease are said to be calmed by certain kinds of music – so long as they are musically sensitive and 'in the right mood'. It must also be the right kind of music, rhythmic and not too harsh or fast, neither too slow. 'Sharp percussive rhythm can make a patient jerk like a marionette, while monotonous crooning proves too flimsy' to have any effect upon the Parkinson's sufferer.

> What's needed is moderately paced, shapely music played in flowing legato, music with a pronounced beat, but beat embedded in rolling melody ... of a kind that suits [the Parkinson's patient's] taste. [This] requires that the patient participate by generating a flux of musical anticipations [himself].[14]

Dr Oliver Sacks, in his book entitled *Awakenings*, talks about his discovery that music was an excellent treatment for a Parkinson's sufferer. Her physical movements suddenly became normal when she listened to music. Another of his patients was able to calm her Parkinson's-addled body by merely thinking of playing the compositions of Chopin. The moment she began to do this, her very abnormal EEG (brainwaves) became normal.

Sacks claimed that a kind of 'kinetic melody' plays out in all our bodies unless we are struck 'deaf' by disease or other limitations. 'Music briefly restores that melody, at least for those sorts of activities that are themselves flowing and "musical".' Music organizes the brain in a way that ordinary experience, which is more chaotic, cannot. One of Sacks' patients who was severely retarded, with an IQ below 20 (100 is average), was suddenly able to perform multistep tasks while hearing music.

The scientist Jacques Benveniste said that high-pitched rapid sounds engender lightness of spirit, and high-pitched slow sounds sweetness. Deep, rapid sounds awaken the fighting spirit, while deep, slow sounds invoke serious emotions, sadness and mourning. These are triggered by defined frequencies. We do nothing more than this when we transmit pre-recorded molecular activities to biological systems. A molecular signal can be efficiently represented by a spectrum of frequencies between 20Hz and 20,000Hz, the same range as human hearing or music. Benveniste hypothesized that biological systems function like radio sets, by co-resonance. If you tune a receiver to 92.6MHz, you tune in to Radio-This, where the receiver and the transmitter vibrate at the same frequency. If you change the setting a little to 92.7, you no longer receive Radio-This, but Radio-That.

For several hundred thousand years, Benveniste said, human beings have been relating sound frequencies to a biological mechanism: the emotions. 'Composers of background music for supermarkets or elevators are practicing neuropsychology without knowing it.'

Healing with the mind

A new type of neuropsychology known as contemplative neuro-science, which examines how meditation affects the mind, is being pioneered by the Mind and Life Institute in Boulder, Colorado. Adam Engle, its chairman and co-founder, says 'people are now realizing you can change your brain, and they want to know what factors or mental events cause these changes'.

Can we change our brains by changing how we think? Can we train our minds to be more attentive and focused, and better at decision-making? Dr Richard Davidson, Director of the Labora-tory for Affective Neuroscience, put the French Tibetan Buddhist monk Matthieu Ricard into a magnetic resonance imaging (MRI) machine to videotape the functions of his brain. Inside the machine, while the monk meditated on compassion, he showed a dramatic increase in activity in the areas of his brain connected with enthusiasm and joy.

This result was magnified in a follow-up study where Davidson charted the normal, emotional states of the brains of 150 people, including Ricard. Most people fell into the middle ground between positive and negative emotions. But Ricard, who had been deeply meditating on compassion when his brain was scanned, nearly soared off the chart of positive emotions. He had the highest level of happiness ever documented.

Ricard describes meditation as a tool for mind training. It helps you to cultivate certain inner qualities that he says change your 'inner conditions' to those of happiness. He says you must stop putting your hopes and fears into outer consciousness so that you can identify what inner factors can contribute to your deep sense of wellbeing. Once we realize the fundamental nature of our mental toxins, they become lost in the space of inner mind. Nega-tive emotions are 'stains on the cloth of the mind' and once we recognize them for what they are, they lose their ability to stain, and the 'I' shines through. But it takes practice to get to know this luminous 'I'.

If 10,000 hours of violin practice can have the effect of teaching or training the mind, muscles, heart, etc., to play beautiful music, imagine what 10,000 hours of 'compassion' [meditation] practice could do to the human heart.

Characteristics like happiness and the capacity to focus attention can be improved with training, Dr Davidson says. 'You can change your mind by changing your ... thoughts. You can intentionally cultivate positive emotions and transform how you react to events in your life.'

Scientists now believe that happiness is a skill that can be learned, just like playing a musical instrument. This idea is being embraced by Christians like Father Thomas Keating of Snowmass, who is pioneering a form of Christian meditation that he calls 'centring prayer'. He has participated in the Mind and Life Institute's dialogue between scientists and the Dalai Lama, building bridges between contemplative religious practice and modern science. MRI experiments at Princeton University (New Jersey) on longtime Buddhist meditators have proven that the human brain does respond to different kinds of meditative practice, he says, adding:

> Science is part of revelation ... The early Christian fathers said there are two books of revelation. One is the Bible and the other is nature.[15]

The Buddhist idea that the first step to acquiring every power is quieting the thoughts goes along with the conclusions of American physicist Russell Targ, who knows from experience that it is necessary to quieten the mind before psi experiences may occur.

Apart from helping to develop the laser with Gordon Gould in the late 1950s and being a Tibetan Dzogchen meditation practitioner, Targ is an expert remote viewer who conducted CIA-sponsored experiments at Stanford Research Institute as part of a programme called 'ESPionage' during the Cold War.

The basis of remote viewing is that we are linked with a 'non-local' or universal mind. This is indicated by quantum physics experiments showing that particles (photons) remain mysteriously connected even when travelling in opposite directions at the speed of light. Targ himself experienced the physical ramifications of this. He was diagnosed with colon cancer in 1985, from which he recovered after surgery, only to see it return in 1992. So he rang Jane Katra, a spiritual healer. After suggesting major lifestyle changes, Katra acted on the theory of 'changing the host so the disease could no longer recognize him'.

Targ improved. Six weeks later, after not taking the prescribed chemotherapy, Targ's CAT scans showed that his tumour was benign. Afterwards he and Katra wrote two books maintaining that 'healing experiences that involve union with a universal consciousness do not arise out of any particular beliefs, rituals or actions, except one: quieting the mind'.

Uri Geller approaches health from a slightly different angle. He suggests that you simply need to recharge your 'mind power' periodically if you want to create health and happiness, which is the result of generous goodwill towards others and the discipline of a positive habit of mind. Geller believes that everyone has mind power, energy, 'or whatever you want to call it – a pool of a certain force' but they don't know how to tap into it. He thinks perhaps he automatically dipped into this force at birth and was able to use it.

Certainly he is striking for his magnetism and the calm, focused gaze with which his eyes settle upon those he meets. But is he a healer? No, he says, although he does believe in healing and that music especially is a powerful healing force. He describes himself as a positive thinker and sees his purpose as being that of a motivator and inspirer. Every day, even when he walks his dog, he does affirmations and meditates, and tries to live a healthy life, exercising physically to keep his powers sharp. His pet charitable activity is working with sick children. He does spoon-bending demonstrations for them simply to prove that he has 'mind power' abilities.

I demonstrate my abilities and then I tell them that that's not really important. What is important is positive thinking. When you tell a child with a brain tumour or leukaemia that they will heal faster if they think positively and are optimistic, in parallel with the medical help – I always make a point to tell their parents never to abandon conventional medicine – they will get better faster. An injured person or a sick person, if they are in a positive frame of mind, they will heal faster.

What stops or weakens his own mind powers? Does he torment himself with self-doubt or worry? He says that he is too busy for that sort of thing.

> What weakens my powers is what everyone feels when they're stressed out, tired or jet-lagged, or they're not in the mood – those are the things that take me out of the mood of doing things. I constantly am busy in many different fields, but I try to make the humanitarian aspects of what I do my number one priority. It strengthens [you] if you can give, not only take.
>
> I get e-mails from people who say to me, 'Dear Mr Geller, I was nine years old when you invited me onto the stage in Mexico City and you told me to focus my mind, go to university, focus on school, never smoke, never touch drugs, and be successful, and today thanks to you I'm a millionaire and I'm exactly what you asked me to be'.

Geller's enthusiasm gives one the feeling that, for him, encouraging children is the pinnacle of all activity. He hopes that one day at least two billion people will take part in some international media event to focus at the same time on some positive thing, as he thinks that would be an enormous positive force.

Mental health and happiness seem to arise from a combination of external social awareness and internal self-discipline, where emotions do not get out of control and are kept in check by an energetic, healthy lifestyle. Together, these make you feel calm and balanced. People who have a strong sense of self-worth and faith in their own goodness do not torment themselves or others. Random acts of kindness result.

A slightly different approach to this is the notion that through prayer one can send healing to others. Dr Peter Fenwick, a British neuropsychiatrist, chairman of Britain's Scientific and Medical Network and an authority on near-death experiences (NDEs), has been conducting studies on the efficacy of prayer in healing for some decades now. He says that in the last 20 years a major change regarding the relevance of prayer to good health has occurred in scientific thinking. One of the earliest papers on prayer (Byrd *et al*, 1988) showed that patients in a coronary care unit who were prayed for had shorter in-patient stays, fewer complications and a reduced drug usage. Since then, positive results have come from a number of high-quality double-blind randomized control trials on inter-cessory prayer. One study by Koenig *et al.* (2001) showed that people over 65 who attended church at least once a week had lower levels of cancer and heart disease. Dr Fenwick states:

> A strong faith, a supportive social network, positive relationships and positive thinking up-regulate the immune system, reducing the risk of cancer and heart disease and improving general health.

Regarding prayer's ability to heal, the evidence thus far leads Dr Fenwick to think that the *intention* to heal is the important variable. However, this needs to be tested further.

> What is clear is that there are sufficient studies now to show that prayer can work, and the evidence suggests that the presence of prayer groups in a hospital setting should be considered.

What healers do

Healers offer their skills to those who need them. This does not mean that they do not suffer from problems themselves. In fact, healers quite often suffer from a cocktail of maladies, occasionally leaving behind a sort of scent of their healing abilities which heal others in some inexplicable, unexplainable way, as St Thérèse de Lisieux (1873–96) did. A Carmelite nun, she suddenly had a stroke at the age of 23 due to tuberculosis. While ill in bed, she requested that roses be brought to her. She then plucked the petals from them and told people to gather the petals carefully, that one day they could give comfort to other people. Shortly after saying, 'Do not lose a single one of them!', she died.

A few years later, a student priest named Charles Ann of Bayeux contracted TB also. He put a locket containing Thérèse's hair round his neck and prayed for her to cure him in order that he might carry on God's work. The next day, his disease was gone. Later still, Ferdinand Aubry, who had gangrene of the tongue, went to spend his last days at Lisieux to be cared for by the convent sisters. One of the sisters persuaded him to swallow a rose petal from Thérèse's deathbed. The next day, the gangrene was gone. Within days, the missing parts of his tongue grew back.

Another case was that of a nun called Sister Louise de St Germain, who in 1915 was dying from a stomach ulcer and had a vision of Thérèse promising her that she would be cured. The next morning, her bed was surrounded by rose petals, which no one admitted to putting there. Within 15 days, she too was cured – a fact her doctors confirmed with X-rays taken before and after her vision.

A special committee of the Catholic Church rigorously investigated these cases, as it does all claims of miraculous cures and paranormal events. Very few pass their tests, as evidence must be watertight, with doctors' medical reports, testimonies, X-rays and other proof. But the events were found to be so extraordinary that the Vatican canonized Thérèse.

Prospero Lambertini, the Chief Inspector of Miracles for the Vatican in the 18th century, remarked that miracles were just as common for the non-religious as for religious devotees. Noting the prominence of dreams in religious miracles, he concluded that much of what he saw was more a product of the mind than God.

Yet for Tibetan Buddhists, *everything* is a product of the mind, and some of the lamas are great healers. One of their most commonly practised meditations is to consciously absorb and transmute other beings' sickness and suffering. When they cannot transmute or clear someone's illness instantaneously, lamas are able to take the illness upon themselves in order to lessen the person's burden. They are said to do this for people who have the capacity and motivation to help others, although why they cannot do it all the time is something of a mystery.

Anyone can do the practice of *tonglen*, also called 'sending and receiving', which means to take or absorb others' suffering and send back healing. Imagine a single living being, or everyone in the world, or universe, and all their suffering, coming towards you in a wave. Rather than absorbing and transmuting the negativity inside yourself, it may be easier to think of yourself surrounded by a golden flame, light or crystal. The moment the negative energy touches your light or crystal, it dissipates and transmutes, changing into positivity, and the goodness bounces back to the person, or to 'all beings'. Even if this takes place only in the imagination, it has positive effects on the person who contemplates in this visual, impersonal manner.

Much folklore surrounds the act of healing. Healers are said to suffer more than ordinary people because they are sensitive. People say they can pick up others' maladies through over-empathizing with those who are suffering and must periodically desensitize themselves, or go out into the 'wilderness' as Jesus did, in order to regain their strength.

When their own families suffer, healers sometimes find it hard to heal them, for strong emotions seem to bar the ability to heal. So when English healer Matthew Manning's wife was diagnosed with cancer, he referred to what he calls Andrew Weil's 'wonderful book' *Spontaneous Healing*, which states:

> When treatments work, they do so by activating innate healing mechanisms. Treatment – including drugs and surgery – can facilitate healing and remove obstacles to it, but treatment is not the same as healing … healing comes from within. Nonetheless, to refuse treatment while waiting for healing can be foolish.[16]

Happily for Manning, his wife recovered from cancer after combining conventional and complementary treatments, including his own form of healing. Manning practises laying-on-of-hands or faith healing.

> When I am healing, I nearly always start by placing my hands on the patient's neck and shoulders. They might immediately feel great heat, [and perhaps] a tingling sensation.

They may also feel nothing, but this does not mean that nothing is happening.

> I am aware that my breathing and my heartbeat slow down, that I become mostly unaware of the external environment and eventually I sense that somehow the patient and I have become linked.

Manning then moves his hands to an area or point to which he feels intuitively drawn. This is often the place where the pain or disease is. He has learned not to be concerned about what the logical part of his brain tells him, allowing intuition to take over.

> I will nearly always get sensations of heat and a tingling rather like a mild electric current, as well as what I can best describe as great energy surges which flow throughout my body. I also experience vivid images that are sometimes very abstract, at other times more literal.

Music seems to initiate these images, during what is for him a kind of 'waking dream state'. He always knows when healing sessions have come to an end because the physical sensations he experiences weaken and the imagery he sees is replaced by conscious thought processes.

> [The sick] need recognition, not just of themselves, but as people experiencing a threat to their lives. It is often difficult for someone else to understand such an important and frightening experience, but it is that understanding that [someone] so often needs.

Manning was tested for five years in the 1970s to find out whether he could affect a range of biological systems. Two tests involving cells were especially significant. The first measured the rate at which red blood cells absorb water and eventually burst, releasing haemoglobin. Placing his hands above a test tube of blood cells without touching it, he imagined the cells surrounded by a brilliant white light. In his mind, he assured the cells that the light would protect them and they would remain intact and resistant to the surrounding solution. The blood cells remained intact four times longer than in the trials where his influence was not present.

> Normally the cells would [die within] a maximum of five minutes … he was able to slow the destruction so that [they] were intact as long as twenty minutes later.

In a second experiment to see whether he could disrupt the electrostatic charge on Hela cervical cancer cells in order to render them inactive, changes in cell numbers were observed in 27 of 30 trials. Manning was declared able to destroy cancer cells.

However, even Manning warns people against trusting faith or medical healers without credentials or recommendations. Conventional treatment must not be abandoned and you must always trust your feelings about what you should do for your own health.

A lighter future

Ethical matters will be the most important issue of the future regarding medicine and science, many scientists believe. Should body-part and brain banks be created they will need to be monitored carefully by independent, scientifically aware, ethical organizations that are not under the jurisdiction of economically-minded interest groups or governments. Those in monitoring positions must act as servants for the general public's welfare and freedom of choice. Systems of international checks-and-balances could be established over managing supervisory groups, and concerned, first and foremost, with humane, ethical action. Systems with morality held uppermost could be maintained by the world's institutions, businesses and governments.

However, moral issues can be complex. Stem cell research is a particularly thorny one today, especially among religious groups, for its use of embryo stem cells and, potentially, babies and clones. Stem cells are different from other cells of the body, and more useful. They have the ability to replace cells that have died in areas that have other types of cells or tissue. Stem cells have been used to replace defective cells and to repair tissues in patients who have many kinds of diseases and ailments.

International pharmaceuticals corporations are known to fund and plant so-called 'experts' in governments as well as complementary and alternative health governing bodies. Through them, money-making businesses influence decisions made about such difficult issues. This makes the matter of ethics all the more complex. Today, what we don't know can harm us.

However, a 'lighter' future is imagined by the American therapist and proponent of light therapy, Dr Jacob Liberman. He says that conventional medical technologies we now use routinely will soon be viewed as barbaric. In future, scalpels will be replaced by lasers, chemotherapy by phototherapy, acupuncture needles by 'needles of light'. Our schools will change from being 'windowless, colourless and inappropriately illuminated' to 'colourful, playful, stimulating classrooms with plenty of fresh air and sunlight'. Our working environments will become healing ones, where fluorescent lights will be replaced by sun-simulating lamps, and daily exposure to sunshine will be scheduled into the day's work.

His ideas are not new. They come from Babylonia, China, Egypt, Italy and Greece, where healing temples for the body, mind and soul used sunlight and coloured light for complaints like skin diseases. The 'cool' sunlight of early morning was used in 19th-century England to cure people of diseases like leprosy. In 1903 physician Neils Finsen received a Nobel Prize for his investigation into the clinical application of light therapy for lesions caused by smallpox and German measles, and so light was used in hospitals in the West until the late 1930s when antibiotics were discovered. When applied in the correct doses at the relevant wavelengths, light stimulates the body's cells to balance, regenerate and re-regulate themselves.

We do not expose ourselves enough to the natural rays of the Sun and Moon, and perhaps miss other forces we cannot see or sense. Our body clocks fall out of rhythm so that we have trouble sleeping at night if our skins aren't exposed to natural sunlight for at least 15 minutes, preferably 30, every morning. It could well be that other factors leading to good health and a sunnier disposition are involved in this exposure to natural light that scientists haven't yet discovered.

Now that bacteria and viruses are beginning to grow stronger in their response to antibiotics, doctors are beginning to look again at light therapy, including low-level laser therapy. Today light therapy is used for chronic and acute medical conditions, from dermatological problems to autoimmune diseases.

Liberman believes that medicine of the future will speak directly to the body, so that its own wisdom can be the foundation for its healing. It will treat *people*, not disease. Light, being both a visible and invisible source of energy, shows us that what we see and cannot see 'are equally important to our development, growth, and evolution'.

Back down to earth

Herbalists claim that all the ingredients of a plant (leaves, seeds, flowers, stems and roots) enhance herbal remedies' therapeutic effects. The whole plant is used as opposed to its active ingredient, diffusing its activity slightly and generally making it safer.

Allopathic medicine producers identify the active chemical constituents of a healing plant, then synthesize and reproduce them. These pharmaceutical drugs target specific diseases or illnesses and, although generally more hard-hitting and immediate in their effect than herbal medicines, can cause severe side effects.

Side effects are less common from plants, although the poisonous ones must be treated carefully, if not avoided. An American who calls herself Granny Earth claims that all the things we need to heal ourselves are around us – weeds, for instance. When we don't know what the useful purposes of a plant are, we call it a weed. 'There are changes we can make to get away from chemicals', Earth says. 'I suspect that 99 per cent of all weeds can not only be used as medicine but also as food.'

Dandelions and ground ivy are viewed as common weeds, but they are useful as natural remedies. Nettles are high in vitamins and minerals, including iron. They taste much like spinach when cooked and may be eaten raw, once you roll the sting out of them. Their sting can stimulate the body to rid itself of arthritis, according to folk remedies from countries like Iran. Granny Earth makes her own child-friendly medicines from plants she purchases from an organic farm in Oregon. She has more than 100 weeds stored in jars.

Scientific data to prove the efficacy of medicinal plants is growing today. The UK Medical Research Council is conducting studies on a plant called *Sutherlandia microphylla*, traditionally used as a tonic in South Africa which seems to increase energy, appetite and body mass for HIV patients. Another herb called

Artemisia annua, used in China for almost 2,000 years, has been proven to be effective against malaria, from which almost one million people die annually, most of them children. Researchers from the world's powerful pharmaceutical drug companies seek potent herbs like these in order to test and copy them.

Notable herbal medical systems exist in China, India, Persia, Europe and the Americas, and among island peoples like the Polynesians and Hawaiians, although foreign diseases decimated much of the latter's population and therefore its knowledge of plant medicine (not helped by the outlawing of it in 1922 by the US Territorial Government). The world's earliest written records of plant medicines were found in Egypt on papyri dated about 1,500 years ago, and South Africa's orally transmitted medical systems are thought to date back to Palaeolithic times. Around 3,000 species of its plants are used in medicines, but more than 30,000 of its species have not been studied or even named by botanists.

About 475 BC, Huang Di wrote Chinese traditional medicine's most important book, the *Nei Jing* (*Canon of Interior Medicine*), in which he carefully noted what the body did after ingesting particular herbs. More than 2,000 documented medicinal plants indigenous to Bolivia's three distinctive geographical regions (the High Andean plateau; the valleys, El Chapare; and the tropical Amazonian region) are utilized by the Kallawayas, who make medicines from plants that grow in the Andes. Today it is estimated that 50 Kallawayas practise their medicine in Bolivia, and that they have the ability to utilize around 900 indigenous medicinal plants. Peru's Institute of Traditional Medicine, whose germplasm bank contains 120 species, has placed its jungles' medicinal plants in 332 botanical categories. Its research director, neurologist and neurosurgeon Dr Fernando Cabieses, believes that private companies and his government must protect Peruvian traditional medicine from investors who want to manufacture and market them because:

> [Knowledge] is beginning to be lost despite the fact that traditional Peruvian medicine gave the world Quinine, which saved Europe from malaria, and later provided Cat's Claw, Sangre de Grado, Maca [and many other herbal remedies].[17]

Unfortunately demand for herbs is endangering plant populations worldwide, although certain taboos and rituals help to ensure that plants are not over-harvested. African healers call upon their ancestors for supernatural guidance before collecting wild medicinal plants, and tend to salvage natural materials, like the bark from trees felled during road construction, most of which can be dried and stored for use as medicines. A similar protection is afforded herbs by Tibetan medicine, for which astrology determines what days are favourable for picking and preparing herbs and when therapies are prescribed. Those who do not have taboos or strictures to follow have only common sense to guide them, in a situation where the uncontrolled over-harvesting of raw materials could destroy the natural habitats and resources of endangered animal species, causing their extinction, and where international standards for patent law do not protect traditional knowledge and biodiversity.

> Chopping down forests, killing animals and treating the human body as a piece of equipment with replaceable parts are no longer acceptable actions.[18]

Our task is to more adamantly appreciate the natural, health-giving things all around us, and to bring them into our bodies and world. What is invisible to us today could lead to a healthier future for us all. Should more natural approaches to health be developed by humanity, they also will have positive effects on the ecology of our planet.

5

ECOLOGY AND THE BUILT UNIVERSE

*The Kingdom of Heaven is spread about upon the
Earth and yet men do not see it.*

JESUS, VERSE 113, 'THE GOSPEL OF ST THOMAS', *THE NAG
HAMMADI LIBRARY*, ED. JAMES M ROBINSON

*Even after all this time
The Sun never once says to the Earth
'Earth, you owe me.'
Look what happens
With a love like that –
It lights up the whole sky.*

HAFIZ (c.1320–90)

IF GALILEO HAD LOOKED into ponds instead of observing the
stars, physics might not be our most prominent science. Had he
done so, perhaps rather than seeking technological methods for
travelling in outer space, we might be paying more attention to our
quality of life down here on Earth. Elizabet Sahtouris suggested
this in a lecture she introduced with the above poem by Hafiz.

We might find solutions to our social and environmental problems, she said, by looking at the way biological organisms work
and how a healthy body functions. Each cell of the human body
has 60,000 recycling centres, while our DNA reorganizes itself in

response to stress. Nature has more efficient inbuilt systems than human beings have ever created.

What might happen if we viewed society as a single organism on a planet that is also a single organism in a vast universe? We once related to our surroundings through stories involving such ideas and mythologies – the stuff of dreams – which became religions. But a great change has happened. Science now tells the story of the universe. Methodology is preferred to imagination and intuition. Scientists see things as if on a spectrum or keyboard, with matter at one end, beyond which is electromagnetic energy. Beyond that is a vacuum or 'Zero Point Energy Field'. Further still – and matter's opposite – is mind or spirit.

In the past, the seasons and the weather decided how things were done. Now it is economics. Economists generally perceive nature as a transformer of resources, making products that are exchanged, distributed, consumed or recycled. Nature is just an economic factor to be considered in the great scheme of money-making. Businessmen believe a viable business must operate like a machine, but healthy bodies do not function like machines. Nor are they healthy from just any kind of food.

The best food is produced by farmers who behave as 'husband-men' to the land. They are the true 'freemen' of the Earth. Theirs is a *calling*, not merely a job. Such farmers know how to wait, how to let things grow in their own time, with the periodic addition of themselves as helpers. They grow and change through the seasons with the plants they tend.

Living things cannot be maintained in dark spaces with no concern for the environment they are placed in, as machines can be. Modern hospitals – built more for machines than people – are a product of mechanistic thinking.

Both business and evolutionary theory are stuck in our historic past, Sahtouris says. Magellan believed the Earth could be owned. Afterwards, Columbus initiated trade between the Old World and the Americas. In 1600, England's Queen Elizabeth I created the East India Company, beginning the habit of using business to ensure control over territories. Later Darwin adopted Malthus' doctrine of evolution through competitive struggle.

The Western worldview derives from that held by physics: the non-living universe is running down through entropy and biology, while an endless struggle ensues due to scarcity. Perhaps science-based ideas such as these should be viewed as suppositions or possibilities – black holes might radiate outwards as well as suck things into them.

Batches of new species appear after each of Earth's critical junctures, so perhaps our world is not doomed in the way we often visualize. Earth will probably carry on whether or not humans destroy themselves.

Dr Sahtouris suggests another way forward. Rather than globalization, the idea of *glocalization* could be developed, where local interest groups work with other similar groups. Self-interest is important in every living system. However, if egocentrism takes precedence, it becomes harmful to the entire system. All the parts of a living system must work in cooperation to ensure that it remains alive.

Glocalized gardening

Indigenous cultures see themselves as guardians of their environment. They are local interest groups. They strive not to upset the balance of their environments. Half the food the world eats today was created by indigenous Peruvians, who had a very advanced agricultural system, from which Sahtouris says we could learn much today.

Most non-Western cultures view every entity as being 'endowed with agency, intelligence and wisdom', the science director of England's Schumacher College, Dr Stephan Harding, says. Rocks are seen as the elders of the Earth, and are sought out for their tranquillity and wisdom. 'Forests are living entities ... consulted before a hunt' by shamans who intuitively sense and communicate with 'the great being of the forest'.[1]

Psychologists have observed that children pass through an animistic phase in which they relate to objects as if they had a character and were alive, but they believe this is appropriate only to early childhood. Most seek to help children realize 'as quickly and painlessly as possible that they live in a dead world in which the only experiencing entities are other humans'.

American journalist Richard Louv believes that many of our social problems come from our separation from nature. A wonderfully honest fourth-grader in San Diego, California, told him, 'I like to play indoors better, because that's where all the electrical outlets are'. Spending time outdoors is essential for the healthy development of children's bodies and emotions. In his book, *Last Child in the Woods*, he says:

> Given a chance, a child will bring the confusion of the world to the woods, wash it in the creek [and] turn it over to see what lives on the unseen side of that confusion. In nature, a child finds freedom, fantasy and privacy.

In his own childhood, he says, 'The woods were my Ritalin. Nature calmed me, focused me, and yet excited my senses'.

Like other Buddhist teachers, the roving Lama Samten says that our physical health depends upon our environment. Healthy surroundings, lakes, mountains, other animal species and so on, are our protection. If these are destroyed, we suffer.

For American Indians, 'everything is alive, not supernaturally but naturally alive' Jamake Highwater says in *The Primal Mind*. The Indian who makes pottery offers songs to the fire which fires it, because she does not want the fire, which has its own will, to burst or discolour her pots. Everything is seen as having spiritual power within it. Even stones contain living, moving entities.

Interestingly, the British crystal healer and inventor Harry Oldfield has photographed beings moving in stones with his Kirlian diagnostic machine. This brings to mind the Arthurian legend that Merlin was encased inside stone by the sorceress Morgana, and the Celtic tales that speak of druids who could put men's spirits into trees and stones. Could these stories be a reference to perceptual abilities we have lost? Could people once see beings in stones?

The relationship of a Northern Californian Wintu Indian with nature is said to be one of 'intimacy and mutual courtesy'.

He kills a deer only when he needs it for his livelihood, and utilizes every part of it, hoofs and marrow and hide and sinew and flesh. Waste is abhorrent to him, not because he believes in the intrinsic value of thrift, but because the deer has died for him.[2]

American Indians did not attempt to control what gave them life. Certainly it would never have occurred to them to destroy the Earth and all its creatures. They might quarrel and fight with other humans, even kill them and burn their houses, but destroying the natural environment around them was simply unthinkable. That would have meant destroying themselves. The wealth of the defeated would go to the conquerors, but for Indians that wealth was in the Earth, its waters, skies and animals. Can we learn to look at our environment in a way that will enable us to live within it more peaceably? An American Indian gives this advice:

> You must learn to look at the world twice … First, you must bring your eyes together in front of you so you can see each droplet of rain on the grass, so you can see the smoke rising from an anthill in the sunshine. Nothing should escape your notice.

After that, you must look again, at the very edge of what is visible, and see dimly if you want to see things that are dim like mist, visions and cloud-people, or animals that hurry past in the dark. Do not look merely for what is physically before you. What you see is an interaction of forces by means of which something else arises. What you see with your eyes is a virtual image that does not really exist. It is similar to a reflection in a mirror, or a rainbow – the 'ineffable made visible'.

This is different from being a spectator of the world – outside nature, yet governed by 'natural law' – as Western people tend to think of themselves. We have devised a metaphysical standard that places everything far away from us. Cut off from nature, our bodies cannot function in harmony with our ideas, feelings and experiences. Writes Jamake Highwater: 'Without a sense of one's whole body, one cannot participate in the world that lies beyond observation.'

Other, older cultures consciously explore what we consider to be the subconscious mind. The Senoi tribe of Malaya instruct their children how to enter actively into and shape their dreams and, in Tibet, learning to navigate within 'lucid dreams' – in which you know you are dreaming, while dreaming – became part of religious training. Primal people 'have not closed themselves off from the non-material aspects of experience' – their 'intuition is capable of existing as apparition, as virtual image'.

Tibetan lamas tell of leading people from danger in the waking world by dreaming, or perhaps astral travelling to where they should go in order to avoid it. The same thing happens in American Indian tribes. Medicine men and tribal elders guide their chief so that he will lead their tribe 'along safe pathways'.

So how far does our influence over our environment extend? Do our thoughts have an impact on what happens and what we create around us? If so, what are we thinking that is making our world more polluted? Perhaps the answer lies in our relationship with the Earth. Britain is full of gardening enthusiasts, but even there many people have never planted anything in the ground. When we depend upon food for survival and most people in cities have never planted anything in the land of the worms, this could be why economist-thinking is taking over the countryside, transforming people-centred villages into neon-lit nightmares and dormitory towns.

Gardens would spread out into a park adjoining a Roman house, and olive gardens were placed west of and inside the city of Jerusalem. But the precedent for creating gardens was set in Egypt and Persia. In the Middle East, settlements were not separate from nature. One recent study of Yemen describes nature as never being extraneous to or different from the settlement. They formed the landscape together. 'The irrigation systems, their elements, the agricultural fragmentation of the territory, the materials and the colour of the houses and … ancillary works' formed an integrated system which comprised the landscape, according to Professor Frank Granger in *Vitruvius on Architecture*.

Settlements were constructed of stone, with residential, public and religious functions in a small area, as if to occupy the smallest possible amount of cultivable land. Tower-houses were placed alone within market gardens behind low, dry stone walls.[3] These enclosures rose 'out of the ground without any discontinuity', fitting into the landscape. Almost all the houses and palaces of the 'one big garden' town of Sana'a were surrounded by large gardens which, irrigated by well water, provided every sort of fruit and vegetable.

Basic gardening is easy. Anybody can plant a seed or pull up a weed. The first lesson for children in every primary school should be planting a seed in the earth itself. We need to meet the worms and insects in their own territory, so that we know that they want to live and have a right to be here as much as we.

When I am gardening, birds sometimes look upon me with a friendly eye, as if they appreciate my stirring up the earth so that they may find wriggling worms more easily. Cats lurk cautiously while I destroy their precious high-grass gardens and sit meditating with me when I rest. Only by working with the earth does one notice the relationships we have with creatures who talk to us through song and sound, blinking eyes, flicks of tails and ears. How can one not be impressed by the way that spiders instantly begin all over again to spin their webs after one destroys them – webs that serve as homes as well as food-traps, which shine so beautifully in sunlight, especially when rain droplets decorate them like rainbow-coloured diamonds? Empathic relationships with living, breathing beings cannot be found with computers in offices. We need inspiration from communicating with other minds down here on the ground living alongside us.

After a 19-year-old girl in England, Emily Cummins, invented a solar-powered refrigerator, she paid tribute to her 76-year-old grandfather Peter Harrison who had inspired her to 'invent'. She was given faith in her abilities by someone she loved and respected and, as a result, managed to create something that could help counteract the most serious problem of our time, environmental damage.

If more people supported others this way, we might just avert ecological catastrophe. If enough of us think we can, then perhaps we can. Our world has ecosystems on every level. When one system

becomes unbalanced, other systems reshuffle and rebalance themselves. Everything is moving all the time.

> In line, in colour, in the changes of the seasons, in the rising and
> falling of the waves, in the wind, in the storm, in all the beauty of
> nature there is constant movement.[4]

Circulation systems and patterns

An invisible constant that moves all things, while moving within
them, is the wind. 'Without wind, most of the Earth would be
uninhabitable.' Air pollution is the most important pollution we
have in the world today, Australian ecologist and explorer Tim
Flannery says. With 100 billion more people added to Earth's
population every year, he doesn't see our planet's stress levels
decreasing measurably anytime soon. A century from now, 56 per
cent of the CO_2 we put in the air today will still be here.

The wind also moves diseases around, and seeds, as well as
birds and insects in their migrations. Explanations for migrations
have been attributed to the wind, but also to ocean currents and
seasonal and food-supply changes.

> [Birds] orientate themselves [by using] the position of the Sun
> during the day, and the stars at night. [They use] clues such as
> visual layout of the land, smell (of the sea), sound (waves on
> shores, winds through mountain passes), [and therefore] can be
> distracted and killed by lit-up skyscrapers, lighthouses and other
> unnatural man-made formations.

Apart from bad weather, hunters and natural obstacles, bird
migratory patterns are being affected today by human actions like
the draining of wetlands and cutting of forests. These have an
impact on their ability to eat and rest.

An intriguing conclusion was reached by the English barrister
Edmund Selous (1857–1934). After retiring from the law courts, he
observed birds and made detailed notes of their movements. In
his most famous book *Thought-Transference (or What?) in Birds*,
he argued that some process of thought transference so rapid as to

amount practically to simultaneous collective thinking sweeps through bird flocks, which sparks them into an instantaneous, communal, cloud-like dance.

> [Telepathy is] a natural faculty, part of our animal nature. [It] usually occurs between closely related animals that are part of the same social group, or those who are 'bonded' with each other, [and] may play an important role in the coordination of the activity [of the group].[5]

Rupert Sheldrake's morphic field theory, based on telepathy, suggests that migrating animals remember things in their individual morphic fields, in a way similar to magnetic attraction. 'Migrating animals often rely on a sense of direction that enables them to navigate towards their goal, to which they are connected through morphic fields' – inherent in which is ancestral memory, although magnetic and celestial clues also help them. Lyall Watson's Hundredth Monkey theory – deemed a fabrication by the scientific community – was the basis of Sheldrake's morphogenetic field theory. After reading about the morphology theory of German scientist and poet Johann Wolfgang von Goethe (1749–1832), Sheldrake developed his theory to explain it.

In 1973, Sheldrake conceived of a universal field encoding the 'basic pattern' of an object, which he termed the 'morphogenetic field'. This pattern superimposes itself repeatedly upon organisms of the same kind, making them take on the same form as others of their species. An organism develops under the guidance of this morphogenetic force – not, as scientists generally agree, according to messages from its DNA, which Sheldrake says also receives instructions from the morphogenetic field. The feedback mechanism, morphic resonance, proves 'the increasing ease with which new skills are learned as greater quantities of a population acquire them' through collective, instinctive memory.

Social groups, like flocks of birds and schools of fish, are likewise organized by fields. A human society has a collective memory that is transmitted through a culture via rituals, festivals, myths and stories, from one person to another – as a kind of resonance passed on through time. Habits of instinct enable animals to survive in the wild, while human beings build successful societies through passing on mental, physical, emotional, linguistic and cultural habits. These build morphic fields of relationship which, Sheldrake suggests, provide an explanation for how telepathy occurs.

> [Telepathy] seems to be a normal means of animal communica-
> tion [and] is normal, not paranormal, natural not supernatural,
> [especially between] people who know each other well.

Mental morphic fields extend beyond our minds. The magnetic fields of magnets extend beyond the surfaces of magnets; the Earth's gravitational field keeps the Moon in its orbit; and the fields of a cell phone stretch out far beyond the phone itself. Likewise the fields of our minds extend far beyond our brains. This intriguing notion implies that if enough individuals imagine naturally beautiful environments with human-sized architecture strongly enough, we will communicate it to others through our collective unconscious, and eventually manifest it.

Morphic fields 'hold together and coordinate the parts of a system in space and time, and contain a memory from previous similar systems'. A social group is a type of morphic field. Groups are held together and structured by a tribal collective memory similar to C G Jung's *collective unconscious*. According to Rupert Sheldrake:

> The process by which this memory is transferred from past to
> present is called 'morphic resonance'. ... Morphic fields [permit]
> telepathic influences to pass from animal to animal within a social
> group ... even over great distances.

Birds, as well as other migrants, could be influenced by other species' thoughts – even humans' thoughts, or by unseen electro-magnetic and sound waves. Everything is subjected to a constant bombardment by millions of conflicting electromagnetic and sound waves. Life protects itself from this turmoil by using sense organs, which let in only a very limited range of frequencies.

Sometimes even these are too much for us, so we have another barrier – our nervous system, which filters the input and sorts it into what is useful or irrelevant to us. Lyall Watson says that cosmic forces recur in cyclical patterns, yet he perceives the cosmos itself as being 'patternless'. That is probably because we live within a chaotic soup we can see only from the inside while being whirled about. The forces pushing us around are part of something much greater and vaster than us – something whose patterns we cannot perceive.

Creating a human-size ecological community

While we are part of a constantly shifting world, it is important to function in a way that is amenable to oneself. Scotland's Findhorn Community is a loose assemblage of people of diverse views who came together for this reason. They work together intuitively to create an ecological environment.

Recently Findhorn has acquired Establishment acceptance. Britain's National Health Service, Shell and BP chose to send their managers on Findhorn training courses, while Price Water-house Coopers sent accountants there to learn about 'emotional intelligence'.

Findhorn's members' core beliefs centre upon the idea that there is one transcendent 'God of Love' that contains both masculine and feminine elements. Some believe in 'non-physical beings such as angels, devas, discorporate human and perhaps super-human souls ... who exercise some kind of dynamic intelligence [and] with whom we can communicate.'[6]

Important for the community is its notion that people can 'manifest' things through faith. Findhorn's policy is to steward and make possible such 'manifestations'. A longtime member and one of its consultants, Alex Walker, says that the key to doing this, in a world with ecological imbalance, unemployment, the nuclear arms race, and Third World debt and poverty is to recognize the potential of every situation we encounter.

> Manifestation is a process of working with natural principles and laws [to] translate energy from one level to another. It is not the creation of something out of nothing, but rather a process of realizing a potential of something that already exists.

It rises from a sense of wholeness and oneness with all life, rather than from separation, lack or fear. They say the following are necessary for positive material results to manifest in the world: right identification, right imagination, right attunement and right action.

Community rules are as traditional as its sustainable energy ideas are forward-thinking. Four wind turbines power Findhorn's bungalows, caravans and eco-houses. A natural sewage plant – consisting of vats with reeds and other plants growing in them called 'The Living Machine' – cleans water to near-drinkable level. Members and visitors tend organic gardens that produce food consumed at Findhorn.

Food and farming

Growing food in individual neighbourhoods seems a good idea at a time when food is transported across the world, wasting energy and creating pollution. Certainly this is thought to be one solution for the problems of hunger and poverty in sub-Saharan Africa, where hundreds of indigenous vegetables are said to be so resilient as to thrive in poor soil on small plots of land.

> [Farming] is becoming ever more specialized, capital-intensive and technology-based, and food marketing ever more globalized. These trends are proving disastrous. [Nonetheless] most governments intend to accelerate the process, with policies that aim for higher exports and lower barriers to trade, more chemicals and more genetic engineering.[7]

They aim to maximize production of a limited range of globally traded commodities, while minimizing human labour. New technologies are promoted to farmers without regard for local ecological and social conditions.

> This has led to the reshaping of agricultural products, landscapes and diverse cultural traditions to suit the available technologies, and the homogenizing of nature and culture to better serve the global economy.

Farms have grown larger while the number of farmers has shrunk. Control over the world's food supply has been tightened by transnational corporations. Corporate farms gobble up small farms that collapse under competitive pressures from supermarkets, and laws support industrial-style corporations – which are less productive than small farms, despite their size. The author of *The Killing of the Countryside*, Graham Harvey, says that the billions of pounds in EU hand-outs, intended to aid small farms, are instead feeding a rampant agribusiness that is rapidly swallowing them up. Peter Rosset of Food First in the USA says that American farm subsidies are basically a transfer of money from the pockets of US taxpayers to large corporate farmers. According to www.primalseeds.org:

> Seventy-five per cent of agricultural crop diversity was lost during the 20th century. Seed resources are shifting from communities into the hands of transnational corporations, who are buying, patenting and investing heavily in biotechnology. Three vast agrochemical corporations, Monsanto, Dupont and Syngenta, now control a quarter of the world's entire seed supply.

Pressures from them are causing millions of acres of land worldwide to be planted monoculturally with genetically uniform hybrids. Farmers are being pressured into industrial agribusiness, which demands uniformity and crops designed for mass mechanization and chemical management. Such uniformity invites crop failure, because pests and diseases spread more easily once the buffer of diversity is removed. Farmers must buy seeds and chemicals, putting many into debt. They cannot survive financially when their crops fail. The highest suicide rate worldwide is now in farming communities. Elisabet Sahtouris in *Earthdance: Living systems in Evolution*, says:

> Diversity is crucial to nature, yet [we] seem desperately eager to eliminate it, in nature and in one another. This is one of [our] greatest mistakes. We reduce complex ecosystems to one-crop monocultures, [and] force others to adopt our languages, customs and social structures, instead of respecting their diversity.

E F Schumacher suggested that corporations should remain small because community spirit is lost as soon as an economic system goes beyond the human scale. He said 'any fool can make things complicated. It requires a genius to make things simple'.

Transnational corporations dictate much of what the World Trade Organization does, and the WTO has a great deal of power over what happens to the world's agricultural systems. Its member states must accept all imports and patents the WTO deems appropriate. This means that we on the grass-roots level must protect seed biodiversity and our food supply. Movements have begun in response: farmers' markets and local organic food providers may be found sprouting everywhere.

Organic farming is known to bring back bird and plant species that disappear when pesticide- and chemical-ridden, intensive, monocultural farming methods are used. Planting certain species beside each other can deter insect attackers. Natural fungicides, organic nutritional additives and rhythmical crop rotation also encourage plant growth.

> The Rodale Institute in the USA found that organically managed soils typically contained between 15–28 per cent more soil carbon than non-organic soils.[8]

The Prince of Wales runs his own estate of Highgrove entirely organically. He states that he witnessed wanton and unnecessary destruction of so much of Britain's ancient, species-rich habitats and landscapes when he was young that he felt he had to do something about it. 'Whole field systems, thousands of miles of hedges, venerable woodlands, wildflower meadows … were ripped up in a mechanized instant in the name of what came to be known as "agri-industry".'

Farmers were merely responding to 'experts' and governments who were addressing the food shortages of the Second World War. The consequences were dire. Since 1945, 186,000 miles of hedgerows, 85 per cent of wildflower meadows, 50 per cent of chalk grassland, 50 per cent of ancient lowland woodlands and 50 per cent of wetlands have been lost.

In the 1970s, an international law was made to outlaw the sale of plant seeds that were not patented or approved. This effectively quashed food plants farmed for centuries worldwide, limiting the promotion of only a few by the world's agribusinesses. For this reason, in Britain the Henry Doubleday Research Association (now Garden Organic) set up a heritage seed library whose seeds are free to members.

Navdanya pioneered the movement for seed saving (including the seeds of medicinal plants and more than 2,000 varieties of rice) in India. Positive effects have already resulted from its efforts. Saline resistant seeds conserved by it helped 1999 cyclone victims in Orissa to re-establish their sustainable agriculture.

Biodynamics and permaculture

One step beyond organic farming is the anthroposophists' 'bio-dynamic' method. In 1924, the Austrian scientist Rudolf Steiner declared that planetary rhythms were important to plant growth. The phases of the Moon and the seasons are taken into account in the biodynamic method of growing and harvesting crops. Regenerative forces, not only light, come from the Sun and Moon, and work through the soil to the plant. When the plant is removed from the soil, not only are its own forces taken out, but also those in the land. Therefore, special therapeutic preparations are added to compost and manure to replenish soil and plant forces. Weeds are controlled through mechanical and organic means.

Biodynamic farmers view a farm as self-sufficient. It provides its own seeds, fertility and feed for a variety of different animals that roam freely within a range of environments, including ponds, hedges, orchards, pastures and woods. A biodynamic farmer is a kind of artist who blends a landscape with animals and crops that attract particular birds and insects, all of which create a sustainable, balanced, harmonious organism. Every biodynamic farm has a personality of its own, shaped by an interrelationship between the farmer, the land and the creatures living there.

The purpose of permaculture is to create thriving, edible eco-systems. Its central premise is that an abundant natural forest made of food plants outperforms a wheat field in yielding edible foods. It requires that certain seeds be put together and particular methods used to grow things in different landscapes. Diversity is key, and cooperation its means. 'Some of the edible ecosystems of permaculture may actually look like a forest. But in others the copy is not so direct.'

One can attach a conservatory to the south side of a house, which helps to heat the house during the day, while the house keeps the conservatory warm at night. Food plants can, therefore, grow there in winter. Its 'design is based on the principle of making useful connections. This is what makes ecosystems work and it is also what makes permaculture systems work.'[9]

Australian Craig Gibsone shows off his own permaculture garden to his students who come to learn about ecovillages and sustainability at Findhorn. He calls himself a 'seed guerrilla'. Fill your pockets with different kinds of seeds and surreptitiously throw them into every well-manicured garden and barren, derelict patch of land you happen across, and you can be one too. That is the most basic kind of permaculture 'farming', he says. His own home, which he made with oak staves from a giant whisky barrel, is surrounded by a wild, burgeoning permaculture garden. This is particularly appropriate to the principles of permaculture since this is whisky country.

A Japanese hill farmer called Masanobu Fukuoka, another permaculturist, gave seeds for 100 kinds of plants to people in Ethiopia and Somalia. Because the desert is so hot and does not have water, seed roots travel downwards very quickly in search of water, which often is around 6–12 ft (2–4 m) underground.

> Chemical agriculture can't change the desert. [To] make the desert green requires natural farming. The method is very simple. You just need to sow seeds.

Masanobu feels it is better to send seeds than food or clothing to the needy, as even children can plant seeds. African governments discourage home gardens and small farms so garden seed has now become scarce. Africans are encouraged to grow export crops to make them money, not the amaranth and succulents that grow so well there. 'Vegetables are just food; they don't bring in any money', he says, and US government representatives 'say they will provide corn and grain, so people don't have to grow their own vegetables'.

A Japanese college professor told Masanobu that Somalia and Ethiopia are 'the hell of the world', but he says, 'No, this is the entrance to heaven'. These 'people have no money, no food, but they are very happy. The reason they are very happy is that they don't have schools or teachers.'

He suggests that the United States throw seeds into the deserts from airplanes or space shuttles instead of going to outer space. Masanobu says that people feel happy in the spring because of the oxygen that plants emit. However, because African land is rapidly being depleted of plants, soon everyone there is going to be affected by a change in the air, so we need to start planting now.

> People in Ethiopia are happy with wind and light, fire and water. Why do people need more? Our task is to practise farming the way God does. That could be the way to start saving this world.

HOW TO MAKE A SEED BALL

The American Indians originally devised a 'seed ball' for seeding dry, thin, compacted soils and waste areas during winter. A penny-sized mixture of clay and soil humus holds seeds together. The soil dissuades predators like mice and birds and stops seeds from drying out in the sunshine or blowing away. Once enough rain has fallen to make the seeds inside the ball sprout, they are protected within soil that contains good microbes and nutrients. A seed ball is said to create a haven for beneficial insects and is particularly useful in arid places with unpredictable rainfall. Just throw a minimum of ten seed balls onto one square metre of ground (derelict land may require more) and a wild garden should sprout by the time spring and summer come.

Contact a local agricultural agency or nursery to find out

continues

what native plant species are beneficial to the area you're trying to restore. Non-native 'invader species that are proven voracious spreaders' should never be planted. Seeds that may be useful include clover, alfalfa, alyssum, nasturtium, yarrow, carrot, dill, daikon, celery, radish, fennel, caraway, chervil, gypsophila, coriander, calendula, mustard, anise hyssop, phacelia, agastache and amaranth. Seeds coated with soil or calcium won't dry out or get eaten by animals. Mix tree and vegetable seeds, and you will sow everything at the same time.
www.pathtofreedom.com/pathproject

Nature's way: biomimicry

What better models could there be for learning how to create sustainable and ecological methods of living on Earth than 'our planet-mates – the fantastic meshwork of plants, animals and microbes' which 'have been patiently perfecting their wares' and 'doing everything we want to do, without guzzling fossil fuel, polluting the planet or mortgaging their future'? American biologist Janine Benyus uses the term 'biomimicry' when referring to copying nature's designs and manufacturing processes to find solutions to problems. Doing things nature's way, we can consult animals and insects, following natural models for growing food and creating new technologies. Solar cells could be copied from leaves. This is not new to the Huaorani Indians of Ecuador, as almost 'all native cultures that have survived without fouling their nests have acknowledged that nature knows best, and have had the humility to ask the bears, wolves, ravens and redwoods for guidance'.

Benyus writes in *Biomimicry* that exams for her forestry degree required study in 'reductionist fashion', so that each piece of the forest was observed separately, without consideration that a forest might add up to something more than the sum of its parts. Forestry students were taught a human-centred approach to management. Only later did she begin to notice the harmony between organisms and their environments. 'In seeing how seamlessly animals fit into their homes, I began to see how separate we managers had become from ours.' It is time that we adapted to the Earth rather than the other way round, she says.

'All our inventions have already appeared in nature in a more elegant form.' Central heating and air-conditioning have already been developed by termites, whose tower is kept at a steady 86 °F (30 °C).

> [Radar] is hard of hearing compared to the bat's multi-frequency transmission ... our new 'smart materials' can't hold a candle to the dolphin's skin or the butterfly's proboscis. Even the wheel [has] been found in the tiny rotary motor that propels the flagellum of the world's most ancient bacteria.

Safeguarding 'the naturalness of nature' will help us find solutions to future problems. This is why it is important to ensure that we do not alter it out of all recognition. Biomimicry will become increasingly important if, as some scientists predict, we begin to lose a quarter of all species in the next decades.

The built universe: the missing master builder

Architecture is frozen music.

GOETHE

Might we mimic nature in the forms of energy we use and the kinds of houses we build in future? City plans that blend and harmonize buildings with landscapes could be created in a way that could incorporate modern sustainable energy sources. We needn't limit ourselves to making everything look like a machine, or as if a computer imagined it.

> The word 'architect' means *master builder* – one who masterminds the complete design concept, construction and costing of a building; one who has studied the art and science of architecture ... a philosopher who has a wisdom and spiritual insight into the nature of humanity and the natural world.[10]

Master builders of the 14–18th centuries include Brunelleschi, Alberti, Leonardo da Vinci, Palladio, Inigo Jones, Christopher Wren and Sir John Vanbrugh. Today such great architects aren't in evidence. Author Thomas Saunders believes the main reason they aren't is that Western schools of architecture do not teach humanistic philosophy alongside the fundamental principles of design. Added to this, architects have allowed their role 'to be eroded to the level where, more often than not, they have become little more than the person who "draws up plans" and designs appropriate facades, much like a cosmetic artist or theatrical costumier'.

Today architectural teams build buildings. Nobody is trained 'to mastermind the grand strategy that transforms a building into architecture'. During the 1990s, 40 per cent of the major new building works in the UK were carried out under a 'design and build' contract. This means that a team including an architect is employed by a building-contractor 'client'. The whole building (design, specification and construction) is under the direction and control of the *builder*. Often the architect is engaged to create a design concept only and is not allowed to have direct contact with the building owner or developer client. As a consequence, the 'master builder has no role to play in the design team of today'.

> [Today] schools of architecture are turning out graduates who do not have the ability (nor the inclination) to draw manually with a pen or pencil – everything is done on computer.

Students aren't learning about history or the history of art and architecture. As a result, many architects do not understand the present is a continuum of the past.

> [We] have witnessed over the past 100 years [a] loss of direction in [design,] philosophy and understanding that has produced buildings and new towns that are not only soulless but have also proven to be bad for our health and wellbeing.

The decline of architecture accelerated near the end of the 19th century due to new technologies that suddenly affected every aspect of our lives.

The architect became overburdened with keeping up with the volume of building by-laws and the latest materials and electronic devices, [and no longer evaluated] their effect on the health and wellbeing [of those who would use the buildings].

In Britain the 1947 Town and Country Planning Act allowed local governing authorities to control building development. This gave property developers the power to employ architects who would squeeze the greatest volume of building out of a site.

When a man is content to build for himself alone taking the natural rights of life, breadth and light and space away from his neighbour, the result is monstrosity like the pretentious sky-scraper. It stands for a while in the business slum formed by its own greed, selfishly casting its shadow on its neighbours.

The users and occupiers of buildings today can change this situation. We can demand that beautiful, people-oriented buildings be created.

Sacred sites

In the past people rose at dawn and went to bed when the Sun went down. Bear-like hibernation was normal during cold weather before electricity came along. With this slower way of life, people were conscious of whether their natural surroundings were beautiful, not merely functional, although even ancient sacred sites had utilitarian purposes. These could have been astronomical or technological devices, cultural, religious or burial sites or places of healing. They are found all over the world.

In the 1980s, I discovered the same kinds of earthworks in upstate New York that I had seen in Ireland. With an intrepid friend who had long investigated these things, I saw one in the process of being destroyed for a highway. It was a minor earth-work, so not important, my friend told me. I had never known such things were being bulldozed all around me.

Later I saw two extremely large cave mounds in a New York state park. One had an interior made entirely of rose quartz. Imagining I felt the healing qualities that folklore attributed to the stone, I wondered whether American Indians had made it.

Stone circles and monuments may be found all over the world. Evidence that sacred sites are linked may be found in the networking rituals that folklorists have unearthed. Chapter 2 mentions Ireland's May 1st ritual in which a bonfire on the island's tallest hill, from which its high king ruled, sparked other fires all round the country.

Earth mysteries photographer Martin Gray believes that such sacred sites hold a transformative power that is one key to resolving our personal and planetary problems. Every sacred place has individual, unique qualities. Gray thinks that ancient people 'encoded' these in myths and legends. Some sites have an 'oracular' nature and inspire precognitive experiences. Having travelled all over the world visiting such places, he likens visions he has had in them to those of the Oracle at Delphi, Moses on Mount Sinai and Buddha under the Bodhi Tree. He has 'seen images' of a world environmentally healthy without hunger or disease, but says that it won't happen until after a period of crisis some time during the 21st century, when widespread famine, terrorism, environmental degradation and socio-economic collapse will awaken people to realize that they must care for and serve all of life and the Earth.

Sacred caves have intriguing acoustic qualities. American researcher Steven Waller found that percussive sounds directed at painted rock walls yielded more echo decibels than unpainted surfaces nearby. Percussive echoes in such spots transformed into sounds suggestive of galloping hooves. These emanated from painted images of herds and bison on the walls as if they had their own soundtrack.

Earth mysteries researcher Paul Devereux undertook an investigation of Neolithic chambered mounds in Britain and Ireland, including Newgrange, with Princeton University's Professor Robert G Jahn under the aegis of the International Consciousness Research Laboratories (ICRL) group in Princeton. They discovered that those sites had resonant frequencies of 95–112Hz (hertz or cycles per second), with most at 110Hz. 'This is in the male baritone range, raising the possibility that male ritual chanting took place in the chambers or that oracular pronouncements were made from them.'

Sounds inside a cave are amplified when made at the same resonant frequency as the cave. Tests at stone circles and inside 'passage graves', show that internal acoustic effects vary according to where you stand. The graves are shaped like a 'Helmholtz resonator' – a cavity in the centre of the mound is connected to the outside world by a narrow passage. A site in Scotland called Camster Round has a Helmholtz resonance of 4Hz, which 'would be felt as a deep vibration rather than heard as a sound', much as one experiences while standing near a bass speaker.

Mayan sites are also known to have unusual sound properties. Tuned stone steps exist at a temple in the Mayan site of Tikal, while at Palenque a normal conversation may be held across the tops of three pyramids. In his *The Illustrated Encyclopedia of Ancient Earth Mysteries*, Devereux states:

> A faint whisper can be heard all around certain Mayan ball courts. [At] Chichén Itzá on Mexico's Yucatán peninsula, [a] screeching echo reverberates … in response to any percussive sound … similar to the primary call of the quetzal bird, which was sacred to the Maya.

Sites all over the world have acoustic oddities like these. Associated with some of them is folklore that may indicate their purpose, such as the oracular pronouncements made at the chambered cairn at Loughcrew in Ireland. Gregorian plainchant may have been sung at Chartres Cathedral in order to make its stones resonate. Other sites may have been used for astronomical purposes, such as Stonehenge in Wiltshire, England. Those of the Hopi Indians in America in the 1930s had 'sunwatcher priests' who observed important agricultural or ceremonial dates according to the Sun's position on mountain peaks.

A sunbeam shines on the face or crown of whoever sits on Charlemagne's throne on June 21st (summer solstice) at Aachen

Cathedral (western Germany), where Charlemagne (Charles the Great, 747–814) held court and was crowned. On his birthday, April 16th, a beam of sun shines on his throne. One might think this coincidence, had astronomical calculation not been taught to the clergy of Charlemagne's time.

> In the 1950s, the Reverend Hugh Benson surveyed almost 300 medieval English churches and found that a significant proportion were ... aligned accurately to sunrise on their patron saint's day.

Building ecologically according to nature

Using sunlight, nature and climate in architectural designs were most important to the famous Greek master builder-architect of Rome, Marco Vitruvius Pollio, who was steeped in an architectural sensibility that had vanished even in the 1st century AD. He considered what style of building suited different body types, whose reactions to temperature and geography governed what kind of comfort they needed in their homes. Locations for Roman towns were chosen geographically, and buildings were planned to assure comfort, warmth and dry interiors. Professor Frank Granger, in *Vitruvius on Architecture*, says that houses included a system of heating by 'hanging floors' raised upon pilasters of brick. Adjustments in planning were made according to the need for sunlight in rooms used for particular purposes at different times of the day and in different seasons. Vitruvius even planned for north light in painters' studios, picture galleries and embroiderers' weaving-rooms.

Something extra must be added to buildings to make them places in which we wish to live and work, just as we must find some extra value in life to make it seem worthwhile. However, as British scientist Richard Dawkins says, 'if everything is judged by how "useful" it is – useful for staying alive, that is – we are left facing a futile circularity'. At least part of life should be devoted to living it instead of just trying to stop it from ending, he thinks.

This is how we rightly justify spending taxpayers' money on the arts. It is one of the justifications properly offered for conserving rare species and beautiful buildings. It is how we answer those barbarians who think that wild elephants and historic houses should be preserved only if they 'pay their way'. [Science pays its way and] of course it is useful. But that is not all it is.

Englishwoman Helena Norberg-Hodge sees traditional houses in Ladakh as being more than just functional. Ladakhis spend much time on purely aesthetic details.

> Windows and doors receive special attention. Some have ornately carved lintels (the work of the village carpenter). [Small] balconies, again finely worked, adorn the upper floors.

House entrances face east, which is considered auspicious. A stone stairway goes to the first floor where people live. The ground floor holds animals. The kitchen and storage rooms take up most of the first storey, into which light beams from a large courtyard on the second floor. Land, which once never cost money, has become a commodity with a monetary value. Instead of simply digging up land to make the mud bricks they used to build their houses with, people now buy them in an urban area and bring them home. Building in mud is slow and the majority of 'educated' people have never learned how to do it. Consequently, Ladakhi housing engineers generally build with cement and steel today. Norberg-Hodge states in *Ancient Futures*:

> As a consequence, the skills required to build with mud [are becoming] ever more scarce and thus more expensive. There is a psychological dimension as well: people are afraid of seeming backward – and everything traditional is beginning to be seen that way.

However, the mud brick of Ladakhi houses has been found to be an excellent medium for absorbing and storing solar energy. The French inventor Felix Trombe invented a simple device for heating houses called the Trombe wall, which is easily adapted to Ladakh's traditional architecture and building materials. A thin, glazed air space is placed in front of a thermal storage wall. A double layer of glass is attached to the outside of a south-facing wall, which is painted black to absorb the sun's rays. The ceilings and other walls are insulated with straw. Solar radiation is stored in this thermal mass behind an air space covered by clear glazing. Warmth radiates into the house evenly. The rays of the low winter Sun heat the room, while those of high summer barely touch the Trombe Wall, enabling it to remain cool.

Many Danish sustainable community buildings have solar 'Trombe' panels on adobe walls (a mixture of straw plus 25 per cent clay, similar to 'cob') – clad in wood to protect them from bad weather. The Danes have also created south-facing geodesic domes with heat-release structures built into them. These attract lots of heat.

Norberg-Hodge and others have begun to educate people in developing countries about alternative energy technologies that will enable them to avoid relying on and being controlled by governments running a 'national grid' system for electricity, heating and running water. Practical self-sustaining, non-electric machines, which people can make and repair themselves, and solar panels for tents, giving Tibetan nomads light and heat, are provided by Applied Technology for Tibetans.

Similar to Ladakhi and Tibetan houses and American Indian adobe huts, the Arab courtyard or patio house is a prototype for many variations used in the Arab world. According to Gianni Scudo, it has the same 'contacts with open space, the same response to shade and to the movement of the air at each hour of the day, as the Arab experienced when he lived in tents'. Without mechanical devices, it creates a temperature regulating system – a microclimate – with heat transfer processes that use the Sun, wind, sky, water, vegetation and local building materials.

Seen as a microcosm linking land and sky in space and time, its courtyard walls symbolize 'four columns carrying the dome of the sky, which is drawn down into intimate contact' with its rooms. In this way, nature and space are brought into the house. Heat is exchanged through the 'inner envelope' of its courtyard walls and the 'external envelope' of its walls and roof. These surfaces are constantly exposed to outdoor temperatures, however their exposure to solar radiation varies depending on time of day. During the daytime, movable shading devices and plants – placed so that they will add dampness to the air and further increase shade – keep the indoors cool. Rooms on the ground floor are used in summer, while upper floors are used in winter.

An external white colour reflects the Sun rather than absorbing its heat, and the roof, considered the most critical component of the building, is flat to maximize heat loss at night. At night people sleep there under the stars while, during the day, people work, eat and sleep in the courtyard and shady areas. A dry earth wall contributes to thermal protection, as do fewer walls exposed to sun and hot wind, together with shady, narrow winding streets around the house.

> A wide street offers no shade and heats up more rapidly than a narrow one. The difference in comfort is clearly felt in all the streets that were widened and straightened during the remodelling of old parts of Cairo. They are extremely hot in summer and are full of dust.[11]

'Wind catchers' or solar towers are used in Iraq, Iran and Egypt to intercept cooler, faster, less dusty air flows and funnel them into houses. To increase their effect, they are often combined with fountains and humid underground tunnels or little streams which also allow the watering of the ground. These act at different times of day and night to create a cooling system which can drop air temperature to 5 °C (40 °F).

Victorian houses in England are also good at keeping cool in summer and warm in winter. They were built to allow air to flow through them, with holes near kitchen floors, in pantry doors and at the tops of walls, above kitchen fumes and bathroom steam, to avoid mould and damp. We need buildings that live and breathe with their natural surroundings rather than ones that are hermetically sealed.

Nature-based architecture

The movement to return to creating buildings made of mud, straw or similar materials, with solar, wind, geothermal and hydro-electric sources of energy, is gathering speed worldwide. Even yurts and tents can now be powered by solar panels.

Ecological buildings are meant to use natural energy sources, and to be in harmony with nature and its elements as well as social and environmental surroundings. For heating or cooling a house, one can use geothermal methods, photovoltaic cells, wind energy, micro-hydro or any number of small methodologies to give the necessary energy to drive a heat pump. Houses in northern Scotland generally have 8 in (20 cm) thick walls and 10 in (25 cm) roofs, but in colder climates like Latvia, one should have thicker ones. Insulation can cut down reflective heat, particularly in hot climates, but in places like Brazil, there is no way to push out all the heat, which concentrates on the roof. An ecovillage in Russia has built log cabins with green logs that, as they age, settle into each other. Spaces between the logs are filled with lichen and straw. These buildings are cool in summer and warm in winter.

To build according to sustainable principles, it is not necessary to embrace the 'aesthetic' of quick-build, light industrial architecture. Sustainable architects need not follow the stylistic diktats of modernist architecture with its standardized techniques, based usually on steel-frame construction.

Things like ornament (or decoration) were virtually *de rigueur* in pre-modernist architecture but are signally lacking in sustainable building today. The vast majority is eclipsed in aesthetic beauty by the merest Victorian railway signal box. This is because the Victorians possessed traditions of integrated and subtle ornament. The new eco-architect might say his prime aim is not to recreate traditional styles but rather to create a sustainable architecture. In that case, he must create his own equivalent beauty of, for example, the Victorian recessed window. The importance of aesthetics, incorporating the beauty of natural organic materials into structures and shapes, must not be underestimated. Many sustainable buildings fail to attract people who prefer earth-coloured brick or stone, with large windows filled with flowers, surrounded by green, hilly vistas.

> At last people are beginning to see that it is possible, and important in human terms, to respect old buildings, street plans and traditional scales and at the same time not to feel guilty about a preference for facades, ornaments and soft materials.[12]

Anti-modernist, classical architects Quinlan Terry and Léon Krier, who usually work in England and Europe, create human-scale environments based on traditional styles. In 1988 Prince Charles commissioned town planner Krier to build 2,400 homes on 400 acres on his estate in Dorset. In 1993, the village of Poundbury began to take form. Deliberately narrow, serpentine streets slow traffic through the village and cars are parked behind houses to avoid congestion. Mews and gravelled lanes have been carefully planned to create the sense of a traditional English village.

> Very great sums are being invested to renovate 1950s and 1960s modernist estates. [They are] the artificial prolongation of failed experiments of social and architectural collectivism. [But, even] the most soulless dumps on Earth can – with the right ideas and people, and sometimes very modest means – be turned around to become places of beauty.[13]

American architects such as Bill Haws and Jim Sargent are developing ecovillages in the United States, while city centres are being renovated by entrepreneurial residents such as Ed Bass who, with his brothers, completely transformed downtown Fort Worth, Texas. According to Fred Koetler, Dean of the Yale School of Architecture, the latter could stand as a model among people who are looking for new ways to bring life to existing cities.

You are lost if you don't like the industrialization of the countryside, however. Even places like Findhorn have white industrial-style windmills, although relatively small. One can hear them whirring only when near them. Friends of the Earth supports wind technology. Now moneylenders are beginning to support ecological ventures. Some are set up to deal specifically with them and lend money to projects that benefit the environment, including small woodlands.

Advocating that people use traditional local building methods and materials that are present and recyclable there, Findhorn's Craig Gibsone suggests that people look at the way buildings were made before World Wars I and II, when mass production changed building methods. Four-hundred-year-old cob, adobe and straw-bale structures may be found in the south of England. Their walls breathe naturally, being made of permeable local materials. A very small amount of moisture moves through them, helping balance temperatures. It's very easy to ruin a straw-bale or cob structure by putting a vapour barrier on it, trying to make it more watertight, or something that will last longer so you don't have to maintain it. When you put an impermeable membrane in the walls of a house, moisture moves inside and condenses there, running down the inner membrane and rotting its internal structures. Many 300–400-year-old houses in southern England lasted a mere 20 years after impermeable membranes were put on them.

For earth-built structures of that period, you should apply natural whitewashes and lime-based coverings to the walls, as high-gloss paint creates a barrier that imprisons moisture. A modern bathroom is a good example of what happens in a house sealed with such paint. It not only traps steam: the toxins in the petrochemical-based paint, curtains, furnishings and building materials are trapped also. Even the glues that hold wood together and the fill between walls usually have formaldehyde in them – a pollutant with a long life. By having a vapour barrier, you are putting a plastic bag around your house and these pollutants, holding in their fumes. A vapour barrier that completely encapsu-lates a house causes dry rot and traps modern materials, mostly petrochemicals, creating 'sick building syndrome'. All the bugs in a house are killed by many cleaning products, and 'you're a pretty big bug yourself', Gibsone jokes. Still, a vapour barrier on the base of your house is important, or you must build on a dry, firm foundation where water can't rise into the structure. When he explains to children how a house should be built, Gibsone says:

[A] house needs a really good pair of boots. When it's raining, what would you need? A really good raincoat, and then a really good hat. [If] you wear a plastic raincoat, you end up getting soaking wet, so that's not a good raincoat. A lot of raincoats don't breathe, so you end up more wet on the inside.

If you can build your house yourself out of recycled materials, you could cut your costs by two-thirds, Gibsone suggests, adding that while it might take one person four years to build a house, four people might do it in four to six months.

Ecovillages and cohousing

Never doubt that a small group of thoughtful, committed citizens can change the world. Indeed, it's the only thing that ever has.

MARGARET MEAD, 1969

Findhorn is part of the Global Ecovillage Network (GEN), linking it with a number of ecovillages around the world. What is an ecovillage? It is a community of people united by common ecological, social and/or spiritual values who work together to consciously diminish their ecological footprint by taking no more from the Earth than they give back. They generally use permaculture methods for growing food and aim to be self-reliant regarding sustainable energy and food production. Ecovillages with a spiritual orientation focus on personal responsibility, self-discipline and self-development, while those of a socially motivated nature experiment with different styles of communal living. The most successful ecovillages will probably eventually combine all three aspects, as Findhorn does.

Cohousing communities are conceived as miniature villages within towns or cities. Inhabitants take part in the world outside the community in which they live. Members live in houses or apartments in the same vicinity and keep to certain communal rules and commitments. Cohousing started in Denmark in the 1970s, and was taken to the US in the 1980s. Individuals are beginning to pool financial resources for ventures like this in order to counteract things like the closing of local post offices and hospitals.

Hospitals are probably the most important buildings within communities. Ecological ideas should be expressed first and foremost in them, for most of us are born and end up in them at some point in our lives. Modern hospitals are little more than 'body workshops' housing high-tech machinery and facilitating the efficiency of medical staff, Professor Keith Critchlow says. Almost everything about health facilities design is based on function or medical technology.

American architect Frank Lloyd Wright believed that hospital patients should have health constantly before their eyes. The view from a patient's window influenced his recovery, Wright thought. A hospital should be 'a sanctuary for renewal … a temple for healing the spirit as well as the body', he said (Thomas Saunders, *The Boiled Frog Syndrome*).

British hospital design in the 19th century was inspired by Florence Nightingale, whose experiences serving as a nurse in the Crimean War helped her to articulate her views. It was clear to her that good health required the opposite of what she saw on the battlefield. Believing that fresh circulating air, warm sunlight, natural surroundings, cleanliness and peace were the most important aspects of healing, she designed hospitals with corridors, balconies and windows that opened. The sick 'should be able, without raising themselves or turning in bed, to see out of the window from their beds, to see sky and sunlight at least, if you can show them nothing else'. [14]

She also instituted the matron system, in which experienced nurses managed wards of nurses who ensured that patients' rooms were kept pristine and well ventilated. On warm days, they wheeled recuperating inmates out into the sunshine in surrounding park-like grounds.

> Put the pale, withering plant and human being into the Sun and, if not too far gone, each will recover health and spirit. Walk through the wards of a hospital … and count how many you [see] lying with their faces towards the wall.

With the mechanization of hospitals today – surrounded usually by buildings, concrete streets and polluting cars more than by flowery, tree-filled gardens – patients are not allowed this connection with nature anymore. Architects have designed functional hospital buildings to house and protect machines, not living, breathing, organic beings. It is important to consider the physical and psychological needs of the animals that we are. Opening hospitals to nature and feeding the sick with fresh, organic food need not be expensive. After all, sunshine and fresh air are free. Providing space for these and plants – to create beautiful, natural, health-giving environments for the sick – should be *de rigueur* in this enlightened age.

Eco-cities

When we build our cities, we remove as much of nature as possible. We start by removing woodland or forest. We level off a hill or even divert a river. Town planners and builders take raw materials from this 'butchered environment', creating artificial flat surfaces on which we construct 'cubed boxes'. Our buildings come from the Greek mathematician Euclid, Harry Oldfield says, and their disharmony is internal as well as external, permeating all physical and mental levels.

> [Euclid's] straight line and perfect circle exist [only] in man-made systems of geometry. [These] are not natural guidelines and their implementation in almost every area of our lives could perhaps explain some of our disharmony with nature.[15]

An attempt to address this disharmony is being made by cities like Malmö and Stockholm, Sweden, which are undertaking forward-thinking ecological projects. Sweden plans to be a virtually oil-free economy by the year 2020 and has already converted much of its domestic heating to geo-thermal power (underground heat). The country has been phasing out its nuclear power since 1980 and taxes companies that produce high-carbon emissions, while giving subsidies to those converting to green energy. Cars running on biodiesel are exempt from some taxes and green fuel is cheaper.

In the northwest United States, the city of Seattle hopes to reclaim and rebuild its waterfront in a way that will bring nature back into the city. It is part of a growing US urban ecology movement. They are regenerating parks, encouraging ecological construction and agreeing to the environmental engineering of streets, roofs and new infrastructures that will capture and filter runoff water and protect streams and habitats. Seattle and Portland, Oregon, are pioneering 'green streets' with more trees, landscaped bioswales (shady spots designed to remove silt and contamination from surface runoff water), and paving materials that will reduce pollution, while Chicago and Los Angeles have replaced old brownfield sites with parks. Many cities are revamping their centres by creating better access between homes, shops and workplaces.

Unfortunately London's leaders are planning ever taller, higher density buildings that are encroaching on parks, hemming in canals and edging out the sky. David Nicholson-Lord, writing in *Resurgence Magazine* in 2007, states:

> Between 1989 and 1999 over 1,000 hectares of open space – an area the size of Richmond Park – were lost to development in the capital. More recent figures suggest that between 2001 and 2005 an area three times the size of St James' Park was built on each year [in London]. However, an east London river is 'part of a multi-million pound regeneration project' and already one park in south-west London has had concrete removed from its river so that wildlife now flourish and heron fish there.

The city of Seoul, Korea, has restored a river that had been concreted over with a motorway that carried perpetually jammed traffic. In the highway's place, a five-mile-long, 1,000-acre park has been created.

> It had taken twenty years to build the roads, but it took just two to tear them down and restore the river. [Cars] just disappeared, drivers changed their habits ... some of them gave up their cars and others just found different routes.

Today, the river acts as a natural air conditioner, cooling the capital during its long, hot summers and more birds, fish, insects and plants are now in the area. This restoration has been so successful that 'other cities in East Asia, such as Shanghai and Tokyo, are taking an interest' says John Vidal, environmental editor for *The Guardian*.

Eco-schools for children: UK developments

US Professor David W Orr, speaking at a conference in London in 2006, says the 'extractive economy' is destroying the world. Mountaintops are being removed at an alarming rate. This is happening because people aren't in touch with nature anymore. People spend only five per cent of their time outdoors. The solution may be found partly through education. Our schools should be more creative about education, more inventive about showing children how to work with nature. In Britain 6,300 schools deemed eco-schools are examples to other countries of the possibilities that exist for sustainable education and regeneration.

One organization, called Solar for London, is helping schools across London install solar hot water and photovoltaic systems. A wind turbine, solar roof panels, natural lighting, a thermally efficient heating system and recycled rainwater and other sustainable systems are planned for a primary school in Hertfordshire. In 2005, with help from the Centre for Alternative Technology and the Shropshire Wildlife Trust, a primary school in Shropshire built an almost completely environmentally friendly eco-lab with a greenhouse facing south for a gardening club, store, bike shelter and science lab. Students were involved in both design and building of the eco-lab, where they monitor the weather, learn about sustainable building and grow fruit and vegetables. They created a compost heap, a shady glade and small woodland area that attract wildlife, a pond with frogs, a garden for vegetables and plants, and a bike rack for students who ride bicycles to school. A waste audit was conducted to help them cut down on what they threw away. Now, even pencil sharpenings are composted.

An organization called Cob organized pupils in Cornwall to build a bus shelter for themselves out of cob, a mixture of clay, subsoil, sand, straw and water. Another cob project is taking place in Cornwall, in which an entire secondary school of 20 rooms will be built of cob with the help of some of its students, which its makers claim will be the largest earth building in the western hemisphere.

Birmingham's Storywood project helped an inner city school create a beautiful woodland and a small wildflower meadow with standing stones in a neglected corner of its school grounds. Staff now go there to prepare lessons, have lunch and relax. It has attracted wildlife and made the area greener and more attractive. Old flowerbeds have been transformed into allotments where students can grow their own vegetables. The school now plans to plant a mixed native hedge along its boundary to encourage wildlife and increase security.

Powergen and Britain's Department for Trade and Industry (DTI) offer grants to schools to install micro-generation technology, such as solar thermal hot water, wind turbines, ground source heat pumps, automated wood-pellet stoves and wood-fuelled boiler systems.

Looking for solutions in nature

Our real school has always been nature. Independent researchers are looking for ecological solutions through conducting their own experiments. Dr Roger Taylor, an English biologist and the science editor of *Caduceus* magazine (UK), is passionate about a substance called Ormus, which he believes could make many medical treatments and agricultural pesticides unnecessary in future.

An Arizona cotton farmer called David Hudson discovered a residue he called Ormus, which has no chemical reactions and becomes superconductive under some conditions. Hudson spent millions on a major research program that found that Ormus consists of a group of mostly precious metals in a non-metallic state. Although his findings have largely been dismissed, a group of scientists and laypeople is repeating his experiments and experiencing many of the same results. Crops sprayed by Ormus are said to taste better, mature earlier, need less fertilizer, and to have greater resistance to pests. Dr Taylor's own Ormus-treated potatoes weighed nearly double that of his control potatoes, and some of his carrots weighed over one pound (454 grams) each. Being easily and cheaply produced, and unpatentable, Dr Taylor believes Ormus could help us produce greater quantities of biofuel crops on smaller areas of land and that large areas of forest sprayed with Ormus from the air would soak up much more carbon dioxide.

Ormus residues are thought to be water-soluble and found everywhere – in soils, water (especially sea water) and all living matter. Dr Taylor believes they have been washed into the sea over time and that humans, land animals and plants may be chronically deficient in them. He urges that field trials be undertaken on them.

New technology and initiatives for the future

In 2006, England's Sir Richard Branson pledged US$10bn over a ten-year period to Clinton's Global Initiative (CGI) to help develop renewable energy sources, including biofuel (presumably to fuel his Virgin airplanes). This money is thought to be ten years of projected profits from Branson's Virgin airline and railway companies.

The CGI comprises a non-partisan group of leaders from political, ideological, religious, ethnic and regional backgrounds who are current and former heads of state, top business executives, scholars and NGO representatives. They seek to improve the world's worst conflicts and poverty, healthcare and environmental problems. Participants are asked to take immediate action in one of the focus areas of the group. The CGI is currently encouraging the building of green homes.

Straw-bale homes are being built by a group called the New Rural Reconstruction Movement in China's countryside, where 60–70 per cent of the country's population lives. They are said to be highly energy-efficient and three to four times cheaper than conventional brick houses. Also in China, the James Yen Institute of Rural Reconstruction offers seminars on eco-building with local materials, organic agriculture, permaculture, community organization and rural cooperative-building. Thus far, graduates have founded more than 30 village cooperatives or other cultural and civic groups across China.

Precious Earth in Shropshire, England offers courses on building structures made of materials like willow, straw and recycled tyres, and useful objects like clay ovens. The Centre for Alternative Technology in Wales educates people about ecological building methods and new technology. It even helped the Findhorn Community check the 'breathing walls' of its houses.

New buildings could be designed to incorporate sustainable and recycling water and heating systems. Thicker walls, built 3 ft (1 m) thick or more, like those of houses in the 17th and 18th centuries, stifle noise while also encouraging the retention of warm or cool air. Passive solar areas can be incorporated into housing designs. The Trombe wall, for example, can replace solar collectors such as conservatories and greenhouses. Simple insulation measures enable temperatures to be better controlled.

Geothermal heat is a natural energy commonly used in homes in Scandinavia. Being found in the Earth, geothermal fluids and gases may be tapped at or near the Earth's surface, or from magma miles below. A system comprising a generator, condenser, cooling tower and turbine draws heat up into houses via vents and pipes linked to underground holes. Certain parts of the Earth are more easily used for this kind of energy than others, for instance where one finds volcanic activity or hot underground springs. Wyoming in the US has many warm underground springs, which people there are considering how to utilize for heat without measurable ecological disturbance.

Chief Executive Louis Armstrong of Britain's Royal Institute of Chartered Surveyors says, 40 per cent of carbon emissions come from buildings, so it is critical to find incentives to encourage people to make them 'greener'. The Royal Institute of Chartered Surveyors (RICS) urges real-estate valuers, property industry groups, appraisers, the green building lobby and financiers to work together to identify and promote the hidden benefits of green buildings, so that their market value can become a serious consideration for the landlord, developer and investor. Once the property and construction industries realize that it is profitable to tackle climate change, we may begin to see real improvements in the way new buildings are built and old buildings maintained. 'A new study of buildings in the UK reveals a clear link between the market value of commercial property and its environmental friendliness.'[16]

Only around four per cent of the UK's energy comes from renewable sources, according to Green Energy UK. They offer people help to use cleaner energy through their company, whose customers they hope will eventually own it.

Were people to equip their houses with sustainable technology, and governments to support them in doing it, the world could quickly become a green one. All that such a seismic socio-economic change requires is a shift in perspective. The necessary laws and business reorganization would follow. We should tailor our buildings and the kinds of energy we use to different climates and environments, which require different types of technology and building styles.

Countries needn't superimpose upon themselves the same industrialized technology that every other country uses, while ignoring their own climates and landscapes. The unindustrialized don't have to make the same mistakes that the industrialized world has made. They needn't cut themselves off from the natural world and its rhythms and cycles. Forests could be replenished for biofuels, while ocean currents and geo-thermal heat could be used as sources of sustainable energy. We do not have to over-industrialize, even with clean, renewable energy technologies. We can become conscious that the earth, air, water and animals need time for rest, inactivity and recuperation, just as we do. Rhythm and balance in all things, including our excitement about new technologies, is the wisest way to handle what is happening today. Many people are doing just this with small experiments, which are now gaining momentum on a grass-roots level.

Living in harmony with the natural world, being aware of our place within it, without imagining that we were in control of it, was how we survived until machine technology gradually separated us from nature. Recycling what we used was simply normal until industrialism took over and economic growth became our dictator.

On a sustainable development course at Findhorn, a young Korean woman became almost tearful when she told that she had come to the West hoping to find answers to the problems of pollution she could see growing in her own country. But she was learning nothing new. Complaining that Korea is moving away from recycling, she said that people in her country had always done all the things recommended at Findhorn, and in fact did them better. Home-made implements were used and reused, housing materials recycled, care was taken over how much water was used, and so on. But now the old ways were dying and bad habits growing.

US Professor David W Orr says advertising has been used to stimulate consumerism and it keeps us in a state of infantile self-gratification which, alongside lack of awareness of nature, leads us into being greater polluters than we already are. Our cities need to be repaired, as half the population now live there. Everyone in society should now be doing things for the environment, not just a few. We must especially 'liberate young people so they do great things now'. He says:

> Let children fall in love with the world first, before we teach them anything. Then free them so they can do what their idealism leads them to do.

In Europe and North America many attempted to retrieve good past habits during the 1960s in the 'back-to-the-earth' movement, encouraging people to become more aware of the link between nature and the mind. Today many innovators are doing it through technology, which is where the great ecological advances will take place in future.

But what we need is more of nature. We need natural materials and a resurgence of appreciation for our cultures' organic histories and natural expressions, particularly our historic buildings. Whatever we are thinking now creates our future. People everywhere could work together to create new clean, sustainable energy technologies suited to the beautiful landscapes we would prefer to live in. Together we might even find new sources of truly clean energy in what is, for now, an invisible part of the universe. It may be a dream, but perhaps it won't always be.

6

TECHNOLOGY TO MAKE
THE DESERTS BLOOM

We learn to live together as brothers – or we die
together as fools.

REV DR MARTIN LUTHER KING

DOWSERS BELIEVE THAT some kind of earth-energy is generated at sites where many medieval cathedrals now stand. They describe these sites as Earth's 'acupuncture points'. Significant interactions are said to occur between them and us on physical and mental levels. Are energies present at such sites responsible for healing and fertility phenomena that occur there? Is some kind of new energy source available to us that we haven't discovered yet?

Current research is aimed at bringing together experimental results with wider cosmological concepts involving the quantum vacuum. Jim Lyons is a chartered aerospace engineer who is currently involved in exploiting innovative energy technologies at the University of York. He says that progress to date is showing a significant correlation with the notion of a holographic universe having a universal fractal geometric structure. It is thought that this could be the source of consciousness. (A fractal is a fragmented geometric shape whose parts on all levels or scales are similar to each other.) Indications are that this energy field is all-pervading and may be accessed for energy generation at localized points.

So much is yet to be discovered. New sources of energy may be all around us. This is why it is important not to alter nature too much. We must keep and restore what we have, maintaining biodiversity despite the onslaught of technology upon it, and upon us. Studies show that new species of animals and plants arise faster on the most biodiverse islands. The more species we lose the more we lessen the possibility that new species will appear – species with the ability to survive as our planet changes.

Alternatives to nuclear energy

Adlai Stevenson said, a few years after the advent of nuclear energy and the atomic bomb in 1952, 'Man has wrested from nature the power to make the world a desert or to make the deserts bloom'. Satish Kumar questions why we need to take such a dangerous route as nuclear power to meet our energy needs when we can have safe, secure and abundant natural energy in the form of sun, wind and water. These will not run out, as the source of nuclear fuel, uranium, will. Nor do they cause population displacement resulting from nuclear waste, uranium mining or pollution disasters.

This is not to mention what nuclear technology does to health. A group of conservative scientists who doubted that France's nuclear tests in the South Pacific made Polynesian islanders suffer thyroid cancers are now saying they may have been wrong. Since the 41 nuclear explosions between 1966 and 1974, islanders have suffered high rates of thyroid cancer. Fallout has often been blamed for this. Now evidence of nuclear radiation's link to illness has been found by Claude Parmentier of the Gustave Roussy Institute in Villejuif, France. 'Thirty people in Polynesia with thyroid cancer had three times as many abnormalities in their chromosomes as people in Europe with the same disease.' Such abnormalities are a sign of radiation damage. Radiation is known to be linked with an increased risk of cancer.

Similar observations have been made in Kazakhstan, where Soviet nuclear tests were conducted in the 1950s. Inhabitants were not told what was going on. Genetic damage was found in the embryos of pregnant women there at that time and cancer has become a common way for people from the area to die.

More than two thousand children in Belarus have had their thyroids removed due to thyroid cancer, a situation never before recorded in paediatric literature. This is near the site of the infamous Chernobyl nuclear station meltdown in April, 1986. It irradiated sheep in Scotland, reindeer in Scandinavia and everyone all over the world. Reports claim that clean-up crews sent to the power station were not equipped with protective gear. Nor were they told how dangerous their work was. Local people found out what had happened only weeks later via international radio news reports, but by then they had been exposed to the radiation, which killed some of them in days. Numbers of casualties vary, and it is likely that the truth will never be known.

With the likelihood of such serious results from radiation, are nuclear reactors worthwhile? When taxpayers become ill and develop extremely expensive medical conditions for which the state must pay, one way or another, in what way is that financially viable? Short-term thinking harms everyone in the long term.

Jonathon Porritt, founder director of Forum for the Future and UK government advisor on sustainability, notes: 'Even if Britain's nuclear capacity is doubled, that would still leave 84 per cent of total energy consumption unaccounted for [and] very little, if any, new nuclear energy would come on stream before 2020.' He believes there should be a moratorium on building new centralized fossil-fuel power plants that do not install carbon-capture technology. Declaring that nuclear power is an old technology that has already benefited from decades of massively wasteful public funding, he adds that no public subsidy, direct or indirect, should go to new nuclear build. Unfortunately his committee's advice – that no new nuclear power stations be built until the problem of nuclear waste is solved – has thus far been ignored.

The health consequences of nuclear reactors are enormous. They emit radioactive isotopes consistently into air and water, and are entirely unregulated. Anyone near them is subject to absorbing isotopes through the lungs, which migrate to the fatty tissues of the body, including around the abdomen and upper thighs near the reproductive organs. Radioactive elements – such as tritium, known to be mutagenic, and plutonium – can last for 5,000 years and even thereafter cause cancer and genetic diseases. They emit high-energy gamma radiation and can mutate genes in eggs and sperm to cause genetic disease. Only 5 kg of plutonium are necessary to make a nuclear bomb, and each reactor produces more than 200 kg per year.

Two coal-fired plants in Kentucky, USA, that enrich a large percentage of the world's uranium emit large quantities of carbon dioxide which, along with another plant in Ohio, release 93 per cent of the chlorofluorocarbon gas (CFC) emitted by the world annually. This is banned internationally, as 'CFC is the main culprit responsible for stratospheric ozone depletion' and is a cause of global warming.[1]

According to Nancy Jack Todd, Britain's New Economic Foundation speculates that nuclear power has only survived for as long as it has because its true costs have been hidden from the public, and because its radioactive emissions are invisible.

New non-harmful possibilities

A more sensible route would be to utilize a variety of new clean technologies all at the same time in a single community. Greenpeace has produced an interactive educational animation about this on its website. Some people still think such 'alternative' technologies are more expensive than polluting ones, but the polluting options are definitely more expensive in the long term. All we need in order to implement this is a change in perspective from short-term to long-term thinking.

Clean renewable technologies are rapidly being developed and becoming cheaper by the day. This is happening so quickly that sustainable technology will have advanced beyond what is mentioned in this book by the time it is published.

The Rocky Mountain Institute (RMI) in Snowmass, Colorado, claims that, in our market economy, private investors determine what energy technologies can compete and yield profits. To find out what they are doing, it says 'follow the money'.

Private investors have flatly rejected nuclear power while enthus-iastically buying its main supply-side competitors, namely decentralized co-generation and renewables. By the end of 2004, these supposedly inadequate alternatives had more installed capacity than nuclear, produced 92 per cent as much electricity, and were growing 5.9 times faster and accelerating.[2]

Furthermore, nuclear plant vendors have never made money, while the renewable power industry earns $23 bn annually. Photo-voltaic and windpower markets double every couple of years and are expected to make renewable power a $35 bn business by 2012. Solar panels are considered by many to be too expensive to be practical. What generally isn't considered is that the cost could be spread out over a number of years, making it less than or equiva-lent to people's current monthly bills. However, soon even that may not be a problem due to a new solar device that is just about to be put on the market.

After ten years of research, a team under Professor Vivian Alberts at the University of Johannesburg in South Africa has developed a thin, flexible, 'photo-responsive' metal alloy that is said to comprise panels only five microns thick. A human hair is 20 micrometres thick, while silicon photovoltaic cells are 350 micro-metres. Reports from 2004 state that the alloy used for these solar panels is copperindium (gallium) diselenide (CIGS), which lasts for about 20 years. The cost of manufacture could be recovered within the first two years they are used, while the materials com-prising them may be recycled to make fresh cells. Estimates are that a standard family home will need around 30 m/sq (perhaps the size of a living room/parlour) of CIGS solar panels to meet its electricity demands. Alberts states that, 'unspecified new storage devices (batteries of some sort) and converters have been created alongside these new cells to store the collected energy'.

Apparently the solar panels can generate electricity even in winter and do not require direct sunlight to function. Most impor-tantly, they don't need silicon, which was an expensive drawback with earlier photovoltaic cell technology. Its makers expect this to lead to the development of a hi-tech solar panel manufacturing industry. Alberts has made a deal with a German firm to produce the panels, as it has the infrastructure to do so. The German government provides 15–20 per cent subsidies for clean energy projects.

New buildings might be designed to incorporate sustainable and recycling water and heating systems instead of the ones commonly used today. Thicker walls, built 3 ft (1 m) thick could stifle noise while also encouraging the retention of warm or cool air, depending on climate.

Water technology

For forty years I have been selling water
Beside the bank of a river. Ho, ho!
My labours have been wholly without merit.

SOGAKU HARADA

Roman systems of aqueducts and pipes for water, sewage and heating may still be seen in the remains of Roman villas and baths around Europe – one notable site in southwest England being the baths in a town called, appropriately, Bath. Aspects of these were used in Victorian building and could be used today in modern ecological housing. Of special interest is the way villas were heated and supplied with water.

Soils that produced the most health-giving and best-tasting waters were paramount to Vitruvius in considering where to site habitations. He said:

> An architect should have a knowledge of the study of medicine [to address] the question of climate, air, the healthiness and unhealth-iness of sites and the use of different waters. For without these considerations, the healthiness of a dwelling cannot be assured.[3]

Water and land must always be tested for the benefit of incoming residents. Satish Kumar, editor of England's *Resurgence Magazine*, suggests that a new kind of urban planning, with a paradigm that creates sustainable cities where living is a pleasure, could transform every rooftop into a water source. When we build 18-hole golf courses in Spain that use as much water in a year as a town of 10,000 houses, it is time to reconsider how we waste water in building our houses, towns and cities. Kumar says:

> There is no reason why we cannot harvest rainwater to use for toilets, clothes washing and irrigating urban gardens.

A technological ecological housing venture in London called BedZed, a high-tech apartment complex whose residents use 25 per cent less electricity than the UK average (4kWh per person per day), originally used a 'Green Water Treatment Plant' designed by David Triggs for Albion Water to clean the complex's grey and black wastewater. The 'green water' was reused to flush toilets and irrigate rooftop gardens, which they say saved 15 litres of mains water per head per day. But it cost so much to operate and maintain the plant, which used more energy than conventional sewage treatments, that they made an arrangement with Thames Water to introduce an experimental Membrane Bio-reactor (MBR) unit to treat sewage and wastewater. The MBR incorporates reinforced hollow-fibre membranes combining clarification, aeration and filtration into a cost-effective process that produces consistent, high-quality effluent suitable for discharge and reuse applications.

'An MBR is a combination of the activated sludge process, a wastewater treatment process characterized by a suspended

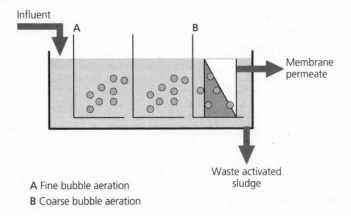

A Fine bubble aeration
B Coarse bubble aeration

growth of biomass, with a micro- or ultra-filtration membrane system that rejects particles', according to the *Science in Africa* online magazine. Along with water-efficient appliances such as low-flush toilets, spray taps, shower heads and washing machines, this has reduced BedZed's demand for mains water from 150 litres per day per person (the UK average) to around 91 litres per head.

The power of the sea's tides and waves is now being investigated by companies working in Wales and Northern Ireland. A marine current turbine called the SeaGen works in principle like a submerged windmill, driven by flowing water rather than blowing wind. The SeaGen is three times as powerful as Marine Current Turbines' first offshore tidal turbine installed off the Devon (England) coast in early 2003. SeaGen is studying the economic and environmental aspects involved in the commercial development of tidal stream energy, with a view to creating a tidal 'turbine farm'. Detractors say a turbine farm will harm marine life.

Another company is pioneering a floating device called a Wave Dragon, trialled in Ireland and Denmark. It channels reservoir water above sea level to turbines generating hydroelectric power. Plans are to place Dragons in the Irish Sea to create electricity for over 60,000 homes, while wind-farms are planned for the North Sea. What toll such large machines could have on sea and water life is yet to be discovered. Could such large operations be made smaller, similar to the old mills that generated energy and milled grain in the past? Surely such massive machine farms are more stressful on the environment than small energy-producers would be. And surely we could use more natural materials in their creation. Stone and bricks made of earth, around which plants could be grown, are friendlier than metal and concrete.

We are being quite unfriendly to ourselves by poisoning the water we use. Researchers discovered that water in Oslo and a remote coastal station in Norway contained traces of perfume chemicals such as synthetic musk, now banned in the EU due to its toxicity. These have been found in rivers and the North Sea, fish, human fat and breast milk. Perhaps this has something to do with the higher infant mortality rate in areas in London where houses are built on waterlogged land. Drugs and chemicals pollute rivers and seas, threatening fish life and getting into our drinking water. The largest consumer of water in Britain, after houses, is the energy industry, which uses it to cool power stations. Carbon emissions are produced from the chemicals and energy-intensive ultra-violet treatments that water companies use to clean this waste water.

However, natural methods are being used these days to remove many impurities from water. The Findhorn Community purifies sewage water by nearly 98 per cent by funnelling it through an aerobic system of tanks in which reeds and other plants remove polluted particles. They call this 'The Living Machine'. Local authorities who came to check the water for purity were so surprised at its cleanliness that they looked for an extra underground water source, which they thought was responsible for diffusing pollutants. Findhorners say the purified water is probably drinkable, but they use it only for watering plants and the nearby forest. The Living Machine consists of big round plastic tanks with open tops called 'aerobic digesters' which contain plants such as lobelia, watercress and mint; willow, tea, larch and gum trees; and anything that grows in a swamp or is in the lily family. These digest or transform and remove pollutants from water.

The flow of sludge moves as a result of gravity via underground polyethylene pipes. It sinks to the bottom of the first two tanks where there is no air. Duckweed shields the water from sunlight to discourage algae from growing. When the weeds die, they join the sludge in the bottom of the tank. Smells are controlled by aerating the tanks. Although most bugs die in this process, viruses can live in treated water for 10 to 12 days. HIV and E. coli bacteria are anaerobic, so they will not be destroyed in an aerobic water purifying system.

The next open tanks are 8 ft (2.4 m) deep and contain plants like Brazilian papyrus, mint and ammonia-tolerant reeds, which process effluents naturally. Bacteria thrive in temperatures of 30 °C or above, doubling with every half degree increase. The ammonia produced is broken down into water and nitrogen, and then into nitrous oxide, which breaks down into oxygen. The system will cope with a certain amount of bleach flushed into it but, to counteract acidity, calcium carbonate lime is added. The water outflow runs off into the nearby woods, to end the recycling process. It takes four days for one litre of sewage to go through the entire treatment, but a similar system exists in London that takes only 30 hours.

Another system of water purification is the anthroposophists' 'flow system'. John Wilkes, a sculptor trained at London's Royal College of Art, established the Flow Research Institute after studying the flow and rhythm of water at the Institute for Flow Sciences in Herrischried, Germany. This led to his invention of the 'Flowform' system. This simple technology steers polluted water through various levels of specially sculptured connecting vessels. It makes the water flow with a rhythmic pulse in a figure-of-eight, side-to-side, swirling pattern. At the end, the water is clean enough to use on growing plants. Tests have shown that rhythmically treated water supports the growth of organisms which clean the water biologically. A vigorous flow of water between opposing vortices also seems to work well, returning water to its natural state. Water is aerated as it moves and gradually leaves behind impurities, which can't keep up with its movement. This system is built on the principle that water that doesn't move stagnates, while rushing rivers, pouring over rocks and vegetation, eventually become clean. Today Flowforms are being incorporated into water treatment projects all over the world.

Grander water

Without clean water, we die. Preferably it should be full of minerals that are good for us rather than pesticides, hormones, chemicals and other pollutants. One person who has been conducting experiments on water for some time is the Austrian naturalist Johann Grander. For years, he has developed systems to revitalize water, his aim being to return drinking water to what it once was. His work is based on the notion that water has a 'memory'.

He says water can 'carry frequency' and transmit information to other bodies of water. When highly-charged water, which he calls

'Information Water', from deep under the Austrian mountains is placed beside ordinary tap water, 'Grander water' proponents say that the molecular and crystalline structure of the ordinary water changes. Tap water becomes like pure mountain water. This works a bit like homeopathy, except that the different waters do not have to mix or touch each other.

Grander's contention is that the water molecules communicate when in proximity to each other. The revitalization is carried out by devices filled with Grander Information Water in sealed tubes, past which water to be treated flows through the field effect emanating from the Information Water. These devices are built into the water supply or immersed directly into the water itself. This Information Water forms the basis for all subsequent applications of the Grander technology. The implications of this are profound. If this works, as it seems to, according to Grander's supporters – who include Austria's Federal Ministry for Education, Science and Culture and the Russian Academy of Natural Sciences – it implies that positive transformations occur in nature via the sympathetic transfer of information on a molecular level.

Grander's claims are significant. Water is supposed to taste better and be enhanced as a result of its altered microbiology. You feel better when you drink and wash in it. Foods washed and cooked in it taste fresher and have more flavour. Plants watered with it grow better and produce more striking, colourful flowers. Smaller amounts of cleansing materials are needed when washing with it. Animals are particularly attracted to it. Fewer chemicals are needed where it is used. Public swimming pools have reduced by one-third the detergent and chlorine they normally use, as the water inhibits bacterial growth and limescale. They use less electricity for heating water. Swimmers find it warmer, more hydrating and kinder to the skin. It has been used to stabilize microbiological conditions in industrial cooling systems without the addition of chemicals. When used on fruit farms, yields are boosted by 40 per cent and fruit becomes heavier and sweeter. Finally, the water returns to the environment still revitalized, so it does nature good. It regenerates ponds and small lakes and leads to the gradual disappearance of algae, which appears when water is contaminated or under stress.

Grander water supplier Jeremy Jones told me about Johann Grander and another Austrian naturalist called Viktor Schauberger (1885–1958). Schauberger called rainwater 'juvenile water', because he believed water needs to flow over rocks and stones before it may be considered 'mature water', which is good to drink and more healing to the body. Jones informed me that every litre of London tap water contains 447 mg of solids. If these solids were minerals that were good for the body, this would be fine, but they are elements from London's sewage, oestrogens and things like that, which one doesn't want to ingest. Jones suggested I try several blindfold taste tests that the Grander technology company recommends to customers. Before we began, I washed my hands in water from faucets attached to Grander technology, and it did seem distinctly soft, which is not characteristic of London tap water.

First, Jones cut a lemon in half, placing one near a glass of Grander water. After some minutes had passed, he asked me to compare the tastes of the two halves of lemon. The one that had been near the Grander water tasted less acidic and easier on the tongue than the much more tart, ordinary lemon. He squeezed the Grander lemon juice into Grander water, being careful to keep it far from the tap water containing ordinary lemon juice. Then I put on a blindfold and tasted each. Without hesitation, I chose the Grander lemon water, as it was much smoother, less tart and sweeter than the tap water.

Then he gave me an organic 'wood smoke' whisky mixed with the two different waters. The difference was remarkable. Although the ordinary water mixed with this very special whisky tasted pretty good, the drink was noticeably harsh. But when mixed with the Grander water, the whisky's aroma and its forest origins became really obvious, without any of the hard edge of the tap water whisky. It almost turned me into a whisky drinker right there and then! Controlled objective blindfold studies should be undertaken to prove that it wasn't the whisky that made me feel revitalized after I left Mr Jones, nor the other water he had given me, which contained special minerals and had been purified via reverse osmosis and charcoal.

New infrastructure to lessen technology's destructive effects

Natural resources such as water are by necessity funnelled to places with dense populations, but linking many cities and towns to one single source of power or 'national grid' is old thinking from our past industrial age. Villages, towns and city neighbourhoods can have their own independent sustainable power technologies. Germany intends to phase out nuclear power by the year 2025. Being the world's largest user of photovoltaic cells, it is on target in its plan for renewables to supply half of its energy needs by 2050.

Sixty-five per cent of energy used in electricity generation is wasted before it ever reaches homes. Large, centralized power plants, whether nuclear or gas, are inefficient. Smaller, decentralized technologies should be used nearer the point of demand – such as micro-renewables and combined heat-and-power plants (CHP), which produce heating as well as electricity. If half of the one million new gas-fired boilers annually installed in the UK were microgenerators (CHP systems that draw on local solar, wind, hydropower and tidal forces), they would produce the equivalent electricity of a new power station every year, removing the need for new large-scale power plants, and they could provide more local jobs, foster new industries and secure energy supplies. By combining renewable energies, such as microhydro, biomass, photovoltaic cells and tidal power, we can move towards supplying energy on the scale we need. Certainly in the short term, it would be better to have individual neighbourhoods sustaining themselves while lessening their demand on the national grid. If power from that grid ever stopped flowing, nearly energy-independent communities would at least be protected from complete collapse.

This is precisely what Woking Borough Council, near London, has done. It now has several sustainable and renewable energy systems that could help protect it in emergencies. Woking Council aims to design, build, finance and operate small-scale CHP stations through its joint venture energy services company,

Thamesway Energy. Already they have begun to supply energy to institutional, commercial and residential customers. Their demonstration fuel cell at Woking Park supports a leisure centre swimming pool and park lights.

> A fuel cell is similar to a battery except that fuel is constantly fed into it to generate electricity and heat by an electro-chemical process, producing pure water. A fuel cell is not, in itself, a storage device but, like a battery, it contains an anode and a cathode insulated by an electrolyte between them.[4]

Hydrogen from natural gas and oxygen from the air combine electrochemically in the fuel cell to produce an electric current. This warms water, which produces electricity and heat. Any excess heat that the cell produces supplies the leisure centre's air-conditioning and dehumidification needs via heat-fired absorption cooling. Surplus electricity from the park's CHP station is exported to the town's sheltered housing schemes.

One unassuming brick building in a residential neighbourhood appears ordinary except for the solar panels on its roof. Its 52 residential apartments and communal area incorporate CHP and photovoltaic technologies, providing low-cost year-round heating, hot water and electricity, which could work in 'island mode' for a while if the national power grid failed.

Woking Council's buildings in the town centre are also supported by a CHP station. Hidden behind a locked door beneath a car-park building, the CHP system seems to be no more than ordinary noisy machines. But it holds the distinction of being the first commercially operating energy station of its kind in England – one with heat-fired absorption cooling with CHP technology and some natural gas. Electricity is distributed via wires hooked up to various commercial customers, while pipe networks send hot and cold water, heat and air-conditioning to them.

Woking's other sustainable ventures include a medical centre with solar panels and CHP link-ups; photovoltaic panels on a canopy that lights the pathway between the railway station entrance and a nearby building; and a demonstration project with eight photovoltaic and vertical wind energy lighting columns called *hybrolights*. A solar battery is placed underground for each stand-alone hybrolight. Once it is fully charged from sunlight, it stores enough energy to keep the column alight for 3–5 days. The battery lasts about 10 years and installation costs around £6,000. Other similar devices may be seen on Britain's country roads, which often combine photovoltaic panels with little windmills.

Nature offers ways to further lessen technology's negative effects. Woking recycles grey-water and harvests rain for land and wildlife regeneration projects. Steel and glass structures meant to be ecological in nature, such as London's BedZed, would benefit from human-scale landscaping with trees and plants and perhaps little natural alcoves or shelters that make a place interesting. Planting herbs like oregano will attract butterflies, while bees are drawn to nectar-producing flowers. Birds gravitate to berry and fruit trees. Those who live and work in high-tech, industrial-style sustainable energy machines are happier in environments containing the natural delights of fragrant plants and small animals like cats (which keep rats and mice away). The sounds of trickling water and wind brushing tree leaves can slightly mask and soften the noise of traffic and computers. Having beauty and living things that need to be cared for surrounding a home or workplace makes people more concerned about what happens around them, and more appreciative of what they have. This also leads naturally to greater neighbourhood harmony.

Efficient farming and transportation

Seeking ways to encourage a harmonious world neighbourhood and supply their own energy needs by acting locally while thinking globally, US entrepreneurs have discovered that they can use their own excess grain and corn to make the clean fuel ethanol. However, many US ethanol producers now go to Brazil to buy sugarcane, which apparently produces a better ethanol than corn and grain. The knock-on effect is that rainforest is being destroyed to grow ethanol crops.

If, as the Manataka American Indian Council chief Arvol

Looking Horse believes, the rainforest is the Earth's lungs, then we are slowly smothering ourselves with our greed. This is also happening to rainforests in Indonesia and Malaysia, and don't forget the animals that live there will die without the food the forests provide. The damage that ethanol could cause to the planet could be extensive. 'Europe would need to convert more than 70 per cent of its total arable land to raise the proportion of biofuels currently used in road transport to a mere 10 per cent.'

The USA – 'despite turning 55 million tonnes of maize into bioethanol, equivalent to one-sixth of the entire US corn harvest' – has managed to distil only enough biofuel from this 'to substitute a mere three per cent of the current oil and diesel used in road transport'.[5] The lesson must be that ideas like this are good only when practised on a limited scale, and only within the country that chooses to use its own produce for a portion of its own energy needs. Using less, still seems to be the key to our future survival on this planet.

Organic farming is one of the means to this end. In 2000, it was found by the UK Ministry of Agriculture to require 50 per cent less energy overall than intensive non-organic agriculture, with organic dairy farming being 74 per cent more efficient.

Another way to use less is to buy a hybrid fuel car. The half-electric, half-petrol Toyota Prius cuts fuel use and CO_2 emissions by around 70 per cent. Scientists say that is the same reduction required of the world by 2050 if we are to stabilize climate change.

Six US states have followed California in requiring cars to emit 30 per cent less greenhouse gas, while similar things are happening elsewhere in the world. A fleet of half-electric hybrids is part of a new private car hire service offered in London. No road tax, congestion or parking fees are charged on electric cars in its central zone. GreenTomato Cars even plant trees to offset their cars' 'unavoidable emissions'. GoinGreen has exclusive UK rights to the Reva G-Wiz, the world's bestselling electric car, which gets 600 miles per gallon of gasoline. France has a fleet of 10,000 electric cars.

Widely used in Europe and America, the biodiesel vehicle runs on vegetable oil made from recycled waste. This is cheaper than an electric car, but the biodiesel fuel may soften rubber fuel hoses in ordinary non-diesel cars built before 1994, so that hoses may need to be replaced every six months. The fuel dissolves diesel deposits, which may help clean the fuel system and reduce engine wear and tear. Vegetable fuel contains no sulphur – sulphur causes acid rain and aggravates lung problems. It is as biodegradable as sugar, less toxic than salt and reduces greenhouse gases and other harmful emissions by 50–90 per cent.

An even more advanced automobile technology is being developed in Europe: the compressed-air Air Car. The engine can run for up to 124 miles/200 kilometres from air cylinders installed in the vehicle and will travel at 68 mph/110 kmph on motorways – more than double the road coverage of the electric car. Recharging takes only 3–4 minutes at service stations supplying compressed air, or 3–4 hours if hooked up to 220-volt electricity.

A lighter, smaller railcar called the Parry People Mover uses fly-wheel energy storage, which allows it to run without overhead wires. It carries up to 50 people and is one-quarter the weight and one-third the cost, using one-fifth the fuel, of the smallest equivalent railway vehicle.

Meanwhile, an effort to revive the old-fashioned clean technology of the bicycle is being made by some towns, which are making themselves safer and more accessible for them. Odense in Denmark and Brighton and Hove in England are examples.

Transportation accounts for about a third of global CO_2 emissions. Land and sea vehicles could be powered so that they do not produce so many emissions. Ships' extraordinarily dirty fuel could be fairly easily transformed by using energy-efficient engines and wind- and solar-powered technology. Set to rise in number are our biggest polluters: airplanes. Running on fossil fuel, their contrails encourage cirrus clouds to form. Because clouds protect us from global warming's impact, environmentalists suggest we develop technology to reduce carbon dioxide in the atmosphere before dealing with airplanes. This could be just round the corner, as nanotechnology is speeding up changes in energy technologies.

[Nanotechnology manipulates] molecules and atoms at extremely small scales, measured in billionths of a metre, or nanometres (nm). These tiny particles and structures are called 'nanoparticles' [which consist] of extremely small collections of atoms of semi-conducting material [called] 'quantum dots'.[6]

Already nanotechnology is helping engineers develop less expensive, more efficient solar and battery storage technology. South African Professor Vivian Alberts' thin, photo-responsive alloy, mentioned earlier in this chapter, is a nanotechnology item. Solar engineers predict that nanotechnology developments could allow a far wider spectrum of solar energy to be captured by future solar cells. These also would enable solar cells to convert solar energy to electricity more efficiently. Most intriguingly, developments could allow solar collectors to be painted on just about any surface thus bringing down the cost of solar technology significantly.

Medical and healing technologies

Nanotechnology used in biomedical areas has a slightly more sinister connotation for many people. They imagine millions of tiny little robots entering their bodies when they hear of scientists proposing that they could one day be used to destroy cancer cells. Nanotechnology is already delivering faster computers, sharper, more efficient electronic displays and lighter-weight solar devices. Scientists are now studying how nanoparticles might transform hazardous chemicals in soils and groundwater into harmless compounds, and how to build intelligent clothing that reacts to heart rate, body temperature and blood pressure. Medical scientists are considering how nanotechnology might deliver drugs to specific parts of the body and be used to construct lightweight, lasting implants such as hip replacements and heart valves.

Nanoparticles and nanotubes that move around freely rather than being embedded in a bulk material could be troublesome, however. They might cause damage to human and animal cells if they enter the body through the skin or are inhaled or ingested.

The chief danger is not what nanomachines might do by accident. It is instead the consequences, both intended and unintended, of what people choose to do with powerful new technologies in a world dominated by economic and strategic competition. That is what we should be discussing and researching today.[7]

Crystal technology

English scientist and inventor Harry Oldfield's approach to health is perhaps safer. His work is significant among researchers now investigating subtle energy or vibrational medicine. Through nature's most stable form of matter, the crystal, Oldfield is seeking to bring back balance to humans and the Earth. Any introduction of energy can disturb the delicate balance that crystals have, which is why they are so effective in energy manipulation, he says. 'From my experience, nature knows best and we should try to copy her at all times.' A body becomes strong enough to heal itself when its 'energy fields' are balanced. Crystals act as conductors for this.

When we met, Oldfield seemed a sort of manic genius-inventor wholly preoccupied with his ideas and their application. Apart from winning accolades for his patented Oldfield Microscope, and teaching and inventing, he runs a clinic south of London where he uses electrocrystal therapy machines for healing. Patients report that his diagnoses of trouble spots in the body are phenomenal. Clients are first photographed with a Kirlian PIP (Polycontrast Interference Photography) scanner, which he invented in the late 1980s using microchip technology. This photographs the body's energy field and shows where energy is 'leaking', strong or weak.

Oldfield first thought about disease detection after noticing that subjects being photographed with a Kirlian camera 'transmitted signals' when in contact with an electrocrystal device. He experimented with various pulses and discovered that the body could be made to emit signals. Then he increased the voltage and invented three-dimensional Kirlian photography and developed transparent electrodes, so you could see through the energies. More sound came from places where there were rapidly dividing cells. This inspired him to work out how to measure the depth of tumours and find areas of inflammation, muscle tension or abnormality, such as old fractures.

With Oldfield's PIP scanner, it is possible to make accurate diagnoses of people's emotional and physical states, and to locate where specific pains and illnesses are – all from reading the electromagnetic energies radiating in a rainbow of colours from various parts of the body and showing on a computer screen hooked up to a Kirlian camera. The differing light intensities are then analysed by a computer. The invention was based upon the notion that the human energy field and surrounding ambient light might interfere with photons – as well as what Oldfield calls 'subtle energy photons'. The PIP scanner shows an object's 'energy interaction with light', providing an insight into the etheric 'organizing' template that keeps our physical molecules in a coherent recognizable form.

> On average, every atom in the human body is replaced every seven to nine years. Think of your body not as a physical structure but as a moving fountain of molecules that are constantly being replaced.[8]

Oldfield balances these molecules through electrocrystal therapy, opto-crystal therapy and crystal sound therapy. He believes everyone needs these as preventive therapies due to the increasing levels of electropollution being created by computers, mobile phones, microwave ovens and other machines we live with. Undesirable internal and external influences upset the delicate balance of our energy field every day. The sea of electromagnetism through which we swim may be having serious effects on our immune defences.

David Wilson, consultant surgeon at Leeds Infirmary, England, recalls that, before WWII, electromagnetism was used to treat patients with ulcers, pain, bone dislocations and breaks. Since then, medical companies have convinced doctors that the only sensible form of treatment is drug-based, even though, unlike allopathic drugs, electromagnetic treatment has no side effects. Oldfield has further developed James Clerk Maxwell's 'unified theory of electromagnetism' and his idea that an electric field forms around any electric charge.

> Both electric and magnetic fields are really just abstractions that
> scientists have made up to try to understand electricity's and
> magnetism's action at a distance. [Electromagnetic] fields interact
> in complex ways that have given rise to much of the natural world.

This is called 'electromagnetic resonance', which once was thought
impossible. Oldfield uses it to heal and balance the body, an idea he
got from his hero, the physicist and electrical engineer Nikola Tesla.
Tesla invented fluorescent lighting, the Tesla induction motor and
coil, and the alternating current (AC) electrical supply system.

Later, Oldfield invented the Kirlian 'gun' for electroscanning.
Doctors thought he had discovered an early warning system for
detecting cancer. For a while, joint research went well, until he began
to realize that some standard hospital treatments might weaken the
body's natural defences and even hamper recovery. After he voiced
concerns, the hospitals distanced themselves from him.

But patients seemed to feel better after being in contact with his
electrogenerating machine, so he began experimenting to find a
healing device based on its principles. By exciting a person's energy
field and cells with controlled vibrations, he believes he can 'put
unhealthy cells back into their normal healthy state of vibration'. In
the 1980s he found that crystals amplify energy and change one
type of energy into another. If you stimulate crystals with electricity, they vibrate, and when you strike them with a hammer, they
produce electrical energy. Thus, electrocrystal therapy was born,
its aim being to balance and normalize the vibrations of the
chakras using pulsed high-frequency electromagnetic energy.

'Most people are unaware that they are literally made of crystal.
Apatite, the mineral part of bone, is composed of microscopic
calcium phosphate crystals.' This makes bone and tooth enamel
hard. 'Some crystals are described as "liquid crystals" and these
are now thought by some scientists to be the basic structure of
brain fluids; and of course liquid crystals are used in portable
computer screens and other digital interfaces.' (*See Harry Oldfield's
Invisible Universe*)

That liquid crystals could be the basic structure of cerebrospinal brain fluids makes the observations of Japanese scientist

Masaru Emoto more intriguing. He claims that physical changes occur in water according to the emotions people near them experience and express. These changes are reflected in the structure of water and ice crystals. He made numerous photographs of these crystals to illustrate his theory that our thoughts and feelings affect our surroundings. These he claims resulted from people's emotions, the spoken word and even thoughts behind words. Water appears to respond to feelings more than thoughts, and to thoughts more than words. Ice crystals' shapes express those words, emotions and thoughts.

Given that most of our body is water, this makes one pause for thought. What are we doing to ourselves and our world with our thoughts, especially if everything is composed of crystals – many observable only on the molecular level? Oldfield says that crystals are everywhere. Soluble crystals are in sugar, salt and soda used for cleaning purposes.

> A crystal of salt (sodium chloride) contains sodium and chloride ions arranged in a regular network that extends throughout the crystal – a 'giant ionic lattice'. A chemical reaction occurs when this crystal structure is dissolved in water, causing the two types of ion to separate and [conduct] electricity.[9]

Salt crystals conduct electricity. Certain crystals, especially quartz, can convert mechanical pressure into electrical energy (as in a record player cartridge) or mechanical vibrations (as in earphones). Oldfield thinks that crystals and gemstones can be used to transform ordinary energies into subtler ones, as they are 'very susceptible to the slightest internal or external influence' and react predictably to electromagnetic pulse stimuli.

Crystals appear to copy a person's individual 'wave-form'. Many respond in precise ways to energies such as electricity, heat, light, pressure, sound, gamma rays, microwaves, bioelectricity and even consciousness or thought. The lattice structures of crystals vibrate in response to these stimuli and can amplify specific harmonics. That is the basis of electrocrystal therapy, in which a crystal receives a correct healthy signal from a cell and rebroadcasts it, counteracting 'out of tune' disease cells.

Oldfield suggests that ancient monuments have geomagnetic properties. It 'is undeniable that our ancestors utilized certain unique properties of crystals and stones in relation to magnetism'. According to him, in 1600 BC an Egyptian scribe gave directions for curing ailments with crystals. The Egyptians' idea was that if you wore crystals, any disease you had would pass out of your body through them and dissipate. Oldfield's idea of using crystals as energy transducers which have an ability to change energy from one form to another is similar to this.

He aims to restore balance to people's energy fields, especially as the 'electromagnetic mire' we live in thickens. Now looking for ways to break down plastics safely with micro-organisms, he also has theories about how to repair the ozone layer, disperse the energy vortex of tornadoes to lessen their destructive power and reduce greenhouse gases using ocean technologies. High levels of electropollution may be having serious effects on our immune defences and could reduce our ability to fight off diseases, he believes.

> Think of the body like a choir. If a few choir members start sing-
> ing [the] wrong notes, then adjacent singers can remind them. In
> some cases, [too] many of the choir start singing out of tune for
> the situation to be contained by the other choir members or its
> master [the brain].

This is similar to discoveries made by sound healers regarding how sound moves one into harmonious or disharmonious psychological states. Oldfield digitally records the melodious sound made by healthy cells and plays it to a person's unhealthy or 'off-key' ones, thus restoring harmony.

'With the correct vibration we may be able to heal a bone.' Since developing his PIP scanner, he has been seeing 'phantom limbs' in the energy fields of amputees. This has drawn him to seek a way to regenerate limbs through activating the body's energy template.

> Many amputees report that they feel pain when someone 'walks
> through' their amputated leg. [Although] the physical leg is no
> longer there, [its etheric template] still exists. I know it does
> because we see it on the PIP scanner sometimes.

The lost limb's cells might grow according to the energy field left behind, provided they are stimulated to do so in the right manner, Oldfield believes, due to cells having an electrical nature. Subtle energy fields may remain after a limb is lost and he wonders whether cells adjacent to the stump could broadcast information to guide regrowth. Might sound vibrations have that kind of effect upon the body – and matter in general?

The effect of sound upon matter

In the 1960s, the Swiss systems theorist and anthroposophist Hans Jenny (1904–72) studied and photographed the effect of sound upon inert inorganic matter (plastics, dust, liquids) and proved that sound alters form. This he called *cymatics*, or the study of wave-form phenomena (from the Latin *kyma*, 'wave' and *ta kymatika*, 'matters pertaining to waves') to describe the way particles of atoms produce wave-like patterns.

Vibrations of sound move sand particles as if they are fluid, rearranging them into repeating patterns. A brass plate may be used for this purpose, with crystal oscillators conveying sonorous vibrations to particles. Sound vibrations may also be sent into liquids like glycerin, in which oscillation patterns can be seen.

The 'tonoscope' is a simple apparatus without any intermediate electroacoustic unit that shows patterns created by the sound, tone, pitch and speed of speech or song. It shows that even vowels have patterns, and patterns metamorphose continually during speech. The first person known to have experimented with this was an 18th-century scientist called Ernst Chaldni, who put grains of sand on glass and vibrated them with a violin bow, creating beautiful symmetrical forms. A strict bilateral symmetry occurs when one tone is played on a brass plate on which particles of salt, sand or powder are sprinkled. When the tone is pure and harmonious, the tiny grains form into symmetrical patterns similar to snowflakes.

Jenny took Chaldni's experiments one step further, observing how sounds made matter move and form shapes. When the sounds stopped, the blobs of matter returned to their former shapeless states. These experiments were positive proof that sound creates form. Everything is in a state of constant vibration, oscillation, undulation and pulsation.

> On the largest and smallest scale, we find serial elements, repetitive patterns. [The] whole vegetable kingdom [is] a gigantic example of recurrent elements, an endless formation of tissues on a macroscopic, microscopic and electron microscopic scale.

A similar principle must operate with music from bowls carved from crystal. Adherents of crystal bowl therapy observe that the body is mostly water, full of crystalline formations. The theory is that when you hear crystal bowls being played, crystalline substances in the body's water 'wake up' to the pure formations of the crystal bowls' vibrational frequencies. The water in the body resonates to mirror them. The sounds create whole, symmetrical crystal shapes within your body, acting as a 'wave of healing' for it.

> Music made from the crystal bowls is very still, very slow. You play them by simply rotating a stick round them. The sounds move through the spectrum of your emotions, but the bowls' tones are basically heart-centred.[10]

In a different way, American sound therapist Barbara Hero has used a laser and scanner system to demonstrate harmonics visually. A mirror placed under a speaker system vibrates when the speakers emit two different frequencies from two sources. When a laser is turned onto the vibrating mirror, which in turn reflects the laser onto a screen, an image created by the sounds shows on screen. Geometrically perfect shapes are projected when the harmonics are pure. These remain on the screen as long as the harmonic intervals remain constant. When they are not, the shapes become imperfect or decay.

Notice how you react to the sound of metal scraping metal or to a screeching voice in comparison to a harmonious chord or the twittering of birds at sunrise. Note how you respond to shouting or the purring of a kitten. Sound has a profound effect upon the emotions, and emotions have been proven to influence the body's circulatory and digestive systems, therefore why should thoughts not have a similar effect upon the material world around us?

How a single consciousness can affect the material world

The thought 'I shall move that chair' can lead us to moving a chair. What we lack is repeatable proof that *thought alone* can move the chair. Emoto's proposition that water reacts to thought and intention may not be so strange when one considers that thought is the foundation from which every action springs, affecting the elemental parts of us on a subatomic level. Thoughts give rise to form figuratively, and apparently literally also. Thoughts may well vibrate. A vibration will move liquid and, since most of the body is water, thoughts could conceivably move molecules, crystals and, ultimately, matter that we can see.

The Israeli spoon-bender Uri Geller appears to have the ability to move or alter material objects with his mind alone, although not everyone believes it is possible, even when confronted with the evidence. Partly this is because some people performing such feats have been caught doing the most simple of schoolboy magic tricks. Parapsychologists associated with the Society for Psychical Research are wise to these tricks, so when one of its most critical sceptics, Guy Lyon Playfair, accepted that Uri Geller wasn't playing games, it was something to pay attention to.

Playfair had ensured that he hadn't allowed Geller to hold eye contact with him, just in case Geller tried to hypnotize him. I determined to follow his strategy when I met Geller in London in 2006. He was a most energetic, magnetic person – not surprising, I suppose! Most striking was his steady penetrating gaze. He probably thought me very strange since most of the time I wouldn't look eye-to-eye with him. But then, being telepathic, he might have realized that I was simply following Playfair's instructions!

Geller spends most of his time publicizing the idea that human beings have the 'mind power' to make their lives and the world a better place. He became a millionaire finding oil through dowsing, but he is also a prolific writer, with an extensive website cataloguing his many activities, not least of which is his work for the Red Cross. Geller has been accused of trickery time and time again, but he told me that 'accusers, debunkers and sceptics' don't interest him anymore. 'They really never actually have', he said.

> I used them. I manipulated them to be my unpaid publicists. Every time they came out with some crazy accusation, they made me more famous. Yes, when I was very young, naïve and gullible, I thought they would destroy me, but they never have. On the contrary, they amplified and multiplied my fame because they made me controversial, and controversy is a fantastic tool to keep yourself out there … so long as you stay on the right side of controversy.

Of his abilities – to bend metal, grow seeds, fix broken watches, make things disappear and open locks without touching them – he says he isn't so sure they are unique. He thinks 'maybe all of us have this power, energy, force – call it whatever'. But he learned how to awaken it. He wouldn't be surprised if we all had certain innate abilities like his, yet he is perplexed as to why other people can't do what he can. 'I keep asking myself how come I'm the only person who can bend spoons or fix broken watches. I simply don't know.' His mother thought it might be something he inherited from her family, perhaps to do with Sigmund Freud, a relation. But Geller doesn't think so, because his children don't have his ability. 'So it's either a fluke or a kind of freakish situation that this energy woke up in me. It could be that I learned how to channel [or] tap into an area of force out there and I'm actually channelling these energies from that outside source, or maybe from inner space.'

When four years old, he was playing in a neighbour's deserted 'Arabic garden' in Tel Aviv, and suddenly heard a loud, high-pitched ringing in his ears. All other sounds seemed to stop. Trees didn't move in the wind. A silvery mass of light appeared above him and struck his forehead. He felt a sharp pain and lost consciousness. Thereafter he started manifesting strange abilities, such as knowing how much money his mother had won or lost at cards. The first time a spoon bent in his hand, he was eating hot soup, which spilled in his lap.

> [My] mentor, an American doctor, Dr Andrija Puharich, [led] me to believe that I was actually having some kind of extraterrestrial encounter and, for me, it was so hard to believe, but we both experienced so many unbelievable phenomena ...

Puharich had gone to Israel in 1971 to check out Geller for the CIA, who were looking for psychics for their Cold War with the Russians – the Americans knew the Russians were training clairvoyants. Geller's Israeli fans had grown bored with watching him bend spoons, so he thought his career was finished. After Puharich ran a battery of tests on him, proving Geller's abilities were real, he invited Geller to be tested by scientists at Stanford Research Centre (SRI) in California. Geller jumped at the chance.

That was how, in 1972, he went to America, where he was tested 'at all the important places', including SRI, the Lawrence Radiation Labs and the American Naval Service Weapons Center. He also was tested in Britain by scientists as eminent as Drs David Bohm and John Hasted, then at Birkbeck College, University of London; Dr John Taylor, Head of the Department of Maths at King's College; A V Cleaver, ex-Director of the Rockets Division of Rolls Royce Limited, and the authors and researchers Arthur Koestler and Arthur C Clarke. After seeing half of a thin crystal disc of vanadium carbide dematerialize due to Geller's efforts, Clarke exclaimed that what he wrote about in his book *Childhood's End* was coming true.

In 1973 Geller felt that unknown energies were being transferred to others after so many people watching his television demonstrations began bending metals. 'There is no question in my mind that the Earth is on the verge of discovering a whole new power, a real and unquestionable power that goes far beyond me ... a power that we can put to good use.'

In Russia, children are now the focus of psychic experiments. Some have the power to read books and see computer screens while wearing blindfolds, according to Russian scientist Dr Konstantin Korotkov of St Petersburg Federal Technical University (SPIFMO).

They cannot read if a room's lights are turned off or if it is dark, so it seems that they can see through the cloth of the blindfold. Geller says that blindfolds 'are no big deal'. Seeing through them is simply telepathy. In his daredevil youth, he would sometimes drive a car while wearing a blindfold, just to prove he could.

Way back in 1974, Prof Taylor of King's College conducted tests on children who seemed to have picked up the ability to bend metals after watching Geller's first BBC-TV broadcast. Taylor was most interested in children, because they seemed better at psychically bending metal, and there was less chance of fraud or trickery with them. He tested 15 children ranging from 7 years of age to the early teens.

Prof Taylor accepted the possibility that metal was being deformed by new energy forces, because he was checking it first hand under controlled conditions. However, if they were new forces, he said, scientists would have to go beyond the laws presently set by physics and find out whether the brain was the source of them and, if so, what kind of radiation was being emitted by it.

Although one of the 20th century's most famous psychics, Uri Geller is far from being the first person to show such paranormal abilities, nor the first to be tested by scientists. The 19th-century Scottish medium Daniel Dunglas Home (1833–86) holds that distinction. He was observed levitating and moving objects around in brightly lit surroundings with many people present, doing things that even Houdini could not replicate. Could this ability be contained in the genes? Home's ancestor was a Gaelic-speaking seer called Kenneth Odhar, born in 1600 on the Isle of Lewis, who forecasted 250 years into the future. Could it be that certain people inherit or have minds that influence matter and events more than most of us?

The power of the mind to affect matter

In 1948, a German research physicist named Helmut Schmidt was inspired by the biologist and parapsychologist J B Rhine to look at the effect an observer might have upon matter at the infinitesimal quantum level. Schmidt thought that there was no cause for anything that happens on the subatomic level. Everything that happens is random until an observer appears. If you see something, you affect how it behaves. The act of measuring or observing something 'freezes' it. Scientists call this the collapse of the wave function, waves being the natural state of matter on a subatomic level. As Louis de Broglie stated, 'subatomic entities can behave [as particles] or waves'. Schmidt wondered, was it true that nothing existed independently of our perception of it?

> Did living consciousness possess some quantum field-like properties, enabling it to extend its influence out into the world? Did we not only stop the butterfly at a certain point in its flight, but also influence the path it will take – nudging it in a particular direction?[11]

Eventually Schmidt built what he called a 'Random Number Generator' (RNG) to test this idea. After running tests from 1965 to 1970 at Boeing Aerospace's research unit, Schmidt lost his job and moved to the Foundation for Research on the Nature of Man, J B Rhine's organization, where he carried out more RNG research with Rhine himself.

Their RNG experiments came to the attention of Robert Jahn, a professor of engineering who since the early 1960s had been busy introducing the idea of electronic propulsion to Princeton University's aeronautical engineering department. After he became Dean of Princeton's Engineering Department in the 1970s, it was awkward being involved in what were essentially parapsychology experiments, but he carried on Schmidt's RNG experiments by setting up a small, privately funded research program called the Princeton Engineering Anomalies Research unit (PEAR). Jahn employed Brenda Dunne, a developmental psychologist from the University of Chicago, to undertake clairvoyance experiments to help him improve the RNG technology.

Jahn invented the Random Event Generator (REG), a 'black box' that ran on electronic noise (instead of atomic decay, as the RNG did) to test whether human thought alone could affect its number readings. Similar to an electronic random coin-flipper, it generated only the numbers one and zero. They picked strangers off the streets whom they asked to make it flip more 'heads' or 'tails' and usually it worked. Rigorous experiments led them to believe that a person's unconscious mind communicates with and influences invisible subatomic levels of the material world and also machines.

Dr Roger Nelson, an emeritus researcher at Princeton University, grew intrigued by this and extended Professor Jahn's work by having groups experiment with RNGs. He found that meditators were able to produce dramatic results and then connected 40 REGs, placed all over the world, to his laboratory computer in Princeton. The machines whirred constantly in a regular fashion until suddenly on 6 September, 1997, the REG's graph shot upwards, recording a massive shift in the number sequence as his machines started reporting extreme deviations from the norm. It was the day that one billion people watched the funeral of Diana, Princess of Wales. To study this phenomenon, Nelson and Jahn formed the Global Consciousness Project in 1998, inviting scientists worldwide to analyse the REG findings.

By 2001, 65 'Eggs', as the REG's were named, were in 41 countries. Before and during some great event that many people took part in, such as the global New Year's Day celebrations, the Eggs began reacting. The biggest reactions occurred on 11 September, 2001 – but started *four hours before* New York City's Twin Towers were attacked. In the weeks before the tsunami struck and killed around a quarter of a million people in December 2004, the Eggs again behaved in the same manner.

These and many other experiments seem to have established that some kind of intuitive link exists between people and world events. When things affect masses of people, random numbers generated by the machines appear to vary in particular patterns and to prove that people begin to react to events before they happen – or in some way *make* them happen. These experiments suggest that a 'world mind' exists.

According to PEAR, people's attitudes have also been found to influence what results come from the experiments. So, not only do we influence our surroundings with our actions – we do so with our thoughts as well. The very act of focusing attention upon something seems to create order. 'We think, therefore we affect.'[12]

When a group's attention focuses the waves of individual minds on the same thing, a type of group 'super-radiance' occurs, which has a physical effect. The REG machine could be a kind of thermometer, measuring the dynamics and coherence of the group. When people experience intense moments of like-mindedness, it seems to gather enough power to impart order on the chaotic purposelessness of the REG machine.

That a group has a more powerful effect than an individual is not a new notion. What is new is that we now have machines that register that the minds of a group, when focused on a particular idea, can affect the material world. This so impressed Dr Nelson that he was moved to declare, 'We're taught to be individualistic monsters. We're driven by society to separate ourselves from each other. That's not right. We may be connected together far more intimately than we realize.'

Physicists have had to adjust their theories as their knowledge of the micro-world has increased, and to go beyond quantum mechanics, relativity and the notion of a 'theory of everything'. Some are now looking for a new definition for what humanity has until now called 'God'. Will technology, in one of destiny's ironic twists, bring the world back to a state of respectful awe for forces, or a force, much greater than ourselves? Is it time to look around us and see clearly that heaven is indeed spread all around us on the Earth? Do we want to avoid creating a machine-dominated civilization where even our thinking processes and feelings grow progressively more mechanistic?

Stories abound in the East of yogis and sages who are able to alter reality and control, heal or harm others with their minds alone. India's ancient peoples perceived the forces of nature as powers of consciousness. Human consciousness might act as a force of nature. Shamans might have power over the weather because they have learned to master and use their own powers of consciousness.

However, Lama Karma Samten Gyatso, whose Tibetan Buddhist tradition is very close to the shamanistic one of ancient Tibet, begs to differ: 'Actually, local deities control the weather. Lamas respect and negotiate with the local deities and that is how they alter the weather.'

It seems that a single mind has only limited power. It must be in collusion with other minds, visible and invisible, to cause movement or change in this material world of ours.

Subtle energy technologies

The way the material world is affected by subtle energy technologies is being studied by the British Society of Dowsers. The scientist Jim Lyons, who is a member, says:

> Dowsers analyse mind effects all the time, though immediately visible results are not always seen. Water divining is the classic immediate effect.

Many researchers are utilizing alternative and traditional medical elements in more technological ways. Acupuncture, for instance, has been proven to work by University College London, Imperial College London and Southampton University researchers, who have shown its bodily effects on imaging scanners. Much research is being done on electromagnetic radiation and cells. Obscure technologies of the past, such as Rife machines – based on German technology but rejected by the medical establishment in the early 20th century – are being used again for healing cancer. They are said to 'resonate' malignant cells to destruction.

The latest evidence regarding homeopathy can be verified by Gas Discharge Visualization (GDV), a scientific procedure developed by the Russian physicist Dr Konstantin Korotkov. His GDV technique analyses the 'glow characteristics' of living organisms, from plants and seeds to blood samples and microbiological cultures. It has gone beyond Kirlian photography by enabling real-time viewing of auras. More precisely, the term GDV refers to the biological emission and optical radiation stimulated by the electromagnetic field, amplified by gas discharge and made visual through computer data processing. A small camera captures the aura and films the energy emanating to and from animals, plants, liquids, powders and inanimate objects. The Russian Ministry of Health has validated it as a medical technology to measure the 'bio-photon field'. It is used by the Russian Olympic team and many hospitals. The effects of drugs, herbs and treatments upon the body can be seen visibly with this technology.

Other subtle energies such as geopathic stress in houses may be measured with Geiger counters, magnetometers, EEG and muscle strength meters. Biofeedback studies are ongoing, as are experiments at stone circles regarding the suppression of detrimental energy.

Pure physics territory: technology inspired by physics

A field of pure energy is now sought by physicists. They want to know why and how matter exists. In 1964, a Scottish quantum physicist called Higgs came up with the idea that a background energy existed in space, called the *Higgs field*. This hypothetical physical field is imagined to permeate space. It is the lowest-energy, natural state of the universe. Elementary subatomic particles do not have mass (or do not become matter) until they interact with the Higgs field.

The most elementary particle (or quantum) of matter is thought not to spin as other particles do, but soaks up energy directly from the Higgs field as paper does ink. It is called the *Higgs boson*. (Some call it the 'God Particle' because it is thought to be the fundamental foundation of existence.) Physicists suggest that a particle's mass depends on its energy-absorbing ability and the strength of the Higgs field. In this theory, energy transfers directly to a particle from a background field of energy.

So far, no one has found the Higgs boson but, at the time of writing, physicists hope to do so during experiments at CERN with a giant particle-boosting machine called the Large Hadron Collider. CERN is an acronym for the Conseil Européen pour la Recherche Nucléaire, the European Council for Nuclear Research, the world's leading laboratory for particle physics in Geneva, Switzerland, where an international collaboration occurs between about 60 countries and 8,000 scientists scattered round the world. CERN was where the World Wide Web was created in 1990. The Large Hadron Collider (LHC) is the world's largest particle accelerator and super-collider, which speeds up particles with a complex system of magnets. Physicists hope it will help them find the Higgs boson. It is built underground, spanning the border between Switzerland and France.

Two beams of subatomic particles called 'hadrons' – either protons or lead ions – will travel in opposite directions inside its circular accelerator. By colliding the two beams at very high speed, physicists will recreate the universe's condition just after the theoretical Big Bang, which they think created the universe.

Using particle accelerators, scientists will be hunting for the hypothetical Higgs boson of quantum theory, which they hope will explain what determines mass in particles, the basic constituents of matter. Theorists suggest that CERN's experiments could make string theory passé. Scientists hope that the LHC experiment will lead them to answers that will help them create a 'theory of everything' and to an understanding of how the universe was created.

What we perceive as empty space may not be empty, according to physicists B Haisch, A Rueda and H E Puthoff. The universe is seething with electromagnetic energy and the vacuum of space is an 'energy reservoir', with energies more dense and powerful than nuclear energy. Puthoff theorizes that energies in the zero-point field (the Higgs field) could supply energy for space propulsion.

> In the old days of classical mechanics the idea of a vacuum was simple. The vacuum was what remained if you emptied a container of all its particles and lowered the temperature [to] absolute zero. The arrival of quantum mechanics, however, completely changed our notion of a vacuum.

Now physicists see all fields, especially electromagnetic fields, as having fluctuations. Astrid Lambrecht says:

Even a perfect vacuum at absolute zero has fluctuating fields known as 'vacuum fluctuations', the mean energy of which corresponds to half the energy of a photon [particle of light].

According to quantum theory, a vacuum contains *virtual particles* which are in a continuous state of fluctuation – they are always moving up and down or in and out, in a wave formation. Objects within this vacuum are drawn together by an attraction between them, which happens as a result of energy from the virtual particle fluctuations in the vacuum.

Electromagnetic fields can propagate in space and therefore exert pressure on surfaces, 'just as a flowing river pushes on a floodgate. This radiation pressure increases with the energy [and frequency] of the electromagnetic field.' Experiments exploring this vacuum 'field' indicate that we may soon be able to create objects that levitate. Already we have a toy called the Levitron which does exactly that. Powered only by permanent magnets, it is essentially a spinning top that levitates.

Progress is continuing in teleportation experiments also. Danish physicists teleported quantum information half a metre through a light beam onto a collection of atoms in 2006. This experiment teleported both light and matter, moving us closer to the goal of transmitting and processing information that will keep it absolutely secure. Previous experiments in quantum teleportation, including one that teleported photons (particles of light) through a fibre-optic cable in an underground sewage pipe from one side of the Danube River to the other in Austria in 2004, were limited to using either light or matter. Replicas of the original photons were created while the original photons ceased to exist. But it's a long way from replicating a human body, which would require a machine to pinpoint and analyse the trillions of atoms that make up the human body.

These are the kinds of matters physicists plan to investigate through conducting the upcoming Big Bang-style collision at CERN. They expect showers of new particles to be created. CERN's chief theorist Professor John Ellis thinks the Higgs field could be the source of 'dark energy', thought to be accelerating the expansion of the universe, and to make up about 70 per cent of it. If a single 'superforce' is found, from which the four forces of nature arise (including electromagnetism), theoretical physicists believe they could discover how the universe was made, why particles behave as they do, possibly even new particles, and even extra dimensions of space.

If their theory of super-symmetry is found to be real (in which every particle has a corresponding 'super-partner' particle that differs in spin by half a unit), it could bridge gaps that exist between scientists' experimental evidence and string theory. The LHC test might reveal something new altogether, as long as they don't blow us all up in the process, of course – a fear I have heard expressed. Some people have suggested to me that recreating Big Bang conditions might upset the balance of the Earth or make openings into other dimensions, through which aliens could enter our world. You have been warned!

The way forward: back down to earth

As we risk bringing the wrath of the heavens down upon us with a big bang, with our experiments on the fundamental building blocks of the universe, we might look again at our home – 'where the Kingdom of Heaven is spread out on the Earth'. Pure physics is now linked with the further mechanization of our lives, and with that comes greater loss of awareness of what is down on the ground and beneath our feet.

Looking too much to physics and the sky for answers, we do not see where we are and miss the squalor and degradation that radicalize desperate people, as Jonathon Porritt observes. The solution to so many problems speeding our way is facing us squarely, as he indicates: 'No terrorist is going to make governments tremble by threatening to bomb a wind turbine, or release clouds of compost over our cities.'

As ex-European commissioner for foreign relations Chris Patten remarks:

The investment we make in sustainable development is as much a part of our global security as the investment we make in our armed forces. And it should offer much better value for money.

If it is true that everything is linked, as REG and other consciousness studies indicate, then through applying science to the problems of our physical world, we could by default find the technological solutions we need. To make the world a better place, technology should be under our control, not vice versa. For that to happen, we must draw closer to nature and the natural things of life, learning to work *with* the elements, evolving consciously in harmony with the intelligence of what is invisible in our universe, following the rhythms of nature and our own seasons from birth to death.

Today even the dying are treated as if they are run-down machines ready to be disconnected. As our concepts of life and death are replaced by a much larger view of the universe, it is imperative that we find ways to become more human and humane towards each other – not less.

7

LISTEN, THE UNIVERSE
IS SINGING

The water in a vessel is sparkling; the water in the sea is dark.
The small truth has words that are clear; the great truth has
great silence.

RABINDRANATH TAGORE, *STRAY BIRDS*, CLXXVI

And God said, Let there be light: And there was light.

THE BIBLE, GENESIS 1:3

EINSTEIN SAID THAT MATTER is 'congealed light'. Physicists are beginning to prove we are made of light. Perhaps, after one shrugs off this mortal coil, one simply becomes lighter-weight particles of light. Harry Oldfield says:

> [We] have discovered there is nothing solid in the universe. What
> we perceive as solid is, in reality, energy of unusual wavelengths
> which creates visible patterns.

So do we, after death, simply move into another dimension of life? The British earth-energies researcher Paul Devereux observes, 'the Land of the Dead, in virtually all traditional cultures, occupies the terrestrial landscape, but in a different dimensional space'.

Does consciousness die, or simply the physical body? People of the past did not hesitate to make rituals surrounding death, nor to have visions about what happens to us after we die. The Egyptians prepared for death, as Tibetan Buddhists still do today. It is considered wise to prepare for 'impermanence', as Buddhists call it, because we experience so many little deaths while we're still alive. One reason Buddhists practice non-attachment to things they like is to train themselves to cope with death, so that they will be able to let go of their body and life more easily when the time comes to do so. As a result of consciously creating a habit of 'letting go', they believe they will suffer less in the dying process. They say our strongest attachment is to our body.

We believe our body is our self, which is why we are so fearful about parting from it. Buddhists say you can drop your fear of losing it by realizing that only this 'illusory' material body dies – illusory in that it has no stable quality and is changing all the time – that even death is a concept our minds have created. It is seen as a transition more than an end. They ask, why fear the future you are imagining – something that isn't happening now, in this present moment, and possibly won't ever happen? The more aware you are of the present moment, the more you can relax into it and experience whatever *is* – good or bad. The Christian, Muslim and Jewish view that you should protect and support what God has given you and be a gardener in God's garden is not different from the Buddhist view except in its self-protective aspects. Buddhism suggests that there is no individual self to protect because we are all part of each other. Vedanta might add 'I am that which I see'.

By focusing on the goodness in whatever we have now, and not exaggerating but simply dealing with the negatives we perceive, we experience peace. Good or bad, nothing lasts very long.

As a Buddhist lama was falling down a mountain ravine with a sheer drop of 300 ft (100 m), he thought of what his teacher had told him: 'Whatever happens in life, it is important to enjoy the experience.' He had been found at the bottom of the ravine, unconscious, but with a serene smile on his face. Weirdly, a PIP scan made by Harry Oldfield did not show injuries as serious as those normally sustained with a fall from that height. The scan showed a large, vibrant aura with dancing lights that seemed like an 'array of symbols' shining all around him. Seeing the interest this aroused, the lama smiled and waved his hand, and the phenomena ceased. His aura became ordinary. Then he said, 'This may be a case of "non-sense", Mr Oldfield. You must see a great deal of such "non-sense" in your work.'

There must be a trick to falling gracefully out of life, as that story describes. How do you die with a smile, or help someone you love die with peace in your heart? The answer comes to each of us in a different way – perhaps through enjoying the goodness in what we have in this present moment. All things cease to be – even pain.

Overcoming pain

Joan Faroughy, an English lady I know in Cambridge, England, was left paralysed along the left side of her body from a disfiguring brain haemorrhage some years ago. She recounts a story of how she experienced the overcoming of pain during a medical examination with the power of her mind alone:

> Having already undergone this medical procedure for a previous thrombosis, I knew what to expect. The procedure involves the injection of radioactive iodine dye into a vein in the foot. This dye is then followed by an X-ray that highlights any blood clots.
>
> My first experience of it was in 1985 after brain surgery, necessary after a stroke. Having spent so much time in bed, I had developed a deep vein thrombosis. As the iodine was injected, I felt an excruciating pain, pain which had me begging and pleading with the doctors to stop. This was not to be. They continued their work. As the pain intensified, so did my cries, reaching a crescendo which must have competed with those from the louder howling hells.
>
> Years later, a second thrombosis was suspected, and I was to undergo the same procedure. I decided that this time I would negotiate with the radiographer to be given an anaesthetic. This was not to be – they never gave an anaesthetic for a venogram, and did not even keep it in the department.

At this time, I was reading *Landscapes of Wonder: Discovering Buddhist Dhamma in the World Around Us*, by Bhikkhu Nyanasobhano, and reflecting on a section dealing with 'the insubstantial nature of the body'. Suddenly it became blindingly clear to me that, if the body were insubstantial, all pain (located in the body) must be insubstantial also.

I continued to hold this as an object of meditation, focusing strongly, steadily, as the dreaded needle went in. As the iodine started to flow, my concentration wavered for a second – ouch! The radiographer smiled – 'Sorry.' I refocused, and she continued. Finally it was all over, and it had been no more painful than a routine visit to the dentist.

Somehow Faroughy had managed to completely detach from her body so that she felt unaffected by the procedure while it was happening. Did she 'go into' the pain and go along with the stress of it instead of trying not to feel it, allowing her to rise above the pain? She said she was amazed that she was able to transcend the pain, but now she realizes how very great the power of the mind is.

Signs of higher consciousness

Magical rumours surround the previous leader of Tibetan Buddhism's Karma Kagyu tradition, the 16th Karmapa, who is reputed to have been able to dissociate from the pain of the final stages of cancer. Knowing he was about to die, he wanted to return to the monastery in India that had become his home after his escape from Tibet in the 1950s, but his American students begged him to stay in the US for treatment in a hospital in Zion, Illinois. Although he had very advanced cancers all over his body, he apparently didn't experience pain – until the doctors gave him morphine. Then he suffered terribly. The Karmapa had to ask his doctors not to give him morphine or sedatives. It is said that, until the moment he died, he unwaveringly showed concern for others, including the nurses and doctors attending him, without seeming to think of himself at all. Stories abound of nurses sitting on his bed and talking to him confidentially of their troubles as he lay dying.

After his corpse had lain in the hospital for three days, nurses came to remove his body, but were asked by the Karmapa's attendants whether it showed the normal signs of death. They had to admit that it did not. His body was warm and the area around his heart was especially hot, so they could not declare him completely dead as they would an ordinary corpse. Soon after, the Karmapa's body was transported to Rumtek Monastery in India, where it was placed sitting upright in a box with a glass window. His body gradually shrank to the size of a child's and, after seven weeks, it was cremated. Observers reported that they saw its heart, tongue and eyes (said by Buddhists to represent body, speech and mind) roll out of the flames as a large rainbow encircled the Sun.

Many kinds of phenomena have been attributed to past spiritual and religious leaders, of course, although a Tibetan lama I know says that sometimes one never knows how spiritually developed someone is until they die. It is not always obvious or related to someone's external role or appearance in the world. Certain 'signs' occur that indicate the deep inner qualities of a dead person. These are usually linked with the natural world, the weather, or the position or appearance of the corpse after the soul has left it. Often something extraordinary happens in outwardly ordinary circumstances or conditions, something unexplainable or unusual, but you have to pay attention to notice it.

Lamas tend to notice quite a lot of things, as that is what they train themselves to do on a daily basis. They, like shamans, are 'walkers between the worlds'. It is said that such people suffer only from perceiving the suffering and unkindnesses of others, which they can experience physically. When one is in a sublimely gentle, loving state where one does not desire anything for oneself, but only others' happiness, it is very hard to be unkind to anyone or anything. But it is said that lamas sometimes do behave unkindly to teach people so that they will learn to avoid mistakes which can harm themselves or others. This can make lamas suffer terribly. But the natural transition between life and the afterworld is for them no problem.

Otherworldly explorations

The Irish clairvoyant Eileen Garrett also saw death as a natural transition. After many years of being a medium and studying psychic phenomena, she stated:

> [Death] is but an exchange of one experience for another, for during all human history there has been a belief, not confined to any particular country, creed, level or culture, that through perceptions beyond the five senses men have been able to get in touch with phases of existence unfamiliar to everyday experience.

Some intrepid explorers have investigated this realm of the dead with a scientific approach, as Garrett did, to find out what happens after the body dies. A few highly respected researchers from the Society of Psychical Research made a study of the activities of a mediumistic group that held frequent séances in Scole, Norfolk, England, during the 1990s. Of the many physical effects they witnessed, the most immediately impressive were light phenomena.

> Points of light would appear from above, dart at great speeds round the small chamber, describe elaborate aerial patterns, alight on our heads, frequently responding to spoken or silent requests, appear to enter bodies, 'dive-bomb' the table top with a sharp 'ping' and emerge from below it.

The lights also illuminated crystals, bowls, the interior of a glass dome and a glass of water.

> On one occasion a light settled on a crystal poised on the edge of the table inches from our hands, spread its effulgence throughout the crystal, which was then levitated before our gaze and gently placed in the base of a translucent kitchen bowl.[1]

Given that experienced and careful members of the Society for Psychical Research observed this over the course of the two-year study – plus spontaneously appearing tape recordings, films bearing images, glyphs, poems, symbols and messages in several languages – it seems unlikely that they would have been fooled by tricks. One especially peculiar thing happened that none of the

researchers, including the late Professor Arthur Ellison, a paranormal expert with 50 years' experience with electrical devices,
could explain away.

A pyrex bowl, normally upside down on the séance table, would
often be illuminated from within by one of the lights, 'producing
an effect like a low-powered light bulb'. It was this way one night
when a dark hand, 'visible only as far as the wrist, appeared to
materialize just above the bowl, turn it the right way up, and
[place] one of the crystals, apparently illuminated from within,
inside it. The hand was withdrawn and then the whole outline of
the crystal was visible in the bowl'.

British psychology professor and paranormal researcher David
Fontana comments that it was bright enough for him to see the
faces of his fellow investigators, whose heads were only inches
above the bowl. They were told by a medium to touch the crystal,
which they did, noting that it was quite solid. Then they were told
to remove their hands, which they did. Immediately after that, they
were told to touch the crystal again but, this time, although it still
appeared as solid as before, their fingers passed through it as if
there was no substance there. Once again, they were instructed to
remove their hands and then immediately replace them. They
found they could touch it again.

Afterwards the 'spirit team' with which they were in contact told
them that they (the spirits) had dematerialized the crystal, leaving
only its 'essence' in the bowl. When the psychic researchers asked
how the small points of light were produced, the spirits said that
they had not brought them, but that the lights had been attracted
to the séances and the spirit-team had found they could make use
of them as aspects of physical phenomena.

It was implied that the lights in some way represented, or were
manifested by, the spirits of departed individuals. What is striking
about this comment is the fact that physicists are beginning to
prove that bodies are composed, fundamentally, of nothing more
than light. Perhaps material things are simply weightier, slower, or
more compressed (or depressed!) forms of light.

Some shamans say that spirit entities exist in realms of the
imagination, dreams and the dead. Apart from human spirits, also

dwelling in our universe are angels and the souls of animals, the Earth, solar systems and stars. According to this view, every plant and object on the Earth also has a spirit. Every object at every level of existence has consciousness. Shamans meet animal spirits like wolves and crows, plant spirits like trees and flowers, and the angelic spirits of stars and planetary systems. The whole universe is seen as 'a system of intelligence' whose members have a bodily aspect in some sense, 'or were at one time in bodies, like the departed'.[2]

Trisha Robertson, the president of the Scottish Society for Psychical Research, says that, most likely, the spirits that mediums speak to are on a very low level. Poltergeists (spirits that throw things around rooms and cause strange phenomena to occur, frequently in the same place) may be caused by spiteful spirits, although there is evidence that the poltergeist phenomenon is influenced by the presence of adolescent angst or problems of pubescent children. She told of a Fleet Street lawyer who thought extrasensory perception was rubbish but who, without being aware of it, periodically slipped into a trance and became a medium. At those times he became possessed by a spirit called Silver Birch, whom Robertson said seemed to be a kind of 'corporate intelligence'. Through the lawyer, Silver Birch said that different portions of a person's consciousness incarnate at different times. In other words, a bit of you is always elsewhere – similar to F Myers' notion of the 'group soul'.

In Tibetan Buddhism it is said that individual lamas sometimes carry one aspect (the body, speech or mind) of a previous reincarnate lama. But what reincarnates – if, indeed, anything does? This is a subject of intense debate among those who consider reincarnation possible.

Dr Archie Roy, also of the Scottish Society for Psychical Research, said that the world's foremost reincarnation expert, the late Professor Ian Stevenson, suggested that 65 per cent of children who remember a past life recall that it was cut short by some violent or tragic event. A high proportion of them carry birth marks in the same spots where they sustained injuries at death in their previous life.

Roy suggested that there may be many forms of survival after death. What mediums pick up may not be a whole personality, and may survive for only a limited period after death. Of course whatever is left behind, after the death of the physical body, could last forever – possibly in the presence of God. But it could also be that a human's individual personality could be left behind simply as a file in a cosmic archive; as a record that is played by a medium in trance; or as 'an earthbound shell of restricted intelligence and confused motivation'. It could also be a conscious, motivated spirit, or something could remain after death in some form that is inconceivable to us.

Archie Roy mentioned that the Swedish scientist, philosopher, mystic and theologian Emmanuel Swedenborg (1688–1772) spoke of there being different levels of heaven and hell, just as the Tibetans do. For the final 28 years of his life, Swedenborg wrote 18 theological works – of which his best known is entitled *Heaven and Hell*, published in 1758 – based on his visions, or perhaps real experiences, of different regions of heaven and hell. He claimed to be able to freely visit both, as well as to talk with angels, devils and various kinds of spirits. Roy observed that Swedenborg must have expected to die when he did, as he paid rent on the place where he was living only until the day he died in his bed.

A living medium's views on death

Mediums like the popular British medium Gordon Smith say that the dead are quite happy where they are. They have none of the problems we have here and are not suffering. We are the ones who have problems with death. During life, the feeling of loss is the hardest thing to overcome. Mainly interested in mediumship as a tool for healing people suffering from the loss of loved ones, he has observed different levels or ways of grieving in the people he 'reads'.

One mother who lost her son suffered a kind of disconnection from her feelings due to the shock of his death. Six months later, she dreamt of him and, for the first time since losing him, cried. In her dream, her son told her to 'switch on the telly'. She did so upon waking and saw Gordon Smith telling a couple about their dead son. As soon as she could, she contacted Smith and, upon meeting him, something he said 'reconnected her with herself'.

Smith thinks people who have suffered great loss tend to get stuck in that state of mind. It's a kind of purgatory, which is very much part of this physical world.

> The dead are free. They aren't bothered as we are by the separation from us. We are spirits just as much as they are. It's just that we are spirits in bodies. We can't move around as fast or easily, nor can we see as much as spirits do. This sojourn on Earth is just a short stopover on an infinite journey of consciousness.

The grieving often think about the dead person's life and their interaction with them, and often look at their clothes and memorabilia. Grief becomes depression where there has been unfinished business between people. Many people *make* themselves feel pain after someone dies, thinking they're taking away the dead person's pain. Smith says that spirits say, 'Don't do that'.

Spirits can put thoughts in our minds. They can even send material objects to the person who is grieving. The grief-stricken often tell him that they repeatedly find feathers, coins, or things that have some sort of connection with the person who has died.

Smith says that, in Tibet, families are given ritual or meditation practices by lamas to help them move on after the death of a loved one. We join the dead as they go through the *bardo* (the intermediate stage between death and rebirth). Death doesn't destroy love. We should see our loved ones as still living. Imagining them dead kills them. Spirit communication is about feeling: that is our bond with others.

After death, spirits go through progressively less dense 'gases' or levels, Smith believes. They must find forgiveness from all the people they have harmed in their lives, plus all the knock-on effects in others of their harmful actions towards one person. But don't think about what frightens you. Be at peace within yourself. You're a manifestation or accumulation of what you have always been, Smith declares, and are not only your actions in this life.

The near-death experience

Evidence for the survival of consciousness after death is increasing dramatically. In the UK, Dr Peter Fenwick (MD) of the Scientific and Medical Network is a clear leader in this area, along with Dr Andrew Parnier (MD) on near-death experience studies. Strong research is going on elsewhere, particularly by physicist Professor Gary Schwartz at the University of Arizona and cardiologist Dr Pim van Lommel in Holland. The near-death experience (NDE) is defined as being a forced out-of-body experience (OBE) caused by organic traumas and/or physical, chemical or psychological agents. It is most common in cases of terminal illness, or situations where the body almost dies, such as by accident, electrocution, surgery, suffocation or drowning. According to van Lommel:

> Near-death experiences occur with increasing frequency because of improved survival rates resulting from modern techniques of resuscitation. The content of NDE and the effects on patients seem similar worldwide, across all cultures and times.[3]

Does brain death really mean death? Does consciousness remain after the body dies? Cells in our bodies die constantly. Each year about 98 per cent of our molecules and atoms are replaced. The body is 'an unstable balance of two opposing processes of continual disintegration and integration. *Is* someone his body, or do we "have" a body?'

Do we have some sort of invisible etheric template around or upon our bodies, which makes them assume the forms they have? Is consciousness in the brain or in the body, or is it just *using* the body, merely 'passing through'? Could consciousness be both within and outside the body at the same time? Can it move around freely within and outside the body?

Dr Van Lommel notes that some theories propose that NDEs are caused by physiological changes in the brain, such as brain cells dying as a result of cerebral anoxia (deficient supply of oxygen to the tissues). So he organized a team in 1988 to start a study of 344 survivors of cardiac arrest in 10 Dutch hospitals. They wanted to know whether particular factors of physiology, pharmacology, psychology or demographics could explain NDEs. They studied patients who survived cardiac arrest, a life-threatening condition. Patients die from irreversible brain damage if cardio-pulmonary resuscitation (CPR) does not take place within 5–10 minutes after they suffer a heart attack. After patients had recovered sufficiently, his team asked them a few standardized questions, probing for memories of the period while their body was unconscious.

Van Lommel found that 282 of the patients in his study (82%) remembered nothing about the cardiac arrest. Sixty-two (18%) reported some recollection of the time of clinical death and, of these, 41 (12%) had a full 'core experience' NDE.

In the core group of Van Lommel's study:

23 patients (7%) reported a deep or very deep experience.

50% with an NDE reported awareness of being dead, or had positive emotions.

About 25% had an out-of-body experience.

30% reported moving through a tunnel. .

About 25% had communication with 'the Light' or observed colours.

About 30% observed a celestial landscape or met deceased relatives.

13% experienced a life review, and

8% experienced a border.

Only those with a good short-term memory appear to have NDEs. NDEs are more frequently reported by people under the age of 60, those who had had more than one CPR during their hospital stay, and those who had experienced an NDE previously.

Interestingly, only cardiac arrest patients who had had an NDE showed long-lasting transformational effects from their experience. Should the NDE have been a purely physiological effect of something like cerebral anoxia, which renders cardiac arrest victims unconscious, then all of them would have had NDEs. But they did not.

NDE-like experiences can be induced through electrical stimulation of some parts of the cortex in patients with epilepsy. They can also be brought on by high carbon dioxide levels in the body or when decreased cerebral perfusion has resulted in local cerebral hypoxia, as happens in rapid acceleration during the training of fighter pilots. Drugs such as ketamine and LSD may also cause them. However, in all of these conditions, if any recollections occur, they consist of fragmented, random memories – quite unlike the panoramic life-reviews that people sometimes have in near-death experiences.

In three studies with identical study designs in different countries, around the same percentage of NDE was found in survivors of cardiac arrest. Van Lommel's 2001 study showed that 18 per cent of 344 Dutch cardiac arrest survivors reported an NDE, while Greyson's 2003 study of 116 survivors showed that 15.5 per cent had an NDE, and Parnia's 2001 study showed that 11 per cent of 63 British survivors admitted they had one. Van Lommel finds it surprising that this can happen when the brain is so dysfunctional. After a heart attack, a patient is deeply comatose and 'the cerebral structures that underpin subjective experience and memory' are severely impaired. Questioning the idea that consciousness and memories are produced by large groups of neurons localized in the brain, he asks, 'How could a clear consciousness outside one's body be experienced at the moment that the brain no longer functions during a period of clinical death?' Even blind people have described truthful and verifiable perceptions during NDEs.

Van Lommel tells one striking, verifiable anecdote about an out-of-body-experience that a patient of his had during an NDE. A 44-year-old comatose, cyanotic man (blue, due to lack of oxygen) had been found in a meadow about 30 minutes before Van Lommel saw him in the intensive care unit of his hospital. He removed the man's upper dentures and placed them in a crash cart before working on him for an hour and a half before he regained sufficient heart rhythm and blood pressure to continue with artificial respiration treatment elsewhere, although still in a deep coma. Van Lommel met him over a week later, awake and in the cardiac ward of the hospital, when a nurse was looking for his dentures. He pointed to Van Lommel and said, 'Oh, that nurse knows where my dentures are.' Then, addressing Van Lommel, he added, 'You were there when I was brought into hospital and you took my dentures out of my mouth and put them onto that cart; it had all these bottles on it and there was this sliding drawer underneath, and there you put my teeth.'

The man had perceived his body lying in bed and all that had happened to him while the nurses and doctors had been busy with the cardio-pulmonary resuscitation. He even described correctly and in detail the small room where it all happened, as well as the appearance of those who had been there. He said that he was no longer afraid of death.

While having an NDE 'life review', people do not experience time or space the way we do ordinarily. Time expands so that many things can happen in only two minutes. People are completely aware and conscious during an NDE, sometimes surveying their whole life in one second, and often experiencing how their thoughts, words and deeds were experienced by other people, and how they were affected by them over time. Van Lommel describes this as a connection with the fields of consciousness of other persons as well as with your own fields of consciousness. One person said: 'All of my life [seemed] placed before me in a kind of panoramic, three-dimensional review, and [in] each event [I perceived] not only what I had done or thought, but even in what way it had influenced others, as if I saw things with all-seeing eyes.'

Van Lommel observed other fairly common significant details of NDEs. People sometimes preview future events during an NDE. When meeting deceased relatives or unknown individuals, thought transfer is often the way they communicate. They recall how they return to their bodies. Usually it is through the top of the head.

Yet the brain does not seem to be the source of consciousness. 'The brain has an absolutely inadequate capacity to produce and store all the informational processes of all our memories.' It does not have enough retrieval abilities for this. Nor does it seem able to elicit consciousness.

Going along with the principles of quantum mechanics, we may receive only some parts of multiple fields of consciousness – as waves – into our waking consciousness. These waves are part of our physical body, which consists of particles.

> During life, consciousness has an aspect of waves [as well as] parti-
> cles, and there is a permanent interaction between these two aspects
> of consciousness. When we die, our consciousness will no longer
> have an aspect of particles, but only an eternal aspect of waves.

Van Lommel says this is complementary, not dualistic. The under-lying reality of both wave and particle is the same. This explains how consciousness is greater than an individual brain. We, and the brain, behave as receivers of information, a bit like a radio, com-puter or television. The information is always present, in the same way that vast electromagnetic fields pervade our surroundings and even permeate us. Yet we are not aware of them unless we turn on a receiver that picks them up.

When the body dies, it doesn't mean that memories and con-sciousness no longer exist. It's simply that the reception ability is lost, the connection or interface is interrupted. Consciousness can be experienced while the brain is not functioning (during an NDE), therefore it is not rooted in the physical body or material world.

> Death, like birth, may well be a mere passing from one state of
> consciousness to another. [Our] waking consciousness, which we
> experience as our daily consciousness, is only a part of our whole
> and undivided consciousness.

We become aware of a greater or 'enhanced consciousness' during critical medical situations; at times where death is imminent; in states of meditation or deep relaxation; or while experiencing changing states of consciousness (for example during regression therapy or hypnosis and while in isolation or under the influence of drugs like LSD); or during the terminal phase of life (eg, in a death-bed vision). This enhanced consciousness appears to be constantly evolving 'fields of information, where all knowledge and unconditional love are present and available [in] a dimension without our concept of time and space'. After the body has died, we become 'part of these eternal and indestructible fields of consciousness'.

Along with Dr Pim van Lommel, the researchers Dr Sam Parnia, Bruce Greyson, Kenneth Ring, Raymond Moody Jr, and Dr Peter Fenwick have published works on the subject of NDEs. Dr Ring did a study of 24 suicide survivors with experiences similar to non-suicide NDEs.

Ring's suicide subjects spoke of having had a sense of drifting through a vast space and feeling good, of hearing music or a comforting voice, or magnified sounds, and seeing flashbacks of their lives. A few people described 'some unsettling hallucinatory images' but did not feel they were in or on their way to hell. Interestingly, whatever they experienced made them wish to continue living. All had 'an awareness of peace, of something beautiful', which had nothing to do with their mental state before attempting suicide, and seemed to undergo some sort of healing.

Dr Peter Fenwick conducted an early survey of NDEs in 1987 with his wife, which became the subject matter of their book *The Truth in the Light* (Fenwick and Fenwick, 1996). This followed the UK's first television programme on NDEs, after which they received 2,000 letters from people telling them of their own NDEs. They sent a questionnaire to 500 people, who described what sounded like 'core NDEs', and received 450 replies. Similar experiences were again reported. Sixty-six per cent had an out-of-body experience, 76 per cent found themselves in pastoral landscapes, 38 per cent saw deceased friends and relatives, 12 per cent underwent life reviews, 24 per cent came to a barrier of some sort, and 72 per cent made a decision to return to life. Only 4 per cent had hell-like experiences. No reports of spiders, gnats, snakes or anything that bites were given. Only a few people reported animals being present in the afterlife, and they were dogs. Many of their respondents did mention birdsong and mainly concordant heavenly music, so presumably birds were about. Meanwhile, 'the dead tend to be seen in the prime of life'.

Moving through a tunnel to a beautiful, flower-filled garden or heaven world is a common experience in Western NDEs. The tunnel seems to be cultural, as Japanese studies reveal that respondents report going into caves or crossing rivers (as the Greeks and hunter-gatherers did) to get to the otherworld dimension.

Bruce Greyson's 2003 study found that patients who had a brush with death 'were found to be less psychologically disturbed than those who did not have NDEs'. Few children have heard of NDEs or have religious views, much less know what to expect at death, yet many have NDEs. Studies of children found the same prototypical experiences: encounters with mystical beings, barriers of no return, bright lights, heightened senses and feelings of peace, harmony and joy.

Studies at the Near Death Experience Research Foundation suggest that the way the brain processes information is much like a holograph. Researcher Dr Jody Long postulates that light can be a carrier of consciousness and describes a man (István Bókkon) who literally sees thought and light as waves and bio-photons. Bókkon has observed that bio-photons generate visible (conscious) and invisible (unconscious, metaphor-like) pictures in the brain. He suggests that biophotons may play an important role in the information processes of the brain during sleep, dreams and wakefulness. The brain may operate by pictures during thinking.

Old concepts of death are dying

C Murray Parkes wrote about a woman who died peacefully after having said, 'I wish I could tell people how nice it can be to die of cancer'. In the foreword to *On Death and Dying* he wrote:

> [People who help the dying] will learn much about the functioning of the human mind, the unique human aspects of our existence, and will emerge from the experience enriched and perhaps with fewer anxieties about their own finality.

The late Dr Elisabeth Kübler-Ross was an early expert on the NDE phenomenon and founded an institution bearing her name which assists terminally ill patients and their families. An English medical doctor, she spent many years helping the dying while encouraging those coming to terms with bereavement to understand that death is part of life and should not be feared. Kübler-Ross herself noted that, the more we achieve in science, the more we fear and deny the reality of death.

> We use euphemisms, we make the dead look as if they were asleep, we ship the children off to protect them from the anxiety and tur- moil [and debate whether people should be told they are dying] – a question that rarely arises when the dying person is tended by the family physician, who has known him from delivery to death.

Kübler-Ross thinks one of the most important reasons we fly from facing death calmly is because dying 'is in many ways more grue- some, lonely, mechanical and dehumanized' than in the past. The dying are often removed from their familiar environments, placed on a stretcher and rushed to a hospital emergency ward amid the noise of an ambulance siren to an uncomfortable emergency ward. 'Only those who have lived through this may appreciate the dis- comfort of such transportation, which is only the beginning of a long ordeal – hard to endure when you are well', much less when you are fighting for your life. We should consider more carefully the patient himself, and pause 'to hold the patient's hand, to smile, or to listen to a question'. Focus should be kept on the patient's experiences, reactions and needs.

> When a patient is severely ill, he is often treated like a person with no right to an opinion. It would take so little to remember that the sick person too has feelings, wishes, and opinions, and [most] important of all – the right to be heard.

In her work with the dying, Kübler-Ross observed that patients were suffering more – not physically, perhaps, but emotionally. She hoped we might begin to combine the teaching of 'new scientific and technical achievements with equal emphasis on interpersonal human relationships'. She did not believe that pro- gressively less interpersonal contact was the way forward, and wondered what would 'become of a society which puts the empha-sis on numbers and masses, rather than the individual'. Doctors should return to the habits of the past and get to know the families and homes of their patients, treating them at home when neces-sary. Perhaps they would treat fewer people and earn less money but, with such human interaction, their work and the lives of their patients would be so much more rewarding. Greater happiness would come naturally to those in such a situation.

Kübler-Ross wondered whether war is 'perhaps nothing else but a need to face death, to conquer and master it, to come out of it alive – a peculiar form of denial of our own mortality'. We might be less destructive if we contemplated our own death and dealt with our anxieties surrounding it, familiarizing others with our thoughts about it.

The way the world was going made her think that life-and-death decisions would probably one day be made by computers. A civil-ization could never be considered great, she believed, as long as science and technology are misused to increase destructiveness, merely 'prolonging life rather than making it more human'.

Science and technology should be used to free people so that they have more time for individual person-to-person contact. Were we to restructure our societies this way, we could help the dying by helping them to live, rather than leaving them to vegetate in an inhuman manner and making them die faster by giving them too many drugs.

Her dying patients stressed that a medical practitioner's empathy with them was more important than anything else when he broke the news of their imminent death. People with even the most advanced cases of illness were reassured when told that everything possible would be done to help them, that treatments were available, that they would not be 'dropped' and there was a glimpse of hope for their recovery.

Patients and their carers go through stages of denial before accepting that a patient's illness is really terminal. First they usually grow angry, then they deny the illness and the course it will take. From time to time after accepting the truth, they will still deny it is true. 'Denial functions as a buffer after unexpected shocking news, allows the patient to collect himself and, with time, mobilize other, less radical defences.'

Family members also experience denial when someone they love is dying. Denial is sometimes so suppressed that it is difficult to realize it is present, especially when a dying person knows and announces he is dying. It is important to listen, to really pay attention when they express this reality, and to appreciate that the dying process is not long, and it is very final. Those left behind after someone dies recover more quickly from grief if they have committed time and effort to ensure the comfort of the loved one before his death.

Kübler-Ross realized that sometimes the best thing you can do for someone who is dying is to be with them through the pain and fear of leaving the world they know. People who have the strength to be with a dying patient in the silence that goes beyond words will know that the moment of death is neither frightening nor painful.

> Watching a peaceful death of a human being reminds us of a falling star; one of a million lights in a vast sky that flares up for a brief moment only to disappear.

Then again, perhaps we go on – we don't disappear at all. We just move into a different dimension. The talents we develop here, we carry with us. As Paul McCartney sings: 'At the end of the end it's the start of a journey to a much better place and a much better place would have to be special.'

In physics an idea is circulating that perhaps at death consciousness simply moves into another dimension, and that many alternate dimensions exist. Rather than a single, universal reality of the kind provided by quantum mechanics, it is likely that there are many realities, many perceptual stances, in the universe.

'More than one complementary or alternative form of knowledge may exist' also, just as certain natural powers such as psychism and telekinesis are possible. Earth's biosystems 'can have more discriminative knowledge of nature than is obtainable by quantum measurement'. The knowledge possessed by biosystems and by science are qualitatively different.[4]

Like the continually moving atoms and particles we cannot see, we could be dancing in a dancing universe to a musical rhythm we hardly notice. The world's healers may not be able to heal all problems, but perhaps the consciousness behind their impulse to heal continues long after their 'essences' have discarded their bodies. Life goes on, from sea to universal sea, from birth to death, ever replacing what is lost. We don't last for very long on this Earth, and where we go after we die remains a mystery.

Perhaps we return to being little lights in the vast universe, or dissipate so that we become part of the winds and the water, the plants and the elements. Maybe we move from better to worse states according to our consciousness and actions, as the religious suggest.

Death reminds us of our fragility, of the finite within the infinite. It shows us what we truly are and what we feel beneath the layers of personality and activity that make up our lives. Nothing is more humbling for the human ego than death.

Choose your universe

With all the knowledge we have about science and the way things work, certain things remain important and are common to us all. When death arrives, even our quarrels may be seen for what they are – a need for love. As often quoted from the French Jesuit mystic and scientist Teilhard de Chardin (1881–1955):

> Some day, after we have mastered the winds, the waves, the tides and gravity … [we shall harness] the energies of love. Then for the second time in the history of the world, man will have discovered fire.

Might love – a force that we generate ourselves – be measurable as other forces are? Or it is immeasurable? Is love the basis of the universe itself – expansive and embracing? Is it the Higgs field of physics?

Perhaps we are on Earth to become more aware that causal effects flow from our ways of thinking and acting. Indulging in ever increasing desires and wants, without awareness, is destroy-ing the natural environment upon which our lives depend. If we did what we perceive as good – what gives us peace – and then just sat back and waited for tiny green shoots to emerge from seeds that we have planted in the Earth, we would soon notice reactions and reverberations in the universe.

Could we, by our actions, be choosing what universe we will move on to after we die? Might we recycle wasteful (and negative) thoughts and feelings that arise in our minds? Machaelle Small Wright of Perelandra, a centre for nature research near Jeffer-sonton, Virginia, began her efforts to recycle her thoughts by gardening a small patch of land organically. Her neighbours were shocked that their gardens withered due to harsh weather while hers blossomed thanks to her organic methods. Wright's philo-sophy is simple.

> You are the creator of your garden, even if you live in an apart-ment. It's up to you to ask your own questions and act on your own answers. Don't be afraid to make a mistake. Take what gardening teaches and use it in all of life!

Nature, by itself, left unharmed, has a way of dealing with its prob-lems, just as the body can often be healed by a mind that is in tune with the natural world and itself. If the mind learns how to be at peace, good physical health will often follow. Humans can help the Earth if they pay attention to what it and its creatures need. For this, it is helpful to notice human beings' needs, not only their deeds.

The musical universe

> The rhythm of music [may] be a manifestation of the basic rhythms of life. [No] living process [occurs] without oscillation, without repetition.[5]

If we attune ourselves to birdsong, to the buzzing of bees and the meditative drone of hummingbirds, the rhythms of the tides, of day and night, of breathing in and out, we may begin to hear a kind of music in the universe. The structures beneath objects, the molecules themselves, are making sounds – a cyclical tune which, if heard, could allow us to live more in tune with what surrounds us.

Music is our way of singing back to the universe. It reflects the poetic grandeur and wonder of the universe in its own way, reflecting them. Music, such as Elgar's, can evoke the country-side and the seasons, as Hindu ragas and Western composers like Vivaldi have attempted. You can attune yourself to your sur-roundings through the sounds you hear around you. If you focus your attention on listening to the sounds and musical tones you hear – a droning siren, sticks clattering, a cardinal singing – you can create a melody from them.

Through becoming aware of the world and other living things around you, you can learn to become more harmonious with them and to move through life a little more easily and gently. Landscapes may be improved by people who are in tranquil accord with them, just as the body can often be healed by a mind that is in tune with nature.

Of course all of us are affected by the poisons and imbalances of those who are unbalanced, so we can't always protect ourselves from harm. However, if enough of us choose to live in harmony with nature, ourselves, and each other, we can, like good bacteria in the body, begin to overcome the disease that threatens the body of the Earth.

How can we do this? By doing what the best singers do: finding what level of the musical scale they sing best, then harmonizing with whatever notes are sung or played by others. We can do this by listening.

So, listen.
Listen to the universe.
It is singing.

ENDNOTES

Chapter 1 Man's Connection to the Universe

1 www.wyrdwords.vispa.com/heathenry/whatwyrd.html (In this passage, I am referring not to Satanists abhorred by Christian fundamentalists, but to the religion linked with prehistory and nature.)

2 Carr, 'Mind and the Cosmos', Lorimer, David et al, *Science, Consciousness and Ultimate Reality*, Imprint Academic, Exeter, 2004, p35

3 Gribbin, John, ed, *A Brief History of Science*, Weidenfeld Nicolson, 1998, p53

4 *Ibid.*

5 Bassett, Bruce and Edney, Ralph, *Introducing Relativity*, Icon Books Ltd, Cambridge, England, 2002, p9

6 Greene, Brian, *The Elegant Universe*, Vintage, Random House, London, 2000, p6

7 Zukav, *Dancing Wu Li Masters*, p63

8 Mayants, Lazar and Zilma, *Beyond the Quantum Paradox*, Taylor & Francis Ltd., London, 1994, p5

9 Capra, Fritjof, *The Turning Point*, Flamingo, Harper Collins, 1982, p4

10 www.lifepositive.com/chinmayamission/index.html

11 Runzo, Joseph, 'Religion and Ethics in a Global World', *Ethics in the World Religions*, Eds. Joseph Runzo and Nancy M Martin, p26

12 *Ibid.*

Chapter 2 Invisible Interconnections Between Us

1 Evans, Joan (editor), *The Lamp of Beauty: Writings on Art by John Ruskin*, Phaidon Press Limited, Oxford, 1959, p232; from *Stones of Venice*, Vol II, Ch VI, 'The Nature of Gothic', II-XIV.A

2 Fiona MacCarthy, 'The Old Romantics', *The Guardian*, London, Sunday, 5 March 2005, www.guardian.co.uk/arts/features/story/0,11710,1430727,00.html

3 Capra, *The Turning Point, op. cit.*, p28

4 www.naturia.per.sg/buloh/birds/migration.htm

5 *Ibid.*

6 One of the best books around about the wind, in biologist-anthropologist Lyall Watson's poetic-realistic style, is: *Heaven's Breath: A Natural History Of The Wind*, by Lyall Watson, Sceptre, 1988

Chapter 3 The Inner Universe of the Human Being: Mind Science

1 Reanny, Darryl, *The Death of Forever*, Souvenir Press, 1995, p106

2 Wilson, Colin, *The Occult*, Granada Publishing Ltd, 1976, p744

3 Zukav, Gary, *Dancing Wu Li Masters: An Overview of the New Physics*, Quill William Morrow, New York, 1979, p65

4 Whitman, Walt, *Song of Myself*, Stanzas 1 & 6, 1855

5 Morehouse, David, *Psychic Warrior*, St Martins Press, New York, 1996

6 www.tcm.phy.cam.ac.uk/~bdj10/stamps/text.html

7 Fontana, David, 'Science, Religion and Psychology', in Lorimer, David, *et al*, *Science, Consciousness and Ultimate Reality*, Imprint Academic, Exeter, England, 2004, p147

8 Mahadevan, Dr T M P (translator), *Why Am I?*, Venkataraman, T N, Sri Ramanasramam, Tiruvannamalai, The Jupiter Press Pvt Ltd., Madras, 1968, p11

9 Mahadevan, Dr T M P (tr), in *Why Am I?*, in *The Rider Encyclopaedia of Eastern Philosophy and Religion*, Rider, London, 1989

10 Dames, Michael, *Mythic Ireland*, Thames and Hudson, London, 1992, p90

11 Wilson, Colin, *Mysteries*, Granada Publishing, London, 1983, p572

12 *Ibid.*, pp570–2

13 Nobbs, Brian, 'Some Reflections on the Hidden World of Nature', written prior to 2004, unpublished and used with permission of the author.

14 Matthews, Caitlin, in Serena Roney-Dougal's *The Faery Faith: An Integration of Science with Spirit*, Green Magic, London, 2002, Foreword.

15 Harding, Stephan, *Animate Earth: Science, Intuition and Gaia*, Green Books Ltd, Dartington, UK, 2006, pp226–227

16 From a talk entitled 'Science at the Crossroads' given by Tenzin Gyatso, the Dalai Lama, at the annual meeting of the Society for Neuroscience on November 12, 2005, in Washington, DC, USA

17 Lutz, Antoine; Dunne, John D.; Davidson, Richard J., 'Meditation and the Neuroscience of Consciousness', *Cambridge Handbook of Consciousness*, ed by Zelazo, P, Moscovitch, M, and Thompson, E, Cambridge Univ Press, 2007

18 *Ibid.*, p5

Chapter 4 The Universe of the Human Body

1 'The Ghost in Your Genes', BBC Horizon,
www.bbc.co.uk/sn/tvradio/programmes/horizon/ghostgenes.shtml

2 Quote by Alan Watts, from James Hewitt's *The Complete Yoga Book: The Yoga of Breathing, Posture, and Meditation*, Rider Books, Random House, London, 1991, p513

3 Sri Swami Satchidananda, from his translation of *The Yoga Sutras of Patanjali*, Integral Yoga Publications, 1997

4 Ballentine, Dr Rudolph, *Radical Healing*, Rider Books, Random House, 1999, p44

5 Sachs, Robert, *Health for Life: Secrets of Tibetan Ayurveda*, Clear Light, Santa Fe, 1995, p16

6 Press Release, 'Dog from the Afterlife Warns Woman of Need for a Mammogram', *PR Web*, Minneapolis, Minnesota, October 19, 2005, www.prweb.com/releases/2005150/10/prweb298670.htm

7 Rubenstein, Micah, 'The Healing Touch of Gentle Giants', *International Magazine for Spiritual Consciousness*, Volume 1/1, Spring, 2005

8 Bowring, Janine, and Dietrich, Joy, 'The Healing Power of Dolphins', www.life.ca/nl/81/dolphins.html

9 Gerber, MD, Richard, *Vibrational Medicine for the 21st Century: A Complete Guide to Energy Healing and Spiritual Transformation*, William Morrow & Co, NY, 2001, and Piatkus, London, 2000, p3

10 Goldman, Jonathan, *Healing Sounds: The Power Of Harmonics*, Healing Arts Press, Rochester, Vermont, 2002, pviii

11 American sound researcher Georgia Neff, PhD, www.biowaves.com

12 Khan, Hazrat Inayat, *The Mysticism of Sound and Music: The Sufi Teaching of Hazrat Inayat Khan*, Shambhala Publications, Boston, 1991, Prologue and pp6–8

13 Trungpa, Chögyam, 'Fear and Fearlessness', *Shambhala – The Sacred Path of the Warrior*, Shambhala Pubs, www.shambhala.com, Boston, Mass., 1984/2007, p49

14 Jourdain, Robert, *Music, the Brain, and Ecstasy*, Quill, HarperCollins, NY, 2002, pp301–2

15 O'Connor, Colleen, 'Willing your way to happiness', *The Denver Post* (newspaper), Colorado, USA, June 4, 2006

16 Manning, Matthew, *The Healing Journey*, Piatkus, London, 2001, p20

17 Lama, Abraham, 'Peru: Traditional Knowledge Enhances Modern Medicine', *TWN Third World Network*, Lima, Peru, 2nd March 2000

18 Liberman, Dr Jacob, *Light Medicine of the Future: How We Can Use It to Heal Ourselves Now*, Bear & Co, Santa Fe, 1991, pp205–6

Chapter 5 Ecology and the Built Universe

1 Harding, Dr Stephan, *Animate Earth: Science, Intuition and Gaia*, Green Books, Totnes, UK, 2006, p20

2 Highwater, Jamake, *The Primal Mind: Vision and Reality in Indian America*, Penguin, New York, 1981, p74

3 Ceccherini, Rita, Gianni Celestini, Fabio Di Carlo & Raffaella Strati, 'The Town as a Garden: The Case of Yemen', *Environmental Design: Journal of the Islamic Environmental Design Research Centre 2*, (1986): 48–55, p48

4 Khan, Hazrat Inayat, *The Mysticism of Sound and Music: The Sufi Teaching of Hazrat Inayat Khan*, Shambhala, Boston, USA, 1991, p2.

5 Sheldrake, Rupert, *Dogs That Know When Their Owners Are Coming Home and Other Unexplained Powers of Animals*, Random House, UK, 1999, p137

6 Walker, Alex, 'Community Beliefs', *The Kingdom Within: A Guide to the Spiritual Work of the Findhorn Community*, Findhorn Press, Scotland, 1994, p187

7 Norberg-Hodge, Helena; Merrifield, Todd; Gorelick, Steven, *Bringing the Food Economy Home: Local Alternatives to Global Agribusiness*, Zed Books, UK, 2002, p3

8 Maynard, Robin, 'Against the Grain', *The Ecologist*, March 2007, p29. (The Rodale Institute is in Pennsylvania.)

9 Whitefield, Patrick, *Permaculture in a Nutshell*, Permanent Publications, Hampshire, www.permaculture.co.uk

10 Saunders, Thomas, *The Boiled Frog Syndrome: your health and the built environment*, Wiley-Academy, John Wiley and Sons, Chichester, West Sussex, UK, 2002, p165

11 Scudo, Gianni, 'Climatic Design in the Arab Courtyard House', *Environmental Design: Journal of the Islamic Environmental Design Research Centre* http://archnet.org/library/documents/one-document.tcl?document_id=4926, p84

12 www.open2.net/modernity/3_16.htm

13 www.katarxis-publications.com/katarxis02-1/id23.html

14 Van der Peet, PhD, Rob, *The Nightingale Model of Nursing: An analysis of Florence Nightingale's concepts of nursing, and their impact on present day practice*, Campion Press, Edinburgh, 1995, pp131–2

15 Solomon, Jane and Grant, *Harry Oldfield's Invisible Universe: The Story of One Man's Search for the Healing Methods That Will Help Us Survive the 21st Century*, Campion Books, UK, 1998, p260

16 'Green for Profit', *The Changing Times: News and Resources for Living and Being*, Christmas 2005, p3

Chapter 6   Technology to Make the Deserts Bloom

1 Todd, Nancy Jack, 'Proposed Solar Field – Reaching the Point of No Return: A renewable energy manifesto', *Guerrilla News Network (GNN)*, 7 November, 2005, www.nuclearpolicy.org

2 *Ibid.*

3 Saunders, Thomas, *The Boiled Frog Syndrome: Your Health and the Built Environment*, John Wiley and Sons, Chichester, West Sussex, England, 2002, p152

4 'Woking's Sustainable & Renewable Energy Installations', Woking Borough Council, pp13–14

5 Maynard, Robin, 'Against the Grain', *The Ecologist*, March 2007, pp28–29

6 Boyle, Godfrey, ed, Ch 3: 'Solar Photovoltaics', *Renewable Energy: Power for a Sustainable Future*, Oxford Univ Press in association with the Open Univ, 2004, p82

7 Vergano, Dan, 'Nano proponents square off against specter of 'gray goo', *USA Today*, Washington, 27 September, 2004

8 'Polycontrast Interference Photography (PIP) Energy Field Video Imaging System', Innovative Technologies and Energy Medicine, www.item-bioenergy.com/pip/

9 Solomon, Jane & Grant, *Harry Oldfield's Invisible Universe: The Story of One Man's Search for the Healing Methods That Will Help Us Survive the 21st Century*, Campion Books, UK, 1998, pp98–9

10 From a private conversation with Jenni Roditi in London, England, in November, 2006

11 McTaggart, Lynne, *The Field*, Element, London, 2001, p137

12 *Ibid.*, p262

Chapter 7   Listen, the Universe is Singing

1 Keen, Montague, 'The Scole Investigation: A Study in Critical Analysis of Paranormal Physical Phenomena', www.scientificexploration.org

2 www.greatmystery.org/newsletters/musings_entities.html

3 Van Lommel, Pim, Rijnstate Hospital, Arnhem, Netherlands, 'Near-Death Experience, Consciousness, and the Brain: A New Concept about the Continuity of Our Consciousness Based on Recent Scientific Research on Near-Death Experience in Survivors of Cardiac Arrest', *World Futures*, Taylor & Francis Group, LLC, 2006, 62: 134–151, p134

4 Josephson, Brian D, Pallikari-Viras, Fotini, 'Biological Utilisation of Quantum NonLocality', Foundation of Physics, Vol. 2, pp197–207, Plenum Press, 1991

5 Clarke, John, 'Time and the Timeless', *Mystics and Scientists*, No 27, Winchester, England, March, 2004

BIBLIOGRAPHY

Attenborough, David, *The Life of Birds*, Princeton Univ Press, 1998

Ballentine, Dr Rudolph, *Radical Healing*, Rider Books, Random House, 1999

Bartholomew, Alick, *Hidden Nature: The Startling Insights of Viktor Schauberger*, Floris Books, Edinburgh, 2005

Bassett, Bruce and Edney, Ralph, *Introducing Relativity*, Icon Books Ltd, Cambridge, England, 2002

Benyus, Janine M, *Biomimicry*, HarperCollins, New York, 1997

Benveniste, J, 'Understanding Digital Biology', *What Is Digital Biology?*, 8 January, 1998

Bonner, John, 'Even in nature, the rich get richer', *New Scientist*, 23 April, 2005

Boyle, Godfrey, ed, *Renewable Energy: Power for a Sustainable Future*, Oxford Univ Press, in association with the Open University, 2004

Bradley, Dr Tamdin Sither, *Principles of Tibetan Medicine*, Wisdom Books, England, 2000

Capra, Fritjof, *The Turning Point*, Flamingo, HarperCollins, 1982

———, *The Hidden Connections*, Flamingo, HarperCollins, 2003

———, *The Tao of Physics*, Flamingo, HarperCollins, 1991

Carr, Bernard, 'Mind and the Cosmos', Lorimer, David, et al, *Science, Consciousness and Ultimate Reality*, Imprint Academic, Exeter, UK, 2004 _etal.

Chambers, John, *Paranormal People: The Famous, the Infamous and the Supernatural*, Blandford, Cassell plc, London

Chisti, Shaykh Hakim Moinuddin, *The Book of Sufi Healing*, Inner Traditions Bear and Company, 1985

Courteney, Hazel, *The Evidence For The Sixth Sense: Divine Intervention 2, The Journey Continues*, Cico Books, London, 2005

Dames, Michael, *Mythic Ireland*, Thames and Hudson, London, 1992

David-Neel, Alexandra, *Magic and Mystery in Tibet*, Rupa & Co, India, 1989

Davies, Paul, *The Mind of God: the Scientific Basis for a Rational World*, Touchstone, Simon & Schuster, 1992

Dawkins, Richard, *Unweaving the Rainbow*, Penguin Books, London, 1998

Devereux, Paul, *The Illustrated Encyclopedia of Ancient Earth Mysteries*, Cassell & Co., London, 2000

——, *Shamanism and the Mystery Lines*, Quantum, W Foulsham and Co, London, 2002

Dorjee, Dr Pema, *Heal Your Spirit, Heal Yourself: The Spiritual Medicine of Tibet*, Watkins, London, 2005

Ellison, Prof Arthur J, *Science and the Paranormal: Altered States of Reality*, Floris Books, Edinburgh, 2002

Emoto, Masaru, *The Hidden Messages in Water*, Oregon, Beyond Words Publishing Inc, 2004

Evans, Joan (editor), *The Lamp of Beauty: Writings on Art by John Ruskin*, Phaidon Press Limited, Oxford, 1959

Fenwick, Dr Peter, 'Scientific Evidence for the Efficacy of Prayer', www.rcpsych.ac.uk/PDF/fenwick %208 4 04.pdf

Flannery, Tim, *The Weather Makers: The History and Future Impact of Climate Change*, Penguin/Allen Lane Books, London, 2005

Fontana, David, *Is There an Afterlife?: A Comprehensive Overview of the Evidence*, O Books, UK, 2005

Ford, Kenneth W, *The Quantum World: Quantum Physics for Everyone*, Harvard University Press, 2005

Fukoku, Masanobu, *The Natural Way of Farming: The Nature and Practice of Green Farming*, Bookventure, India, 2006

—— *The One-Straw Revolution*, Other India Press, 2006

Garrett, Eileen, *Adventures in the Supernormal*, Helix Press, New York, 2002

Gellatly, Angus, *Introducing Mind and Brain*, Icon Books Ltd, Royston, England, 2003

Geller, Uri, *My Story*, Robson Books, London, 1975

Gerber, Richard, *Vibrational Medicine for the 21st Century*, Piatkus, London, 2000

Godwin, Jocelyn, *Cosmic Music*, Inner Traditions, Rochester, Vermont, 1989

Goldman, Jonathan, *Healing Sounds: The Power Of Harmonics*, Healing Arts Press, Rochester, Vermont, 2002

Gott, J Richard, *Time Travel in Einstein's Universe*, Phoenix, Orion, London, 2001

Granger, Prof Frank, *Vitruvius on Architecture*, Loeb Classical Library, Harvard Univ Press, and William Heinemann Ltd., London, 1985

Greene, Brian, *The Elegant Universe*, Vintage, Random House, London, 2000

Gregory, Lady, *Visions and Beliefs in the West of Ireland*, Colin Smythe, Gerrards Cross, Britain, 1920/1979

Gribben, John, *The Search for Superstrings, Symmetry, and the Theory of Everything*, Little, Brown, 1999

——, ed, *A Brief History of Science*, Weidenfeld Nicolson, 1998

Griffiths, Bede, *The Marriage of East and West*, Templegate Publishers, Illinois, 1982

Hamel, Peter Michael, *Through Music to the Self*, Lilian Barber Press, 1987

Harding, Stephan, *Animate Earth: Science, Intuition and Gaia*, Green Books Ltd, Dartington, UK, 2006

Hawking, Stephen, *A Brief History of Time: From the Big Bang to Black Holes*, Bantam, 1988

Hersey, George, *The Lost Meaning of Classical Architecture*, MIT Press, Cambridge MA, 1989

Highwater, Jamake, *The Primal Mind: Vision and Reality in Indian America*, Penguin, New York, 1981

Jacobi, Michael; Schwenk, Wolfman; and Wilkins, Andreas; *Understanding Water: Developments from the Work of Theodor Schwenk*, Floris Books, 2005

Jenny, Hans, *Cymatics*, MACROmedia Publishing, NH, USA, 2001

Josephson, Brian D, & Pallikari-Viras, Fotini, 'Biological Utilisation of Quantum NonLocality', *Foundations of Physics*, Volume 21, pp197–207, Plenum Press, 1991 (*see also* Professor Josephson: www.tcm.phy.cam.ac.uk/~bdj10/

Jourdain, Robert, *Music, the Brain, and Ecstasy*, Quill, HarperCollins, NY, 2002

Kaku, Michio, *Visions*, First Anchor Books, Random House, New York, 1997

Khan, Hazrat Inayat, *The Mysticism of Sound and Music: The Sufi Teaching of Hazrat Inayat Khan*, Shambhala, Boston, 1991

Krishna, Gopi, Kundalini: *The Evolutionary Energy In Man*, 1967 (Shambhala Publications Inc, New edition 1997)

Kübler-Ross MD, Elisabeth, *On Death and Dying*, Routledge, London and NY, 1997

Liberman, Dr Jacob, *Light Medicine of the Future: How We Can Use It to Heal Ourselves Now*, Bear & Co, Santa Fe, 1991

Lambrecht, Astrid, 'The Casimir Effect: a force from nothing', *Physics World*, Sept. 2002

Logan, Kahuna Bula; Fukuda, Miho; Baldwin, Celeste Mulry, 'Hawaiian Medicine, Where Did It Come From? Where Is It Now?', *Journal of Multicultural Nursing & Health*, Summer 2006

Louv, Richard, *Last Child in the Woods: Saving Our Children from Nature-Deficit Disorder*, Algonquin Books, NC, USA, 2005

Lutz, Antoine; Dunne, John D; Davidson, Richard J, 'Meditation and the Neuroscience of Consciousness', *Cambridge Handbook of Consciousness*, ed by Zelazo, P; Moscovitch, M; & Thompson, E, Cambridge Univ Press, 2007

Mabey, Richard, *The Unofficial Countryside*, Pimlico, Random House, 1999

Maclean, Dorothy, *To Hear the Angels Sing*, Findhorn Pubs. Scotland, 1980

Manning, Matthew, *The Healing Journey*, Piatkus, London, 2001

Mayants, Lazar and Zilma, *Beyond the Quantum Paradox*, Taylor and Francis Ltd., London, 1994

McElroy, Susan Chernak, *Animals as Teachers and Healers: True Stories of the Transforming Power of Animals*, Rider, Ebury Press, Random House, London, 1997

McGarry, Gina, *Brighid's Healing: Ireland's Celtic Medicine Traditions*, Green Magic, Somerset, 2005

McMoneagle, Joseph, *Mind Trek: Exploring Consciousness, Time, and Space through Remote Viewing*, Hampton Roads Pub Co, Inc., 1993, 1997

McMoneagle, Joseph, *The Stargate Chronicles: Memoirs of a Psychic Spy*, Hampton Roads, 2002

McTaggart, Lynne, *The Field*, Element Books, HarperCollins, 2001

Mitchell, Dr Edgar, *The Way of the Explorer: An Apollo Astronaut's Journey Through the Material and Mystical Worlds*, New Page Books, 2008

Mourkioti, F, & Rosenthal, N, 'IGF-1, Inflammation and Stem Cells: Interactions During Muscle Regeneration', *Trends in Immunology*, 26(10): 535–542, October 2005

Narby, Jeremy, *The Cosmic Serpent: DNA and the Origins of Knowledge*, Phoenix, Orion, 1999

Nobbs, Brian, 'Pan, ROC and the Findhorn Garden', Network News, Findhorn Community Newsletter

Norberg-Hodge, Helena; Merrifield, Todd; Gorelick, Steven, *Bringing the Food Economy Home: Local Alternatives to Global Agribusiness*, Zed Books, UK, 2002

——, *Ancient Futures: Learning from Ladakh*, Rider, Random Century, London, 1991

Norfolk, Donald, *The Theraputic Garden*, Bantam, Transworld, 2001

O'Rourke, James, 'People healing dogs, and vice versa', *The Journal News*, Nyack, New York, USA, December 4, 2006

Patten, Leslie and Terry, *Biocircuits: Amazing New Tools for Energy Health*, H J Kramer, Inc., California, US, 1988

Pearsall, Paul, *The Heart's Code*, Broadway Books, Bantam Doubleday Dell, US, 1998

Pearson, Ronald D, *Origin of Mind* (pamphlet), 1992

Peat, F David, *Blackfoot Physics: A Journey into the Native American Universe*, Fourth Estate, London, 1994

Playfair, Guy Lyon, *Twin Telepathy, The Psychic Connection*, Vega Books, 2002

Ricard, Matthieu, *Happiness: A Guide to Developing Life's Most Important Skill*, Little, Brown and Co, New York, 2006

Roney-Dougal, Serena, *Walking Between the Worlds: Links Between Psi, Psychedelics, Shamanism and Psychosis*, www.psi-researchcentre.co.uk

Rubenstein, Micah, 'The Healing Touch of Gentle Giants', *International Magazine for Spiritual Consciousness*, Volume 1/1, Spring, 2005

Runzo, Joseph, 'Religion and Ethics in a Global World', *Ethics in the World Religions*, Eds. Joseph Runzo and Nancy M Martin

Sachs, Robert, *Health for Life: Secrets of Tibetan Ayurveda*, Clear Light, New Mexico, 1995

Sahtouris, Elisabet, *Earth Dance: Living Systems in Evolution*, iUniverse.com, 2000

Satchidananda, Sri Swami, trans, *The Yoga Sutras of Patanjali*, Integral Yoga Publications, 1997

Saunders, Thomas, *The Boiled Frog Syndrome: your health and the built environment*, Wiley-Academy, John Wiley and Sons, UK, 2002

Schuhmacher, Stephan, and Woerner, Gert, editors, *The Rider Encyclopaedia of Eastern Philosophy and Religion*, Rider, London, 1989

Schulz, Andreas, *Water Crystals: Making the Quality of Water Visible*, Floris Books, Edinburgh, 2005

Schumacher, E F, *Small Is Beautiful, A Study of Economics as if People Mattered*, Vintage, New Ed edition, 1993

Schwartz, Dr Gary E, and Simon, William L, *The Afterlife Experiments: Breakthrough Scientific Evidence of Life after Death*, (foreword by Deepak Chopra) Simon & Schuster Int'l, 2003

Schwenk, Theodor, *Sensitive Chaos: The Creation of Flowing Forms in Water and Air*, Rudolf Steiner Press, 1996

Scruton, Roger and Barnett, Anthony (eds), *Town and Country*, Vintage, Random House, 1999

Sheldrake, Rupert, *Dogs That Know When Their Owners Are Coming Home*, Random House, UK, 1999

——, *The Sense of Being Stared At: and other Aspects of the Extended Mind*, Arrow Books, 2004

Shiva, Vandana, *Biopiracy: The Plunder of Nature and Knowledge*, South End Press, Cambridge MA, 1997

Solomon, Jane and Grant, *Harry Oldfield's Invisible Universe: The Story of One Man's Search for the Healing Methods That Will Help Us Survive the 21st Century*, Campion Books, UK, 1998

Spangler, David, *The Laws of Manifestation*, Findhorn Publications, 1977

Stone, J, 'Ask the Experts: Why do cats purr?', *Scientific American*, 20 March 2007 (originally published on 27 January, 2003)

Sylvia, Claire, *A Change of Heart*, Warner Books, US, 2006

Szekely, Edmond B, (ed. and trans.), *The Essene Gospel of Peace*, Academy of Creative Living, US

Talbot, Michael, *The Holographic Universe*, Harper Perennial, 1991

Targ, Russell, and Katra PhD, Jane, *Miracles of Mind: Remote Viewing and Spiritual Healing*, New World Library, 1998

Tulku, Ringu, *Mind Training*, Dhi Publications, London, 2003

Van der Peet, PhD, Rob, *The Nightingale Model of Nursing: An analysis of Florence Nightingale's concepts of nursing, and their impact on present day practice*, Campion Press, Edinburgh, 1995

Vines, Gail, 'Psychic Birds (or What?)', *New Scientist*, 26 June 2004

Wales, HRH the Prince of, with Stephanie Donaldson, *The Elements of Organic Gardening: Highgrove – Clarence House – Birkhall*, Weidenfeld & Nicolson, 2007

Walker, Alex, 'Community Beliefs', *The Kingdom Within: A Guide to the Spiritual Work of the Findhorn Community*, Findhorn Press, Scotland, 1994

Warrier, Gopi, and Gunawant, M D, Deepika, *The Complete Illustrated Guide to Ayurveda: The Ancient Healing Tradition*, Element, England, 1997

Watson, Lyall, *Gifts of Unknown Things*, Simon and Schuster, New York, 1976

——, *Heaven's Breath: A Natural History Of The Wind*, Sceptre, 1988

——, *Supernature: A Natural History of the Supernatural*, Hodder and Stoughton Ltd, Coronet edition, 1974

Whitefield, Patrick, *Permaculture in a Nutshell*, Permanent Publications, England, 1997

Wilkes, Jonathan, *Flow Forms: The Rhythmic Power of Water*, Floris Books, Edinburgh, 2003

Willard, Terry, 'The Magic of Medicinal Mushrooms', Herbal Education, *Vitamin Retailer*, US, June, 1997

Wilson, Colin, *The Occult*, Granada Publishing Ltd, 1976; first published by Hodder & Stoughton, 1971

——, *Dreaming to Some Purpose: An Autobiography*, Century, Random House, London, 2004

——, *Mysteries*, Granada Publishing, London, 1983

Wright, Machaelle Small, *Perelandra Garden Workbook: A Complete Guide to Gardening with Nature Intelligences*, Perelandra, 1993

Xu, Dr Guang, *Chinese Herbal Medicine: A Practical Guide to the Healing Power of Herbs*, Vermillion, Ebury Press, London, 1996

Zukav, Gary, *Dancing Wu Li Masters: An Overview of the New Physics*, Quill William Morrow, New York, 1979

RESOURCES

Organizations and charities

Biodynamic Agricultural Association, Painswick Inn Project, Gloucester Street, Stroud, Gloucestershire GL5 1QG, UK www.biodynamic.org.uk

The Campaign for Nuclear Disarmament, CND, 162 Holloway Road, London N7 8DQ, UK
TEL: +44 (0) 207 700 2393, membership@cnduk.org www.cnduk.org

Centre for Alternative Technology (CAT), Machynlleth, Powys, SY20 9AZ, Wales, UK
www.cat.org.uk

The Committee to Bridge the Gap, 1637 Butler Avenue, Suite 203, Los Angeles, CA 90025, USA
TEL: +1 (310) 478 0829, www.committeetobridgethegap.org

Consortium of Academic Health Centers for Integrative Medicine (CAHCIM), 420 delaware Street SE, Minneapolis, MN 55455, USA, cahcim@umn.edu

Environic Foundation International, 3503 Hutch Place, Chevy Chase, MD 20815-4738, USA
TEL: +1 (301) 654 7160, info@environicfoundation.org
www.environicfoundation.org

The Findhorn Foundation, The Park, Findhorn, Forres,
Moray IV36 3TZ, Scotland
www.findhorn.org

Forum for the Future, Overseas House, 19–23 Ironmonger Row,
London EC1V 3QN, UK
TEL: +44 (0) 20 7324 3630, info@forumforthefuture.org.uk
www.forumforthefuture.org.uk

Foundation for Integrated Health (FIH), 33–41 Dallington Street,
London, EC1V 0BB, UK
www.fih.org.uk

International Forum on Globalization, 1009 General Kennedy Avenue
#2, San Francisco, CA 94129, USA
TEL: +1 (415) 561 7650, ifg@ifg.org www.ifg.org

Friends of the Earth, (HQ) 1717 Massachusetts Avenue, NW, 600,
Washington DC 20036-2002, USA
TEL: +1 (877) 843-8687 – toll free in US; foe@foe.org

Friends of the Earth UK, 26-28 Underwood Street, London N1 7JQ
TEL: +44 (0) 20 7490 1555;
for campaigns information, TEL: Freephone 0808 800 1111
www.foe.org

Greenpeace, Canonbury Villas, London N1 2PN, UK
TEL: +44 (0) 20 7865 8100, info@uk.greenpeace.org

Hawaiian Healing Institute, PO Box 726, Ashland, Oregon 97520

The Institute for Energy and Environmental Research, 6935 Laurel
Ave., Suite 201, Takoma Park, Maryland 20912, USA
TEL: +1 (301) 270 5500 www.ieer.org

The Institute of Noetic Sciences (IONS), 101 San Antonio Road,
Petaluma, California 94952, USA
TEL: +1 (707) 775 3500, www.instituteofnoeticsciences.com

Mind and Life Institute, 589 West Street, Louisville,
Colorado 80027, USA
TEL: +1 (303) 665 7659, info@mindandlife.org www.mindandlife.org

The Nuclear Age Peace Foundation,
TEL: +1 (805) 965 3443, www.wagingpeace.org www.nuclearfiles.org

Nuclear Policy Research Institute, 1925 K Street NW, Suite 210,
Washington DC 20006, USA
TEL: +1 (202) 822 9800, www.nuclearpolicy.org

Physicians for Social Responsibility, 1875 Connecticut Avenue, NW,
Suite 1012, Washington, DC, 20009, USA
TEL: +1 (202) 667 4260, psrnatl@psr.org www.psr.org

The Prince's Foundation for Integrated Health, 33–41 Dallington
Street, London EC1V 0BE, UK
TEL: +44 (0) 20 3119 3100, contactus@fih.org.uk www.fih.org.uk

The Research Foundation for Science, Technology and Natural
Resource Policy, Environmental Law Alliance Worldwide (E-LAW),
Avenue, Eugene, Oregon 97403 USA
TEL: +1 (541) 687 8454, elawus@elaw.org www.elaw.org.

The Royal Institution of Great Britain, 21 Albemarle Street, London
W1S 4BS, UK
www.royalsociety.org

The Royal Society, 6–9 Carlton House Terrace, London SW1Y 5AG
www.royalsociety.org

The Society for Psychical Research, 49 Marloes Road,
London W8 6LA, UK
www.spr.ac.uk

The Soil Association, Bristol House, 40–56 Victoria Street,
Bristol BS1 6BY, UK
TEL: +44 (0) 117 314 5000, info@soilassociation.org

Soil Association Scotland, 18 Liberton Brae, Tower Mains,
Edinburgh EH16 6AE, Scotland
TEL: +44 (0) 131 666 2474, contact@sascotland.org

Third World Network, 131, Jalan Macalister, 10400, Penang, Malaysia
TEL: 60-4-2266728 / 2266159, twnet@po.jaring.my www.twnside.org.sg

The United States Public Interest Research Group, 218 D Street,
SE Washington, DC 20003, USA
TEL: +1 (202) 546 9707, uspirg@pirg.org

Whale and dolphin conservation society
www.wdcs.org

Women's Action for Nuclear Disarmament, National Office,
691 Massachusetts Avenue, Arlington, MA 02476, USA
TEL: +1 (781) 643 6740, info@wand.org www.wand.org

World Future Council, www.worldfuturecouncil.org

World Wide Fund for Nature, Panda House, Weyside Park,
Godalming, Surrey GU7 1XR, UK
TEL: +44 (0)1483 426 444
or contact Supporter Relations TEL: +44 (0)1483 426 333, wwf.org.uk

Journals and online publications

Atlantis Rising magazine and online www.atlantisrising.com

The Ghanaian Times website www.newtimesonline.com

Grail World magazine and online www.grailworld.com

Green Futures magazine and online www.greenfutures.org.uk

Hallowquest online newsletter for Caitlin Matthews and the
Foundation for Inspirational and Oracular Studies.
www.hallowquest.org

In Context: A Quarterly of Humane Sustainable Culture
www.context.org

In Motion online magazine about democracy
www.inmotionmagazine.com

Katarxis architectural online magazine
www.katarxis-publications.com

Life Positive magazine and online www.lifepositive.com

National Geographic and online news www.nationalgeographic.com

Natural Life magazine and online www.naturallifemagazine.com

Nexus magazine and online www.nexusmagazine.com

Organic Foodee online magazine www.organicfoodee.com

Physics World magazine and online www.physicsworld.com

Positive Health magazine and online www.positivehealth.com

Positive News quarterly international newspaper and online search www.positivenews.org.uk

Proceedings of the National Academy of Sciences of the USA www.pnas.org

Resurgence magazine and online search www.resurgence.org

Science in Africa online magazine www.scienceinafrica.co.za

Scientific American journal and online search www.scientificamerican.com

Sleep and Hypnosis journal and online search www.sleepandhypnosis.org

The South African Journal of Natural Medicine www.naturalmedicine.co.za

World Futures: Journal of General Evolution, published by Taylor and Francis

Websites

Science and technology

www.biowaves.com

www.britishdowsers.org

www.cern.ch: European Organization for Nuclear Research CERN

www.glam.ac.uk/roccoto/people.php: Professor Mark Brake, Professor of Science Communication, Univ of Glamorgan, Wales

www.grandertechnologie.com

www.janegoodall.org

www.livescience.com

www.national-academies.org: website for the National Academies of Science, Engineering, Institute of Medicine and National Research Council

www.newscientist.com/home.ns

www.ornithology.com: ornithology website

www.redorbit.com: website covering interests in space, science, health and technology

www.sciencedaily.com

www.scitalk.org.uk: Sci Talk

www.sheldrake.org: Rupert Sheldrake

www.stemcellscience.info: information website on stem cell science

www.superstringtheory.com: for an answer to the question: what is theoretical physics?

www.tcm.phy.cam.ac.uk/~bdj10/: Professor Brian Josephson

www.waterwheelfactory.com

Medicine and health

http://altmed.creighton.edu/AmericanIndianMed/: American Indian medicine

www.bna.org.uk: British Neuroscience Association

www.cafescientifique.org: Cafe Scientifique

www.drgrotte.com/BalineseMedicine.shtml: Balinese medicine

www.dana.org/edab/welcome_en.cfm: Dana centre

www.digibio.com: homeopathy

hesas.glam.ac.uk/news/en/2007/apr/03/science-workshops/: Science workshops

www.hghmagazine.co/archives/belfast-homeopathy-results.html: homeopathy

www.library.wellcome.ac.uk: Wellcome Science Library

www.pubmedcentral.nih.gov: U.S. National Institutes of Health (NIH) digital archive of journal literature for biomedical and life sciences www.rife.org: website of the life work of Dr Royal Rife

www.wddty.co.uk: What Doctors Don't Tell You

www.who.int: World Health Organisation

The environment and sustainable living

www.clintonglobalinitiative.org: Clinton Global Initiative founded by Bill Clinton

www.eco-schools.org.uk: sustainable schools programme run by the Foundation for Environmental Education

www.ecovillage.org: Global ecovillage network

www.ecovillagefindhorn.com: the Findhorn ecovillage

www.envirolink.org: Envirolink

www.gardenorganic.org.uk: Garden Organic website

www.le.ac.uk/archaeology/image_collection: archaeology

www.navdanya.org: Started by physicist Vandana Shiva's Research Foundation for Science, Technology and Ecology.

www.nnfcc.co.uk: The National Non-Food Crops Centre

www.oceanarks.org: Ocean Arks – the website of Nancy Jack Todd

www.pathtofreedom.com: website on sustainable living

www.primalseeds.org: Primal Seeds

www.sacredsites.com: Martin Gray

www.sustainable-energy.org.uk: website for Sustainable Energy Action and Renewable Energy in the Urban Environment

Psychology and parapsychology

www.c-far.org: Centre for Fundamental and Anomalies Research C-FAR

www.electrocrystal.com: website of Harry Oldfield

www.iands.org: website for International Association for Near-Death Studies Inc.

www.irva.org: The International Remote Viewing Association

www.koestler-parapsychology.psy.ed.ac.uk: Koestler Parapsychology Unit

www.korotkov.org: website of Konstantin Korotkov PhD

www.lfr.org/LFR/csl: Cognitive Sciences Laboratory

www.mysteriouspeople.com

www.near-death.com: Near-death experiences and dreams

www.nderf.com: website for The Near Death Experience Research Foundation

www.parapsychology.org: Parapsychology Foundation Inc.

www.spr.ac.uk: website for the Society for Psychical Research

INDEX